M000100549

# CULT VEGAS

# CULT VEGAS

## The Weirdest! The Wildest!
## The Swingin'est Town on Earth!

Mike Weatherford

Huntington Press • Las Vegas, Nevada

# CULT VEGAS: The Weirdest! The Wildest! The Swingin'est Town on Earth!

Published by:
    Huntington Press
    3687 South Procyon Avenue
    Las Vegas, Nevada 89103
    (702) 252-0655 Phone
    (702) 252-0675 Fax
    e-mail: books@huntingtonpress.com

Copyright © 2001, Mike Weatherford

ISBN 0-929712-71-4

Library of Congress Catalog Card Number: 00-112333

Cover photo: Brian J. Smith
Cover design: Patrick Tierney
Interior design: Maryann Guberman and Lynne Loomis
Illustrations: Maryann Guberman
Production: Kaleidoscope Publishing Concepts

First Printing: January 2001
Second Printing: April 2002

All rights reserved. No part of this publication may be translated, reproduced, or transmitted in any form or by any means, electronic or mechanical, including photocopying and recording, or by any information storage and retrieval system, without express written permission of the copyright owner.

*To Bill and the other Las Vegas entertainment journalists before me—both the legitimate and the less so—who captured some peculiar history and left a fun trail to follow.*

# Acknowledgments

Writing a book is the dream of nearly every newspaper journalist. Writing it without giving up the day job becomes a long ordeal. Even with many signs that this was meant to be, a lot of people came through with help or encouragement at just the right time.

First and foremost, grateful thanks to my wife Joan, who was still my girlfriend when all this began in April 1997 and had to live with "the damned book" through the milestones of marriage, home-buying, and the entire pregnancy/birth/infancy of our first child, Gillian. But she knew this book was as much a dream as all those things.

Also to my parents, Joanne and Carl Weatherford, for never pushing me toward a real job and for keeping the martinis and cool records in the house.

To Joe Sehee for starting me down this twisted road and helping me discover what was in my own backyard. And to Joe Guercio and Penny France for a lot of things along the way.

Special thanks to those who had an active hand in making the book happen: publisher Anthony Curtis and editor Deke Castleman, who both "got" the concept before the cigar-swing revival was full-blown and stuck with it long after it peaked (great suggestions from Deke throughout the entire process); Huntington Press' Bethany Coffey Rihel and Laurie Shaw for their assistance; Lynne Loomis for being the special someone who fit all the pieces into a coherent whole; and Maryann Guberman for the design I had always envisioned.

Also to (Dang Ol') Mark Antonuccio for all his slave labor, Coco Kiyonaga, Carol Cling for her collaboration on *Fear and Loathing*, Don Knepp, Susan Jarvis, and Kathy War. And to Brian J. Smith and Pat Tierney—arbiter of all taste—for the awesome cover.

Some of this material has appeared in altered form in the *Las Vegas Review-Journal*. Thanks to Sherman Frederick, Allan Fleming, Thomas Mitchell, Charles Zobell, and even Frank Fertado for many years of employment and a clear path on the book.

And thanks to all who took the time to share their stories within these pages, particularly those who granted special interviews without the immediate results of a newspaper article: Pete Barbutti, Freddie Bell, Shecky Greene, Cook E. Jarr, Norman and Mary Kaye, Sonny King, Claude Trenier, and Jerry Vale.

The biggest regret of the book taking so long to come to fruition is that Nicky Blair and Bill Willard did not live to see the finished product. Posthumous thanks to Nicky for his Elvis photos and to Bill for allowing me to be the first person to actually use the celebrity interviews he and Joe Delaney taped for UNLV's Arnold Shaw Popular Music Research Center—which at the time existed only in Bill's garage. Now it's due to become a reality in the Lee and Thomas Beam Music Center at the University of Nevada, Las Vegas. Visit and support the center if this book inspires you to go deeper.

Additional thanks to: Señor Amor, Sam Butera, Eric Caidin, Tina Clarke, Susan Darnell, Joe Delaney, Lamar Fike, Bert I. Gordon, Buddy Hackett, Clint Karlsen, Bruce Kotzky, Jim Laurie, Nick Lewin, Ted V. Mikels, Art Nadler, Nick Naff, Mojo Nixon, Michael Paskevich, Jeff Scheid, Jim Seagrave, Sam Sherman, George Sidney, John L. Smith, Keely Smith, Dyanne Thorne and Howard Maurer, Rob Vale, Don Weiner, and anyone else to whom I owe drinks for forgetting.

Mike Weatherford
September 2000

# Cult Vegas Presents

# INTRODUCTION

It's almost gone now, the old Las Vegas. What remains of it hides—sometimes in plain sight, sometimes under camouflage—trying to evade the heavy hand of progress wielding dynamite or a wrecking ball. Anyone who's visited Las Vegas in the past few years knows the story. The land has become too valuable, each square foot along the Strip too prized, for history. Every inch of space can be developed to the density of an urban skyscraper and crammed with more shops or slot machines—bad news for the tree-lined driveways, the two-story hotel wings, and the rolling lawns of the old Vegas. Names once synonymous with the city—the Dunes, the Sands, the Landmark—have tumbled in celebrated "implosions" staged for the amusement of giddy tourists and locals who've come to know the city too recently to feel any sense of loss.

The new Vegas is a vertical skyline of monolithic hotel towers and casinos mutated into shopping malls. Even some of the classic names that are still in business—Caesars Palace, the Sahara—have done their best to remove any vestiges of their old garden rooms or poolside cabanas in the name of bigger, better and newer. At this writing, the latest casualties were Caesars' Circus Maximus showroom—where the phrase "playing Caesars" was defined as having conquered a particular realm of show business—and the entire 50-year-old Desert Inn. Not that much of Wilbur Clark's original construction remained, but it still was nice to see the name.

Finding what remains of the old Las Vegas, places to stand and feel the physical history, takes some determination. There's the El Cortez casino downtown, where the original 1941 building still lies in front of a newer tower. Walk up to the second-floor barbershop, look out the window past the neon canopy, and imagine what Fremont Street must have looked like in the '40s. Or drive by the Moulin Rouge on Bonanza Road to see the rare example of a 1955 hotel preserved because its land did *not* become valuable on a street now patrolled by the homeless.

On the more inviting Strip, the first nine stories of the Riviera and the three-story room wings to the Tropicana were blended into newer construction. For a better feel of how things used to be, go to the south side of the Stardust and stroll the rectangle of two-story room wings surrounding the swimming pool from the old Royal Nevada. These remnants of the failed 1955 casino were annexed by the Stardust long ago, but they outlasted the Stardust's original motel wings, which were torn down in late 1999. Each downstairs room boasts its own sitting porch and French doors, serving as reminders of the oasis once found along a thirsty desert highway. And just north of the Riviera Hotel, behind an ugly strip mall facade, the Algiers Motel rests in most of its resplendent 1954 glory. For years you could peer through a chained gate to the north and see a real ghost town, complete with blowing tumbleweeds and buildings branded with Wild West names, such as Carson City and Dodge City. The room wings to the original Thunderbird Hotel, they were the oldest standing pieces of the original Las Vegas Strip. But they, too, have recently fallen victim to the wrecking ball so as not to sully the view from new luxury condominiums going up to the east.

With the original buildings disappearing fast, the rest of the old Vegas is all attitude. And that's most of what you'll be reading about here. Not Las Vegas the place, but *Vegas,* the state of mind. The Vegas that never went away, but faded in politically correct times only to resurface as a backlash to Big Brother telling you that you can no longer drink, smoke, or laugh.

This book being an entertainment history—and a fairly specific one at that—it's not the place to read a detailed history of Las Vegas. But a selective overview will help put some of the insanity that follows into context. I'll make it as simple as possible.

The Dunes sign becomes a fallen giant in the wake of the hotel's implosion in October 1993. During the street party, thousands of people cheered as the hotel was brought down, launching the makeover of the Strip.

2

Vegas, at least as it's discussed here, was born on September 4, 1951—the day Frank Sinatra came to town.

Before that, everything sort of set the stage. In 1907, the first electric lights (not yet neon) illuminated Fremont Street. A drilling company discovered that the sleepy railroad town rested on an underground water supply, reason enough to incorporate a city four years later. In 1931, the dusty valley was blessed with a Depression-busting project called Hoover Dam. That same year, Nevada eased its divorce laws and sanctioned wide-open gambling to sweeten the incentives for those dam tourists.

In 1941, the El Rancho Vegas became the first hotel to open along U.S. 91 to Los Angeles, now known as the Strip. It was soon joined by the Last Frontier. No matter what the movie portrayed, Bugsy Siegel did not get the idea to build the Flamingo by stumbling into a barren desert to be imbued with a divinely inspired vision. He was a gangster, not a visionary, or he surely would have tried to buy more of the surrounding land. But he and Meyer Lansky knew a good idea when they saw one. They rescued the financially stalled brainchild of *Hollywood Reporter* publisher Billy Wilkerson, after pulling a quick cash turnover on the El Cortez and trying unsuccessfully to buy the El Rancho Vegas.

The *Bugsy* movie was right about Siegel's cost overruns on the lavish project, which in late 1946 changed the image of Las Vegas from frontier gambling town to big-city sophistication. "The town has been converted to an opulent playground," Associated Press reporter Bob Thomas proclaimed after visiting the Flamingo on December 30, 1946. And Siegel did design his own suite in the Oregon Building so there would be only one way in, but several trap doors and hidden escape hatches out. That's why his

The Stratosphere towers above room wings from the 1948 Thunderbird Hotel. The oldest remaining pieces of the original Las Vegas Strip, the room wings met their demise in the summer of 2000.

still-unknown killer, believed to have represented his disgruntled investors, chose his girlfriend's more accessible bungalow in Los Angeles as the place to put a slug in the 41-year-old gangster's eye.

The Vegas-begins-with-Sinatra theory should be self-explanatory to all true believers and will be addressed in more detail in the Sinatra chapter. But one reason this theory rings so true is that Sinatra's takeover in the '50s coincided with two significant trends: the development of the Strip and the dawn of television.

The Strip was still not much of one, with only three places along the highway featuring nightclub entertainers when Sinatra debuted at the year-old Desert Inn. (Sinatra was competing with Rudy Vallee at the El Rancho Vegas that first engagement.) The Sands, which was to become Sinatra's home, did not open until December 1952. But when the Strip started to grow, it took off quickly: The Sands, Sahara, Dunes, New Frontier, Riviera, Royal Nevada, Hacienda, Tropicana, and Stardust all arrived between 1952 and 1958. All of them to some degree abandoned cowboy kitsch for the sleek supper-club architecture and atmosphere that Wilkerson's Hollywood crowd had come to expect in Los Angeles, not to mention in New York—Sands impressario Jack Entratter was imported from the famed Copacabana—Miami, and Havana.

But the little boomtown in the Nevada desert had the twin advantages of deep-pocket investors (regardless of where the investment money came from), who spared no expense to get big-name attractions into their casinos, and a proximity to "Television City" on the West Coast. As TV started to become a fixture in American homes, Las Vegas could promote its own neon mystique at the same time it capitalized on stars who were crossing back and forth between the nightclub and television worlds. Reigning names such as Danny Thomas, Milton Berle, and Red Skelton may be neglected in this book to focus on cooler characters, but they can't be denied their roles in building the city's importance and legitimacy.

Did I say "legitimate"? Such a (dirty) word would never have come up in the roaring '50s if it hadn't been for those comforting faces from the picture tube. The celebrated murders of Siegel and, later, Gus Greenbaum—who'd "rescued" the Flamingo after Siegel's death, then moved over to run the Riviera before his throat was slit in Phoenix— fueled the public's imagination about the organized crime figures behind the swanky casinos. James Bond's creator, Ian Fleming, wrote a series of travel essays in 1959 and 1960 (collected as the book *Thrilling Cities)* and calmly spelled it out for his readers: "Some of the hotels and casinos in Las Vegas are owned in a considerable proportion by gangster money. These syndicates, as they are politely named, are four—Texas, Cleveland, Detroit, and Chicago."

In truth, the web of ownership was much more tangled, and investigative journalists Ed Reid and Ovid Demaris attempted to sort it out in their landmark 1963 exposé, *The Green Felt Jungle.* "The big guessing game in Las Vegas is 'Who owns whom,'" they readily admitted. "Though there are many big hoodlums in Las Vegas operating openly as licensed owners in plush Strip casinos, there are many more who operate behind legitimate or semilegitimate fronts. ... It is a baffling and curious game that confuses police, the Gaming Control Board, and not a few casino owners along the Strip."

Business continued to boom, as evidenced by the hotel towers of the new casinos and hotel tower expansions to the older ones. Depending on how you view it, the best or worst thing that ever happened to Vegas was the vision of an entrepreneur named Jay Sarno. It was he who created the first "themed" casinos on the Strip, starting with Caesars Palace in 1966 and following it with Circus Circus in 1968. Until that point, any themes suggested by the exotic hotel names and giant neon signs stopped at the doorways of the interchangeable casinos. But the $25 million Caesars Palace made a real attempt—albeit a '60s bachelor-padified attempt—"to re-create the mood of the great 'Golden Age of Rome,'" as press releases touted the opening of the 34-acre resort.

Circus Circus was an omen in more ways than one. Memorably described by Hunter S. Thompson as "what the whole hep world would be doing on Saturday night if the Nazis had won the war," the big-top themed casino opened the door to Vegas as a place that even a fit parent would contemplate as a family destination. Not that the original notion of a "family casino" couldn't still be a little warped. An opening-week ad touted one of the games: "Hit the target and knock a nude girl out of bed and make her dance!" Kids shot water pistols at a target, trying to dump a bikini-clad babe from her perch. "Younger kids really liked that one," remembers Steve Izenour, an architect who crashed the grand opening while visiting Vegas on a field trip from Yale. "But I don't think it lasted very long."

Anyone who visits the Strip today might find it hard to believe that the International (now the Las Vegas Hilton) could actually open without a theme, other than its claim of being the largest hotel in the world, in 1969. However, it can be argued that the 1,500-room monolith might not have drawn so much attention if Elvis Presley had not put it on the map. The MGM Grand Hotel (now Bally's), which opened in 1973, was further architectural proof that the mob days had given way to corporate dreams of mega-hotels, though its Celebrity Room still relied on traditional headliners such as Dean Martin.

"Jumpsuit Elvis" straddled the line between the early social upheaval of rock 'n' roll and the Sinatra-era Vegas mystique that stood for a more subtle rebellion—a boozing, gambling getaway from the bland post-war responsibilities of raising families in the suburbs. Teen-age fans from Presley's breakthrough days were now, like their idol, on the far side of 30. Elvis was hip enough to lure this '50s rock generation to town, but not so hip as to seem completely at odds with the traditional headliners who still thrived here. He was backed up by an orchestra along with his rock band, and he favored current pop hits such as "Proud Mary," or show tunes like "The Impossible Dream," over his '50s rockabilly.

But of course it didn't last, and Elvis' tumble from "Comeback King" to bloated self-parody paralleled the outside world's view of Vegas. The hotels continued to flourish as Howard Hughes and other corporate "big-picture" guys took control in the '70s, but hotel entertainment did not keep up as well. Rock and related pop music evolved from a social movement into an industry. Rock promoters were refining the new business of sports arena tours at the same time that the acts themselves were squeezing the nightclub entertainers out of the pop-culture limelight. Gradually, between 1968 and 1975, Vegas found itself pushed across the generational line that divides cool from laughable.

By the late '70s, Vegas icons such as Wayne Newton became the objects of a new humor honed by irony, as best summed up by Bill Murray's Nick the Lounge Lizard on *Saturday Night Live*—"Star Wars, nothing but Star Wars, if they should bar wars, let them keep Star Wars. ..." Without a new generation of headliner types to draw from, Vegas became an elephants graveyard of has-beens or dependable B-teamers. By 1988, the town was so unhip to touring rockers that Allan Bregman, then president of Caesars World Entertainment, lamented: "Sometimes you can't even get into the money factor. You never even get to that plateau. They just will not do it." This may not sound so bad until you realize that one of the acts that had to be swayed was the Beach Boys, who hadn't been a significant pop music force since the '60s. "They were very reluctant," Bregman said.

A random look at the showroom lineup in May 1982, the dawn of the MTV era, reveals the dog days of entertainment inertia. A couple of celebrated veterans, Sammy Davis Jr. and Shecky Greene. A quartet of younger but out-of-phase traditionalists—Robert Goulet, Crystal Gayle, Neil Sedaka, and Paul Anka. Two journeymen making valiant attempts to become homegrown "stars" in the Wayne Newton mode: singer Lovelace Watkins and female impersonator Jim Bailey (both of whom had been working the Strip for at least eight years). The rest of it was dinner theater comedies or showgirl revues, ranging from famous extravaganzas *(Lido de Paris)* to low-budget burlesque.

The salvation this time did not involve any single name such as Elvis—unless you count Walt Disney. The opening of the Mirage on Thanksgiving weekend 1989 returned the fantasy architecture of the hotel itself to the center of attention, more than any entertainer or attraction within. Self-styled visionary Steve Wynn wisely restored some of the Strip's faded luster by steering the Mirage away from old casino clichés and embracing a colorful tropical motif. A year later, the Excalibur, a crackerbox purportedly resembling a castle, revived the theme concept for the family crowd. The idea was that if all the other casino interiors were interchangeable, maybe you'd go out of your way to see a few suits of armor and a puppet show.

This trend of the casinos themselves replacing celebrity names on the marquees reached its apex in late 1993, when Circus Circus finished a fully functional pyramid called the Luxor and Wynn opened Treasure Island, complete with a full-scale pirate battle out front every 90 minutes. The Strip had become "a kind of sentimentalized Disney World," observed architect Robert Venturi, who has studied Las Vegas since the late '60s. Venturi co-authored the 1972 book *Learning From Las Vegas* after helming an expedition of Yale School of Art and Architecture students, who studied the commercial strip as a social phenomenon. But 25 years later, he found that the motels and gaudy road signs that were "designed essentially for connecting with a moving automobile in a hot desert" had evolved into "a kind of Disneyland where you're walking through a scenographic, a kind of stage scenery where you're on the stage."

> " I remember when Las Vegas was dirty and sleazy. Now it's just cheesy. "
>
> Chrissie Hynde
> 1994

The Strip now sports a hotel fashioned after the New York skyline directly across the street from the Lego castle Excalibur. The visual contrast can be found nowhere else, but both hotels are still more theme-park fantasy—trying to give gambling a wholesome facelift—than the unique piece of Americana that Vegas embodied in the '50s. "It's kind of ironic that in a way [the Strip] is becoming less radical, even though in some ways it's more spectacular," Venturi says.

After the Mirage, the whole city just exploded. The Yale architects and students were drawn to the Strip in 1968 because it was an extreme and isolated example of that automobile-age phenomenon known as the commercial strip. "At a certain level [Vegas] was unconscious architecture," said *Learning From Las Vegas* co-author Denise Scott-Brown. "That doesn't mean that architects didn't design it ... but the overall that was so wonderful hadn't really been thought through."

Now, the corporations have seen just how many hotel rooms can be crammed onto each lot fronting the Strip. The accountants deem anything less than 3,000 rooms an inefficient use of the land. The grand old Sands was blown up and replaced by the Venetian, a Y-shaped knockoff of the Steve Wynn resorts across the street. You can imagine hearing Venetian owner Sheldon Adelson saying, "Wynn got his, I want mine," as he signed the Sands' death warrant to make way for his copycat. Later, the Aladdin's implosion showed how ridiculous all this destruction has become: The Aladdin's hotel tower was built in 1975.

The happy accident that was Las Vegas is now "large and mass-produced and thought through to the very last inch," notes Scott-Brown. "It's part of the largest building scale that society manages." The urban density now forms an uneasy alliance with the return of "class" to the Strip. The new wave of projects—chief among them Wynn's Bellagio—takes its design from upscale Mediterranean resort-hotels. But the Bellagio aspires to a taste level that seems at odds with the hotel's overwhelming size, not to mention that instinctive compulsion of a Vegas casino to go over the top. At the very least, however, the new century found Las Vegas well on its way to shedding the last of its old image as a polyester sea of nickel-chipping seniors and trailer trash.

In fact, it's safe to say Las Vegas is fun again. That much must be freely admitted, especially by an author who covers entertainment for the city's morning newspaper. Toward the end of the '90s, the Strip was pulling in young, attractive people in a way that didn't seem possible 10 years earlier. Try to get past the modern-day fixation on logos and franchising, and it's possible to imagine the relatively cozy Hard Rock Hotel as being what the Sands was in the late '50s—attuned to the pop culture of its day and packed with well-dressed, well-heeled, beautiful people.

Entertainment in the new Vegas has made peace with the modern music industry by opening venues—the Hard Rock and House of Blues, and arenas at the MGM Grand Hotel and Mandalay Bay—to host touring concert acts. And, since rock 'n' roll lived long enough to have a history, the old headliner rooms finally have a new wave of aging has-beens—Huey Lewis, the Moody Blues, and so on—to step into place for today's graying boomers. Finally, there are those Vegas stalwarts, God bless 'em, who simply refuse to go away until time snatches them away: Sam Butera, the Treniers, Don Rickles, Tom Jones.

> "I remember when Vegas was called an elephants graveyard. I remember when all the acts who now play the Hard Rock said they wouldn't find themselves in Las Vegas. It's silly. ... We're past that stage where we make that comparison and put people in little boxes."
>
> Tony Orlando
> 1996

The sin, if there is one, is that the Strip is not that much different now than, say, the theme meccas in Orlando, Florida, or the CityWalk at Universal Studios in California. There's more to do, but less that's unique. No matter what becomes of the town, this book is a reminder that Vegas has always been about change. You can't stop it, so get out of the way. But it's impossible to completely snuff out the feeling that underneath its corporate, homogenized veneer, the Strip is still a little bit nuts.

And perhaps that old spirit just can't be extinguished. Time can take away the entertainers who put the town on the map, and the forces of so-called progress can blow up the fondly remembered places. But they can't take away the warped thrill of *Vegas* as long as true believers hold their shot glasses high and keep their cigarettes burning as brightly as the irrepressible souls who await them in the rest of these pages.

# Frank's Room

Hard to imagine now, but Frank Sinatra's first gig in Las Vegas was a low point in his life. His marriage was almost history, and the gorgeous movie star he had sacrificed everything for wasn't too cooperative either. Sinatra had just wrapped a Reno gig and was vacationing at the Cal-Neva Lodge in Lake Tahoe on August 29, 1951, when he and Ava Gardner had another one of their fights. This was especially disconcerting, since Frank's reason for being in Nevada in the first place was to establish a six-week residency that would allow him to file for a divorce from his wife Nancy.

On this night, strong words flowed with the drinks. Ava jumped in a car and headed for home. As she later recounted it, Frank's manager, Hank Sanicola, summoned her back by breathlessly describing "an overdose." Frank mocked her from his sickbed: "I thought you'd gone." Sinatra denied a quarrel—even though a huffy Ava had been stopped for speeding in Carson City—and he dismissed the so-called "suicide attempt" as an allergic reaction to a sleeping pill. "I just had a bellyache," he assured a reporter. "Suicide is the farthest thought from my mind." He would cite the episode as yet another case of the press hounding him and fueling the public scandal the Ava affair had created. In truth, however, the *Las Vegas Morning Journal* phrased the episode in the speculative from its first report—"Did Frankie Take Overdose of Sleeping Pills?"—and quoted a Washoe County deputy as saying, "I did not consider it serious as there was no question of suicide. ... I did not even consider it serious enough to notify California authorities."

Public outrage about Ava was the most obvious shackle on Sinatra's career, but his slump was so severe that the problems had to run deeper. His records weren't doing well; his movies weren't causing a stir. His foray into network TV, with his own CBS variety show, found him pitted against the more popular *Your Show of Shows* on Saturday nights—and television was only starting to tighten its grip on the nation anyway. Even

Sinatra's beaming face says it all in this *Las Vegas Morning Journal* photo that ran after his Las Vegas debut at the Desert Inn on September 4, 1951. His career had seen better days, but having Ava Gardner at his side made all the hardships worthwhile.

his famous voice was buckling under the stress. Perhaps it was the collective karma of all those World War II soldier boys, who may have resented the hormonal meltdown the lanky singer had touched off in their bobby-soxer girls. With everyone grown-up and reunited after the war, there was no market for false idols.

Welcome to Vegas. Most likely following a path from Reno paved by his Atlantic City nightclub connections, Sinatra made his debut at Wilbur Clark's Desert Inn on September 4, 1951. Ava's presence overshadowed the entertainment details of the event: The next day's *Morning Journal* featured a front-page photo of the singer displaying a beaming smile, clasping her hand. Sinatra was more newsworthy as front-page gossip than as the kind of prestigious performer the city was just starting to attract. The Desert Inn, open a little more than a year, was only the fifth hotel on the highway to Los Angeles, which didn't yet deserve the name "the Strip." Frank's competition that week included Rosemary Clooney at the Thunderbird, the Vagabonds at the Flamingo, and the Sportsmen at the Last Frontier. Instead of taking in the casino action, Sinatra told a reporter, he and Ava planned to boat and fish at Lake Mead on his new 24-foot cabin cruiser.

*Las Vegas Sun* publisher Hank Greenspun reflected the prevailing sentiment in his rundown of opening night, which recalled that Sinatra used to be "a homely kid with a sweet, natural appeal. … That Frankie was a skinny, funny-faced guy who raced home to his wife and kids to tell them of his triumphs." Though Greenspun acknowledged "a good show" with "signs of greatness," it was the *Sun's* entertainment reporter, Bill Willard, who better read the signals that pointed toward the era to come. "The guy is one of the greatest showmen seen in these parts," Willard wrote, particularly impressed by "I'm a Fool to Want You"—the all-too-revealing song Sinatra recorded earlier that year—and "Soliloquy," the *Carousel* tour de force that "KO's the whole place, but good."

And Sinatra got what he came for. His Nevada divorce was granted November 1, when "the spindly crooner," as the *Journal* described him, flew back into town to spend 15 minutes in the courtroom of District Judge A.S. Henderson. Going in, Sinatra was all piss and vinegar: "This has nothing to do with my public life. ... I ought to give a cocktail party for the press and put a mickey in every glass," he announced to the collected media. But he emerged to mumble, "Everything's all right now." The Desert Inn's publicity director, Merwin Travis, served as the mandatory witness. Within a week, Frank and Ava were married in Philadelphia.

Sinatra played the Desert Inn once more, in July 1952. A modest newspaper ad proclaimed him "America's foremost balladeer ... singing the songs you love to hear." The newspapers otherwise ignored him.

When he returned on October 7, 1953, things had changed—for Sinatra and for Vegas. Still just a town of 25,000 during the crooner's first visit, Las Vegas was beginning to experience the hyperactive growth that would continue until today. The Sahara opened, followed by the Sands. Opening in mid-December 1952, the Sands was the most elegant carpet joint to unfold along Highway 91. Designed by Hollywood resort architect Wayne McAllister, it spread leisurely across the desert, its 200 rooms graciously clustered in two-story motel units around a tiled and heated pool. The main bar, according to press releases, was 108 feet long and would "accommodate 520 tipplers at one standing."

The centerpiece, however, was the Copa Room. For this 395-seat (later expanded) supper club—the room that would lift the Sands above anything yet seen in Vegas— owner Jake Freedman needed a secret weapon. He turned to a charismatic, 240-pound former club bouncer named Jack Entratter.

A native New Yorker, Entratter was introduced to the hospitality business as a 14-year-old desk clerk at the French Casino in Florida. He grew into a 6-foot, 4-inch man who nonetheless knew he could do more with charm and diplomacy than with brawn. At New York's Stork Club, Tallulah Bankhead took the young greeter under her wing, introducing him to the celebrity circle. When publicity agent Monte Prosser bought New York's Copacabana club in 1940, he named Entratter as its general manager. By 1949, Entratter had a controlling interest in the club.

In 1952, the impresario, now 38 years old, cashed out to embrace a new vision as general manager of the Sands. Entratter had been responsible, to varying degrees, for the nightclub successes of Johnny Ray, Jimmy Durante, and the team of Dean Martin and Jerry Lewis. Now it was time to tap their loyalty—as well as that of Lena Horne,

Advertising for Frank Sinatra stints in the '50s tell the story of his Las Vegas ascent. Modest display type announces his second Desert Inn engagement in July 1952 (right). Though legend has it that *From Here to Eternity* restored Sinatra to full stardom, a 1954 Sands gig well after the movie's release shows the hotel still found it necessary to bill him as part of the *Ziegfeld Follies* (bottom left). By March 1956, however, the Sands shows were advertised in conjunction with hit Capitol albums such as *Songs for Swingin' Lovers.*

WILBUR CLARK'S DESERT INN
Presents An Outstanding Entertainment Event!
**A SHOW TO THRILL YOU!**

America's Foremost Balladeer in Person!

# FRANK SINATRA

Singing the Songs You Love to Hear

**PAUL GILBERT,** The Laugh Specialist

**SINCLAIR & ALDA, exotic dancers**

**ARDEN-FLETCHER, dancing darlings**

BILL JOHNSON, Singing MC —— CARLTON HAYES and Orch.
Show Times 8:30 p.m., 11:30 p.m. Late Show Saturday 1:30 a.m.

**EXTRA!**                **EXTRA!**
CHUCK GOULD & MICHAEL SOMOGYI in the Sky Room
DANNY CASSELLA & ORCHESTRA in Lady Luck Bar
RIST BROS. TRIO with Gene Corry in Lady Luck Bar.

WILBUR CLARK'S **DESERT INN**
PHONE 6000 FOR RESERVATIONS

THE SANDS PRESENTS
THE ZIEGFELD FOLLIES
produced by JACK ENTRATTER
starring
FRANK SINATRA
GEORGE TAPPS & his DANCERS
THE MARTIN BROS.
THE SANDS' OWN ZIEGFELD GIRLS
WRITTEN AND STAGED BY SID KULLER
RAY SINATRA AND HIS ORCHESTRA
For reservations phone 7100 Two shows nightly 8:15 and 11:15

The Sands, Las Vegas, Nevada

Danny Thomas, and other Copacabana stars—to return the favor in Vegas. Within six months, if you believe the hype, Entratter spent a million bucks booking a diverse mix of stars with publicity value, including Tallulah Bankhead, Edith Piaf, and the ingenious teaming of opera star Robert Merrill with jazz legend Louis Armstrong.

Lorraine Hunt, Nevada's lieutenant governor, spent many of her teen-age years hanging around the Sands as a friend of Entratter's daughter Carol. "We were just dazzled with this coolness. ... We came from this cowboy town to ultrasophistication," Hunt recalls. "I remember I was so attracted to those shiny shoes. That was an era when the hotel owners were all walking around in cowboy hats, and all these guys came in with the mohair tuxes with the black satin shoes. That look was so cool."

By October of the Sands' first year, Sinatra was back on his feet and could pick any hotel he wanted. But there was only one choice. "Sinatra's allegiance to Jack Entratter was because Jack stood by him through all his troubles," says veteran lounge singer Freddie Bell, who often worked the Sands the same time as Sinatra. "Jack stood by him when Frank was down and out. Jack was the one man who stood by him and still played him. You can't imagine Sinatra getting canceled at Danny the Beachcomber's in Miami. He got canceled, second night."

But no one was canceling Sinatra now. Earlier in 1953, he had filmed his hard-won role as Maggio in *From Here to Eternity*. The movie opened that summer as a blockbuster: "16,342 Las Vegans have seen it," a November ad from the Fremont Theater would claim of the "all-time record holder." Moreover, Sinatra signed with Capitol that spring and teamed with young arranger Nelson Riddle for what would become a historic reinvention of his sound. As Sinatra shed the image of fallen teen idol and adulterer, the sarcastic tone of hardened newspapermen began to soften.

After witnessing Sinatra's opening-night performance, *Sun* publisher Greenspun revised his earlier opinion: "Ooooooh Frankie, you almost gave me goose bumps last night ... not quite, but it's an improvement because two years ago you left me oooooh so cold." Greenspun went on to explain how at the Desert Inn, Sinatra had tried to bluff his way through the performance: "Your head was too big for your heart and your heart was not in your work." The 1951 Sinatra "carried a big chip on his shoulder and stood ready to punch anyone in the nose who spoke the truth about him—the fact that he had slipped badly."

Now, having clawed his way back—"almost to the point where you were ten years ago when the world loved you"—Sinatra appeared to Greenspun more like "the prodigal son who returned, which proves humility is, after all, an unconquerable virtue." During his 68 minutes onstage, Sinatra coached and coaxed the house band of older cousin Ray Sinatra through "All of Me," "Don't Worry About Me," "I've Got a Crush on You," and "One for My Baby"—all songs he would sing for the rest of his career.

But the *Sun* had a little Siskel and Ebert-style debate within its pages: Columnist Sean Flannelly called the same show "a failure" and found Sinatra "arrogant, ill-tempered, and downright insulting." The review claimed that Frank sang his opening

**T**oward the end of Sinatra's first Sands stint, Shelley Winters—his co-star in *Meet Danny Wilson*—began working at the Flamingo. During one Sinatra show, a gag met with only mild response. "If it's screams you want, catch Shelley Winters or somebody!" he told the crowd.

Tri✳Via

number, "I Get a Kick Out of You," with "one big grimace," and when it was over he dressed down the musicians: "Don't be afraid; play it. They [the crowd] want to hear it." The singer, Flannelly claimed, "told the assemblage they weren't paying enough attention to him" and kept telling the band to "relax, just relax."

The contrasting reviews reveal that Sinatra was again important enough to tie up the attention of multiple newsmen, but also that his image was still in transition. He would forever remain surly and hot-headed, but the Capitol records soon would establish him as a vocalist with great sensitivity to musicians and a player's ear for an arrangement. "He was a great musician; he had perfect pitch," notes Jerry Vale, the Italian balladeer who became a Sands headliner in his own right. "He could read a lyric like nobody in the world. Nobody even came close to what he did."

As Frank cemented his marriage to the Sands, he lost his grasp on Ava. Her absence was noted at his Sands debut: "I really don't know if she'll come up," he admitted to one reporter. On October 27, the day before Jeanette MacDonald came in to replace Frank at the end of his first Copa Room run, Ava's publicists at MGM issued a press release informing the world of the couple's final separation.

But Sinatra and the Sands—now that would be a swingin' affair. Granted, it took its time to simmer. When Sinatra returned in the summer of 1954, the hotel somehow felt the need to package him as the headliner of "The Ziegfeld Follies starring Frank Sinatra." Still another *Sun* columnist, writing under the single moniker Delyle, suggested the Ziegfeld trappings were unnecessary. "Never before have we heard such thundering applause for a performer," the columnist wrote of a star who related "the feeling of wanting to please that he lacked before. ... Sinatra possesses a rare quality for humor and plays it just right."

Sinatra became so synonymous with the Sands, legend would have you believe he performed there all the time. Fact is, he was so busy making movies and records that he did not play Vegas at all in either 1955 or 1957, and did only one engagement in 1958. But when he was there, the hotel fully exploited the success of the Capitol albums. Nelson Riddle's band came in for a March 1956 stint that was given the same billing as a just-released album—*Songs for Swingin' Lovers*—which is now considered one of Sinatra's best. It included the classic "I've Got You Under My Skin."

When he wasn't performing, the Sands was his personal playground. If Frank acted like he owned the place, it was because he actually had a piece of it. Within days of his debut engagement, the singer was granted a 2 percent interest in the hotel that would increase to 9 percent by the time Freedman died in 1958 and Entratter became the top man. "Entratter was wise," noted singer Sonny King, a longtime lounge fixture and stage partner for Jimmy Durante. "Entratter was the first guy to give [the entertainers] points in the hotel. If you messed up and didn't show up, you would lose money."

A 1959 hotel publicity release stated: "Sinatra avers he is only three hours away from [the Copa Room] at any time. ... The Sands is Sinatra's home away from home." It wasn't such an exaggeration. "He really loved Las Vegas," King said. "Because it was small, he could do whatever he wanted and not be bothered. He could walk outside and not be bothered—which he couldn't do in any other city—because they were so used to seeing celebrities in Las Vegas."

"He'd always be there," remembered Freddie Bell. "You'd never know when you were gonna see Frank. It was a close-knit group in those days. Fly in and fly out, you know? You gotta understand, he partied pretty heavy in those days."

Gambled, too. Some biographers claim the hotel tore up Sinatra's markers for his losses but let him walk away with his winnings, knowing the high-roller action he brought to the tables was worth it. Bell, familiar with the practices of the day, said Sinatra was probably just shilling. "I'd work jobs in those days where the boss would say, 'You don't win; you don't lose.' The old bosses used to do that. It was a standoff which a lot of guys had. We used to be allowed to deal [blackjack], too. The only guys who would get in trouble were Martin and Lewis, because they would really give the money away. Dean was originally a dealer."

Sinatra's circle of friends helped promote Las

In November 1954, Sinatra cut out between shows to sell tickets to his movie *Suddenly* at the Fremont Theatre. He was dressed in the same outfit he wore in the picture.

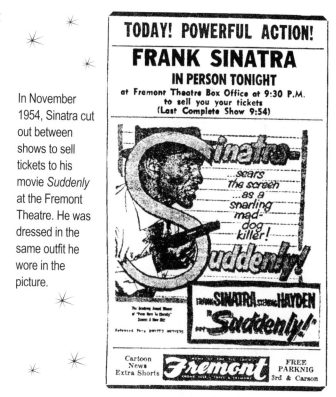

TODAY! POWERFUL ACTION!

## FRANK SINATRA

### IN PERSON TONIGHT

at Fremont Theatre Box Office at 9:30 P.M.
to sell you your tickets
(Last Complete Show 9:54)

...sears
the screen
...as a
snarling
mad-
dog
killer!

*Suddenly!*

SINATRA starring HAYDEN
*Suddenly!*

Cartoon News Extra Shorts

Fremont

FREE PARKNIG
3rd & Carson

Vegas among an influential crowd. "The minute he stepped in town, money was here," King said. "He drew all the big money people. Every celebrity in Hollywood would come to Las Vegas to see him, one night or another." Any mode of transport could deliver a party. In October of 1958, it was a chartered railroad car full of celebrities for Judy Garland's opening. In late 1963, it was a movie theater in the sky: Newsmen saw *Come Blow Your Horn* on a chartered jet from New York that touched down as a "surprise" in Vegas.

"He used to bring everybody," says Keely Smith. "When I say everybody, I mean everybody. No matter who was in town—Spencer Tracy, Gary Cooper, Natalie Wood, Robert Wagner." A table would be reserved in the Sahara's Casbar lounge for Smith's legendary shows with Louis Prima. "I met John Kennedy through him. Any star that was in town when Frank opened, they used to come in here when he would get offstage at the Sands."

## Come swing with me

Until 1960, Sinatra had always worked alone (given the floorshow format that allowed for the Copa Girls and opening acts). But Vegas was a small town, and soon the fraternal atmosphere of stars catching each other's acts spilled over into the formal billing. A young comic named Joey Bishop worked the Desert Inn four months before Sinatra did; Bishop was opening for Beatrice Kay at the El Rancho during Sinatra's second Desert Inn visit in July 1952. In December 1953, when Sinatra headlined an all-star first-anniversary bash at the Sands, another comedian named Buddy Lester was working the Last Frontier's Ramona Room. In early 1956, Sinatra's opening night fell immediately after the closing night of Martin and Lewis, who had worked the Strip from the days when the Flamingo was the only plush nightclub on the highway. Entratter

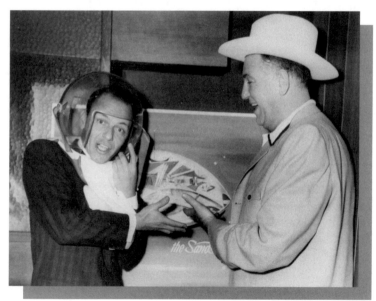

Since Sinatra was a Sands investor as well as performer, no publicity stunt—such as spoofing the Sputnik launch with "Sands-nik"—was too silly for him or for legendary Sands Entertainment Director Jack Entratter.

brought them to the Sands in 1955 and cut separate deals to retain the two as solo acts when the partnership soured the next year.

Sammy Davis Jr. was no stranger to either Sinatra or Vegas. Frank had known and supported the young dynamo since 1947, two years after he began playing the Strip with his father and uncle in the Will Mastin Trio. Davis' autobiography, *Yes I Can,* recalls the stark contrast between the star's greeting he received in the showroom and the segregation in the rest of the casino. Barred from the hotels, black entertainers of the postwar era were housed in a shantytown boarding house west of downtown.

By November 1954, however, the Will Mastin Trio had commanded full run of the Last Frontier's casino and VIP suites. By now it was clear who was the star; the billing was basically a gesture of loyalty. While Mastin and Sammy Sr. "assisted not too strongly"—in the tongue-tied prose of columnist Ralph Pearl—young Sammy tore up the place: imitating Nat King Cole, Tony Bennett, and even Sinatra; singing "Hey There" in his own voice; dancing a Bill Robinson tap routine; pounding out a drum solo; and, finally, knocking 'em dead with "Birth of the Blues." "Sammy is definitely a one-man show," Pearl concluded, noting that the Ramona Room would be a tough ticket for the three-week run.

Unfortunately, three days after the opening, the young star had to interrupt his Vegas winning streak with a late-night ride back to California. Davis' friend Charles Head drove so that Sammy could stretch out in the back seat and rest up for a recording session in Los Angeles. Somewhere near San Bernardino on that night of November 19, the car collided with one driven by a 72-year-old woman from Van Nuys, California. Davis lost his left eye and suffered a broken jaw and facial injuries. Sinatra offered his Palm Springs home for convalescence and (according to *Yes I Can*) told his younger buddy: "Relax. You're going to be bigger than ever, Charley. Bigger than ever."

Another of Frank's pallies decided to step out on his own in March 1957. Suave Italian crooner Dean Martin finally had enough of playing straight man to comedy partner Lewis and worked the Sands for the first time as a solo act that March. The final Martin and Lewis movie, *Hollywood or Bust,* was still playing a couple of miles away at the Huntridge Theater, but it took Dino only one night to assure both audiences and Entratter that he didn't need any annoying partners. Martin was quick to establish his languid, loose style—"If he gets any more relaxed, he'll collapse," the *Review-Journal's* Les Devor observed—dashing off his hits "That's Amore" and "Memories Are Made of This," but slowing down to woo the ladies with "I Don't Know Why."

More important, Martin proved he could hold up the comedy end as well. The show unveiled what would become a key prop: a Copa Girl wheeling out a mobile wet bar full of bourbon and scotch bottles. "I don't drink anymore ... and I don't drink any less," he told a crowd of first-nighters that included Jack Benny, Phil Harris, Lucy and Desi Arnaz, and Debbie Reynolds. "I spill more than you drink," he told Harris. The first night's show was good enough for Entratter to sign Dino on as a solo act in a five-year, six-weeks-per-year contract.

When Judy Garland summoned Frank Sinatra and Dean Martin to the stage on her opening night at the Sands in October 1958, the audience got a preview of the seemingly improvised, anything-goes clowning that would become a trademark of the Rat Pack.

But Martin didn't jokingly suggest he be billed as "the last of the red hot partners" for nothing. Judy Garland's October 1958 opening night at the Sands was a hint of things to come. Garland called two audience members—Frank and Dean—to the stage for 20 minutes of music and mirth. "It was automatic that whoever the star was, the star that was following would show up closing night," Freddie Bell says. And as often as not, the schedule had the buddies trailing each other: Frank before Dean in January 1959, then Frank after Dean in April.

It took a movie to put the team that would become known as the Rat Pack all on one stage together. The year 1960 saw the Rat Pack at its peak and Vegas witnessing the finest hour of its golden age.

Sinatra, then 44, was at the height of his movie popularity and unchallenged in his mastery of the standard. Equally important, he was a model of cool living for the postwar generation that now embraced life in the suburbs. Elvis had threatened their teen-age daughters, but the rock 'n' roll danger had been dealt with: Banished to Germany with the Army, Elvis would come back with his wings clipped. (In May 1960, the Rat Pack would meet Elvis on its own terms with the "Welcome Back" TV special from Miami.) An older, wiser Sinatra, on the other hand, turned his maturity into high theater: a single focused pin spotlight, a cigarette, a drink, and "One for the Road."

"Sinatra perpetuated this music of Gershwin and Porter, and gave it a longer life than it should have had in terms of that kind of intensity," singer Paul Anka noted. "First of all, pop music was at its infancy stage and just growing. … It was just a bunch of us kids," said Anka, who first played the Sahara in 1959 when he was only 18. "Now you've got the greatest, cool, hippest entertainers around. … I think timing is everything, obviously in this business. And those guys were it. They put the glamor, they put the buzz in it."

In January 1960, the Sands marquee said enough: Frank Sinatra, Dean Martin, Sammy Davis Jr., Peter Lawford, Joey Bishop, in equal (if descending) billing. "Which star shines tonight?" asked the newspaper ad, which explained that from January 20 to February 16, the Rat Pack would be onstage every night together, or in satisfying combinations of two or more, while in town to film *Ocean's Eleven*.

The "Summit at the Sands" took its name from an upcoming Paris summit that would bring Eisenhower, Khrushchev, and DeGaulle to the same table. The Copa Room would do the same for pop culture's Rat Pack, the name lifted from Humphrey Bogart's Holmby Hills Rat Pack. (It was a better name than "the Clan," which despite its racial connotations still turned up in print as late as 1961.)

Opening night brought the usual eyebrow-raising flock of celebrities. Peter Lorre, Dinah Shore, Zsa Zsa Gabor, and Lucille Ball on the same guest list? The mind boggles. There was even a celeb parking cars: Edd "Kookie" Byrnes, who wasn't a valet but played one on TV in *77 Sunset Strip*. (This was the rare case where Al Freeman, the Sands' publicity director, had to downplay a great angle: Byrnes was in a salary dispute with Warner Bros., which was releasing

It was a pop-culture zenith: the Rat Pack at its peak and Vegas in its golden age. Never was so much star power packed onto one stage as on January 20, 1960. As the Sands ad explained, the filming of *Ocean's Eleven* guaranteed only one star each night. But as everyone now knows, the absentee rate was low.

*Ocean's Eleven.* Though Kookie thought he would generate public sympathy by parking cars on a night when the national press was in town, the stunt didn't go down well with the real valet parkers union. The Associated Press "complied with our request about not saying that Byrne parked any cars," Freeman wrote the next day in a memo to Entratter found in the Sands Collection at the University of Nevada, Las Vegas.)

Sinatra opened with six or seven tunes, shocking those who expected Bishop first: "Gee, what an opening act to follow," the lowest-billed comedian quipped. Lawford— who became a member of the gang after co-starring with Sinatra in 1959's *Never So Few*—joined Davis for "Shall We Dance." Martin took it all in quietly, glass in hand at the rear of the stage, until it came time to thank "Srank Finatra" and glide through a few ballads. "Together" they all stood at the end, until Bishop rode out on Entratter's back. "That was clearly the best show in the history of this community," said former Nevada Governor Bob Miller, who saw one of the Copa Room dates as a teen-ager. "It was like being backstage with them."

The fun continued at virtually the same pace until mid-February. "The five or six bosses would fly in all the big players. All the big tables were sewn up," said Jackie Heller, who worked as a Sands "greeter" and introduced the shows. "People would ask me if I could get them in. If I didn't know them, I'd say, 'Sir, there isn't a chance in the world.'"

The shows cost "more as a toke than it cost you at the table," comedian Buddy Lester, one of the movie's "Eleven," recalled in 1987. The dinner and show usually cost less than $10 per person, but "it was nothing for a guy to slip the maître d' a hundred for a table."

The legend about the making of *Ocean's Eleven* is as famous as the movie itself. The Rat Pack kept a grueling schedule—self-imposed—of two shows per night, followed by an extended stretch of boozing in the lounge while the film crews set up for the day of filming, which was usually done either in the pre-dawn hours or in the early morning when the casinos were at their sleepiest.

"They wouldn't let anybody into the lounge after the second show," Sonny King recalled. "They knew that the boys would come in." The maître d' "used to put reserved signs on every table. There wasn't a soul in the place because [people] were waiting in line outside to get into the lounge. He would practically charge them, like a hundred dollars, to get closer to Sinatra."

The more private parties carried on in the suites. One retired singer-dancer, who appeared as a showgirl in one of the movie's showroom scenes, remembers Lawford inviting her to a late-night party. Naively, the Oklahoma girl didn't understand what kind of party it was until two prostitutes arrived. She was so upset, she spilled her drink on her dress. Sinatra, the perfect gentleman on this night at least, saw her trying to clean up the stain with paper towels and brought her a real towel to help with the mess.

Daylight brought sleep for those lucky enough not to be needed on the set. At

The date and circumstances of this tantalizing photo session aren't certain, but Sinatra did subject himself to a variety of "Arabian night" publicity photos for the Dunes in 1956, helping out Las Vegas gambler Bill Miller and Chicago oilman Major Riddle after they acquired the struggling new hotel.

dusk, the Sands' fabled steam room became the epicenter of the hotel. "That's where you went to sort of get yourself together to go back to work," said Freddie Bell. "The guys would come there to recover. ... We used to meet there about five. They would have hors d'oeuvres and booze, then everybody would shower, put on their clothes, and go to work." Even before *Ocean's Eleven,* it was not uncommon for lounge singers to "get done with work some nights at five or at six a.m. and go right to the golf course. I would play golf and come back and lay by the pool, go to the steam room and get a steam and rub, lie down and take a nap there."

One time Jerry Vale was taking a shower and vocalizing: "Frank banged on my door and said, 'Nobody warms up in this group. We go on cold.'"

Everyone special had a bathrobe with his nickname on it. If you had a robe, you could stay in the place after it was closed to the public. Every robe was white except Sammy's, which was brown. Sinatra's embroidered nickname was "The Pope." Sammy was "Smokey." Dean was "Dago." Entratter was "Jew Feet," Don Rickles was "Rhino," Jerry Vale was "Golden Throat," Vic Damone was "Little Dago," and Bell was "Little Little Dago." The small spa had two massage tables and eight beds in the back, where the guys could grab an hour or two of sleep. The steam room itself was the royal meeting place for movie stars, sports figures, and hallowed guests from all walks of life.

"The things the guys would do to each other, my God," Bell says. "Dean would come in from golf and automatically go to the john with a newspaper. And he'd be there thirty-five or forty minutes. One night we got tape and taped the door closed

# Vegas Goes Legit

Newpaper columnist Don Usherson used to call Vegas "The Great Bright Way"—and with good reason. During the month of January 1977, would any discriminating theatergoer really have wanted to freeze his butt off dodging panhandlers in Times Square, when Vegas showrooms offered the following theatrical alternatives?

✻ Mickey Rooney starring in a three-act comedy called *Alimony* at the Tropicana's Fountain Theatre

✻ The 20th week of *Natalie Needs a Nightie* at the Union Plaza

✻ Linda Lovelace—yes, *the* Linda Lovelace—starring in *My Daughter's Rated X* at the Aladdin's Bagdad Theatre

Patrons had to hurry to catch the latter, as it closed well before the end of its four-week run. Even then, Lovelace missed her first Sunday due to illness, provoking columnist Forrest Duke to quip, "No truth to rumor she was felled by 'Vegas Throat.'" Linda, who later disowned all her X-rated exploits, claimed the show failed because she kept her clothes on.

But that was a feeble excuse, since three years prior—in October 1974—Marilyn Chambers drew positive critical notices for her theatrical debut as Divina in the "pre-Broadway engagement" of the catchily titled *Mind With the Dirty Man* at the Union Plaza. The theatrical outing with Phil Ford and "Trixie from *The Honeymooners*" Jane Kean was a big enough hit that Kean and Chambers reteamed for *Last of the Red Hot Lovers* in early 1978, before Marilyn triumphantly returned to porn.

If nudity was what the tourists wanted, then *Hair* at least gave them a glimpse of it in the International Hotel's Legitimate Theater in 1970. After initial concerns about whether the Fuzz would let the fuzz go on in the signature nude scene (unveiling of "pubic areas" was illegal in this topless showgirl mecca), *Hair* ran for more than 200 performances. Six cops attending opening night made no arrests. "Identification of the performers is difficult from any vantage point in the audience," an undersheriff explained. Besides, he added, "What would it look like if we busted in there and hauled off

UNION

**Plaza**
Hotel/Casino
LIVE IT UP

Presents

"Natalie Needs A Nightie"

A Comedy Sleeper of Sheer Bedlam

By
NEIL and CAROLINE SCHAFFNER

a bunch of screaming nudists? ... We would be playing right into their hands." Those wily hippies.

During the '69 Summer of Love, the always open-minded Caesars Palace hosted *The Boys in the Band,* Mart Crowley's gay-themed comedy about a birthday gathering, in the intimate Caesars Roman Theatre. "This play is unsuitable for children," ads warned of the 8:40 p.m. and midnight shows.

Not all of Las Vegas' theatrical history is confined to smirking dinner-theater farces or once-controversial fare. The Strip has a long legacy of hosting legitimate Broadway musicals, even if the so-called "tab" versions were cut to 90 minutes to meet the two-show-a-night schedule. The movie adaptation of *South Pacific* ran 171 minutes, but Monte Proser's "New Look" production at the Thunderbird in 1963 offered "a streamlined version" with "all of the songs made famous on Broadway" and "more comedy scenes added during the last month" of a six-month run, according to a publicity release.

Some stars did bring the roles they became famous for to Las Vegas. Stubby Kaye sang "Sit Down, You're Rockin' the Boat" in a 1963 Dunes adaptation of *Guys and Dolls* with Dan Dailey and Betty Grable, who lived here as the wife of trumpeter and lounge fixture Harry James. Theodore Bikel first played Tevye in a 100-minute *Fiddler on the Roof* staged at Caesars in 1968. And a year earlier, in 1967, Caesars Palace cast Tony Randall as Felix in *The Odd Couple* before he played the part on TV in 1970. It was an odd cast indeed, with the ubiquitous Mickey Rooney as Oscar, and Sugar Ray Robinson and *Ocean's Eleven* co-star Buddy Lester among the poker buddies.

For other TV stars, Vegas theater signaled a reverse career path. Yvonne "Lily Munster" DeCarlo starred in *Little Me* at the Sahara in March 1968. James "Book 'em, Danno!" MacArthur worked in a T-shirt and boxer shorts opposite Bambi Jr.—who was a stripper before she married talk show host Montell Williams—in *A Bedful of Foreigners* at the Union Plaza in 1990. "Surprisingly enough, there's not one dirty word in it," MacArthur, the son of Helen Hayes, said of the slamming-door comedy by Dave Freeman, a writer for the British TV comedy "Benny Hill."

Nowadays, the line between Vegas and Broadway is blurry; both '80s-era hits of Andrew Lloyd Webber and Las Vegas revues such as *EFX* and *Notre Dame de Paris* are equally reliant on spectacle and special effects. Andrew Lloyd Webber's *Starlight Express* turned Elvis' showroom at the Las Vegas Hilton into a skating rink during the mid-'90s, even though Webber's production designer, John Napier, said he "just nearly vomited" after seeing a "tribute" to *Cats* in the *Splash* show at the Riviera. "I was apoplectic," he commented.

with Dean in there. He started screaming and yelling, then *boom!* Here comes the toilet top through the glass door. ... If you went to sleep on the table, you woke up with shaving cream all over your body."

"One time Don Rickles was berating everybody, as he usually does," Vale remembers. "And Jack Entratter said, 'Let's throw him outside.' I said, 'Jack, he doesn't have any clothes on.' He said, 'So what?' So we threw him out in the nude for a few minutes, then we let him back in. But it was five o'clock in the afternoon, in the daylight."

Despite the high jinks, the "Summit" still managed to include an extra February 7 benefit concert at the Convention Center to raise money for a local monument to the "Four Chaplins," who died in World War II when their transport was torpedoed. The very next day, the Convention Center—and later the Sands—was visited by Lawford's brother-in-law, a Massachusetts senator running for president. In Frank Sinatra, Senator John F. Kennedy had "a showbiz campaign manager already hard at work," observed *Sun* columnist Tab Tabet, in the only newspaper account to link the Rat Pack to the senator.

Since he had yet to win a primary, no one knew Kennedy's visit would become a part of history and launch into play a long soap opera, one that only incidentally involved Vegas and is better told elsewhere—a complicated entanglement that would inspire questions beyond Kennedy's death about the degree to which Sinatra used the influence of mob boss Sam Giancana to get Kennedy elected. Sinatra's affiliation with Giancana unquestionably cost him his friendship with both Kennedy and Lawford, and his casino license for the Cal-Neva Lodge at Lake Tahoe three years later.

But those events would play out slowly over the '60s; there were still some very good years to enjoy.

Dino's 44th birthday on June 7, 1961, served as reason enough for a Rat Pack reunion at the Sands. The boys were again shooting a movie, *Badlands,* which was renamed *Sergeants 3* by the time it was released. But this time they were shooting in Kanab, Utah, and the commute dictated that Sinatra, Martin, Davis, and Bishop perform separate but consecutive weeks in what Entratter labeled "Jackpot Month." On the night they all came together for Dino's birthday, the United Press claimed that more than 2,000 people were turned away from the Copa, where the crowd inside was two deep along the walls. Ringsiders included Marilyn Monroe—Frank's suitemate and longtime soulmate—Elizabeth Taylor, Eddie Fisher, Andy Williams, and two of the "Eleven," Richard Conte and Henry Silva.

Sinatra "relaxed his way" through four cigarettes, a cup of coffee, and 13 tunes, according to the UPI writer, before the real fun began. Lawford, Bishop, Damone, and Eddie Fisher were summoned to the stage to serenade Dino with original birthday lyrics by Sammy Cahn. Then the boys wheeled out a five-foot-tall birthday cake, shaped like a J&B Scotch bottle. Dino threw the first slice at Sammy. Sammy fired back, and all hell broke loose.

Food fights were a constant threat at the Sands. One night, Sonny King recalls, "Sinatra stayed until my last show and said, 'I feel like eating pizza. Let's go to my room and I'll order a nice pizza.' But by the time the pizza came, he got really drunk. My ham and cheese sandwich came and I started eating it, and he said, 'Have some pizza.' I said, 'I don't like pizza.' And he says, 'What kind of Italian are you?' I said, 'I'm a very good Italian, but I just don't like pizza. I don't like fried oil.'

"Well, he took the pizza tray and hit me over the head with it. I took the ham and cheese plate, and I shoved it in his face. Before you know it, a battle ensued—a friendly battle, but he ripped the telephone off the wall and really trashed the place. He said, 'You better sleep in that other room, Sonny; you're too drunk to drive home.' So I slept in the room, and Jack Entratter came in the next day because he heard the complaints. Sinatra said, 'Look what Sonny King did.' Jack said, 'Not only are you fired, but you're barred from this hotel.'" Sinatra made Entratter apologize, "which I wouldn't accept because it wasn't his fault at all. Jack Entratter was too much of a gentleman."

The Sinatra, Martin, and Davis shows, which began as something unique, became semi-regular affairs, whether they were official—such as the "Three Coins in the Copa" in January 1963—or drop-ins. "Dean Martin, Maybe Frank, Maybe Sammy" read the Sands marquee that September. An announcer stated the agenda on January's opening night: "Mr. and Mrs. Sinatra, Mr. and Mrs. Martin, and Mr. and Mrs. Davis present their sons—the Drunkards."

Typically the three would perform separate sets—interrupted to varying degrees by the other two—before going into the homestretch together. The illusion of anarchy was expertly affected. If something funny happened spontaneously, it went into the act permanently. Other "ad-libs" were written by Bishop. Sonny King claimed to have come up with one of the most famous sight gags: Martin hoisting the diminutive Davis into the air and announcing, "I'd like to thank the NAACP for this award."

"Sammy was the most beautiful little imp, and he'd always jump in somebody's arms," King recalled. "Anybody could hold him, he was so tiny. When he was in Dean's arms one time, he looked like a trophy. ... Sammy had a beautiful sense of humor, and he could always come back at you," King added.

They were high-flying times, literally. In November 1961, Sinatra swooped in for his Sands engagement on "El Dago," a $100,000 "flying hotel" equipped with an electric piano, sofas, a cocktail bar, and two restrooms. Jerry Vale remembers Frank wanting to show it off: "I said, 'Frank, you get through at one-thirty in the morning. I gotta do a show at two forty-five.' He said, 'No, no, we'll wait for you. Don't worry about it. ... You come back to my suite. We'll wait for you.'

"I did my last show. ... I run and change my tux real fast, and my wife and I go back there to his suite. They're all sitting there waiting. [Baseball manager] Leo Durocher said, 'Whatta you got on this guy? He don't wait for anybody.'

"He [Frank] had a way of trying to get you to go on the plane. He used to close the door, and if he flew somewhere, you had to go with him. So I said to my wife, 'Stay near the door. Don't let them close the door, because he's gonna go to Mexico and we'll have to go to Mexico with him.' He said, 'Where're you going?' I said, 'I'm leaving.' I ran out the door, because I knew how he was."

During that same engagement, *Sergeants 3* was being edited for its debut the next February. Sinatra secured a Las Vegas theater for a late-night screening and invited Jerry Vale along. There was just one catch, Vale recalled: "I said, 'Frank, I've got to do a last show.' [Later] he comes in and walks over and says, 'C'mon, let's go.' I started to walk out, and the fellow in charge of the lounge says, 'Where're you going? ... You can't leave. We've got a whole bunch of people here to see you.'

"So I grabbed Frank and said, 'Bobby [Entratter, Jack's nephew] doesn't want me to leave.' He said, 'Wait a minute.' He called Bobby over and said, 'Look here. If those people like him so much, tell 'em to buy his records.' And we walked out."

The "Maybe Frank" stint of September 1963 fell just after the Nevada Gaming Control Board moved to revoke Sinatra's gambling license at the Cal-Neva, claiming Chicago mob boss Sam Giancana had been given the "red carpet" treatment at the resort. Two months later, Kennedy was assassinated. The next year, the Beatles began an invasion of the United States that included a stop in Las Vegas in August 1964. At some point along the way, perhaps imperceptibly, the Rat Pack began its long slide into irrelevance.

# Cycles

The live album *Sinatra at the Sands* with Count Basie's big band was almost a coda to Frank's years at the hotel by the time it was recorded in January 1966. Following up on a one-night "concert performance" of November 27, 1964, the Basie-Sinatra teaming captured the end of an era without even knowing it. It's one of the few non-bootlegged recordings that contains all the showroom patter, from the opening salutation, "What are all these people doing in my room?" to the wind-down, in which Frank responds to an audience member, "One more what? I'm goin' to the bar. I'll be sayin' that to the waiter in a minute: 'One more, please.'"

The opening-night

"When you're drinkin' ... when you're stinkin' ..." The booze cart became the key prop in the Rat Pack's stage shows during the first half of the '60s. Though audiences seldom realized it, the joint performances became more ritualized and less improvised over time.

guest list included Liza Minnelli, who was making her Vegas debut with Jackie Mason at the Sahara. Frank also introduced "a lovely girl" named Mia Farrow. "I'll have you know I cut her hair," he said of the boyish new *Rosemary's Baby* 'do that had shocked the producers of her soap opera *Peyton Place* and no doubt her older boyfriend as well. That July, the 50-year-old singer and 21-year-old actress tied the knot in an afternoon wedding in Entratter's suite at the Sands. *Sun* reporter Harold Hyman found the singer "visibly nervous."

Some considered Sinatra's Las Vegas wedding to Mia Farrow in July 1966 as a struggle to remain in step with the rapidly changing times.

"We were both out West; it seemed right and we're in love and it was logical," Frank explained. Something else seemed logical, too: After vows were exchanged, Sinatra turned to those assembled and announced, "Let's break out the wine and caviar." Sinatra's third marriage of four probably seemed like a single sweet glass of champagne; he and Mia were separated by late 1967 and divorced in August 1968.

In September 1967, Howard Hughes, an old beau of Ava's, bought the Sands. Columnists began to speculate that Sinatra was about to jump ship to Caesars Palace, a decadent new $25 million resort that suddenly made the Sands look quaint. With the rumors flying, the Sands management was skittish about Sinatra's E-Z credit terms in the casino, particularly his tendency to keep his winnings but ignore his losses. One night a pit boss informed the star that his credit had been denied.

Sympathizers say the matter could have been dealt with later, when it came time to square the paycheck for the hotel's top draw. Others say he had bullied Sands employees long enough. Either way, the events that unfolded that night brought Sinatra the worst local publicity of his career from a media that had always handled him with kid gloves. "Sinatra Loses Teeth in Strip Hotel Brawl" shouted a giant *Review-Journal* headline.

Okay, it was just the caps of two front teeth and a bruised lip. Still, the incident in those early morning hours of September 11 found the King of Cool at his most unglued. The sequence of events varies in different accounts, but Paul Anka, who was performing down the Strip at the Bonanza Hotel, claims to have been there. "He got up on that table and started yelling and screaming right in the middle of the casino," Anka said. "I took him to the coffee shop with Jilly [Rizzo, Sinatra's longtime bodyguard and coattail holder]. He was livid—'We're gettin' the fuck out of here! We're going to Caesars!' He was really mad."

Hotel management decided to wake up casino boss Carl Cohen, who was known around town as a patient and benign man. "It was like three in the morning," Anka remembers. "[Cohen] was in his bathrobe in the back of the coffee shop. We took him [Frank] in there and he really got after Carl." When Sinatra tipped over the table between the men and threw a chair that hit a security guard, "Carl got up and punched him and all his teeth flew."

A Sands floorman told the newspaper that Sinatra then "went into the room where the switchboard is and yanked all the telephone jacks out. He was yelling at the top of his voice, and everyone in the place was jittery." Then the coup de grâce: Frank jumped in one of the golf carts used to shuttle baggage and, with a petrified Mia onboard, aimed the cart straight for a plate glass window.

*Ka-baam!* Sayonara, baby!

"I built this hotel [the Sands] from a sand pile, and … before I'm through, that is what it will be again," he reportedly declared. And he would never set foot in the place again.

The Caesars deal was announced the next day. Hotel press releases proclaimed the coming of "the noblest Roman of them all" on November 22, 1968, and gave Sinatra a conqueror's welcome. The black-tie guests began their evening in the 25,000-square-foot convention area, which had been transformed into "an Italian marketplace" buffet, before heading into the Circus Maximus showroom, which seated more than 1,100—nearly twice that of the Copa.

A parade of acts both veteran and contemporary built up to the main attraction. The Harry James big band was first, followed by the Fifth Dimension. Then it was flamenco guitarist Jose Feliciano doing his groovy version of "Light My Fire" and veteran comic Pat Henry. If this seemed like a deliberate attempt to confront the generation gap and position Sinatra in the present tense, then it was entirely in keeping with the singer's new album *Cycles,* which had him covering such current hits as "Little Green Apples" and "Gentle on My Mind." No square was he, the man who nonetheless treated the crowd to "This Is All I Ask" and the moving, authoritative "Soliloquy" from *Carousel.* The next year, he even opened his show with "Mrs. Robinson."

The Rat Pack, for the time being, defied the turbulent changes of the late '60s. But Vegas did not. The hotels that were once individually owned by front men for questionable "investors" were now being snapped up by corporate players: Howard Hughes (the Sands, Frontier, Castaways, and Desert Inn, where Hughes holed up in solitude), the Del E. Webb Corporation (the Sahara, Thunderbird, and Mint), and Kirk Kerkorian, who bought the Flamingo and then built the world's largest hotel, the

International, which brought Elvis to town in the summer of '69.

Vegas remained an oasis from harder rock for those not swept into the tide—remember, Dino's No. 1 hit, "Everybody Loves Somebody," came during the height of Beatlemania in the summer of '64. For a few years the city managed an uneasy alliance with the mods, simultaneously providing shelter to the Establishment while incorporating go-go boots into its stage revues for the open-minded and the old "swingers" trying to get groovy. *Psychedelic Topless* was a succinctly named show playing the Lucky Nevada Club in the fall of 1967.

And the grooviest thing on TV was *Rowan & Martin's Laugh-In,* hosted by a second-tier comedy team that had worked Vegas since 1953. Rowan and Martin owed Entratter for pulling them out of the El Cortez downtown and giving them a high-profile opening slot with Nat King Cole in 1956. When *Laugh-In* caught the frantic pulse of a schizoid

Caesars Palace proclaims the arrival of "the noblest Roman" after the Sands era came to an end in 1968.

nation in 1968, Rowan and Martin (the least interesting elements of the show) brought Alan Sues, Ruth Buzzi, and Jo Anne Worley to the Sands that December. The duo "must be as astounded by their sudden rise to enormous popularity as those of us here on the Las Vegas scene who remember the lads plugging earnestly for the past sixteen years ... without setting worlds or audiences afire," Ralph Pearl sniffed.

Dino ended up leaving the Sands, too. But he took his time, lest anyone think he bailed out of the hotel where he had a 3 percent interest just because Frank told him to. In early 1969, Martin cut a deal that gave him 10 percent of the Riviera, paving his way for a showroom debut that June. The Versailles Room was expanded by 300 seats to hold 1,000 people, including the va-voom-acious Ann-Margret and Connie Stevens on opening night. Dino's act hadn't changed much, though he threw in "Little Green Apples" along with the usual boozy shtick.

Afterward, the party ended up in Dino's Den, a rechristened restaurant where, according to a publicity photo caption, Dino and Frank were "yucking it up at paintings by the old masters with one slight variation: Dino's face was painted into every picture." By this point, Dean's four Matt Helm movies had run their course. But he had just finished working on a little picture called *Airport* that became one of the biggest movies of 1970. And his NBC variety show had been going strong since the fall of '65, offering a martini and innuendo haven from all things hippie and trippy.

Las Vegas claimed an occasional victory in the revolution. During Dino's debut stretch at the Riviera, Sonny and Cher shed their fur vests and love beads, changing into tuxes and sequins to work the Flamingo as Pat Boone's opening act. Sonny told the *Sun,* "I used to be considered a liberal. But now I'm probably a conservative." Cher noted: "We haven't changed our material. But we sing some of the older songs. I like the songs of the nineteen forties that my mother likes."

No one dug the whole *Laugh-In,* flower-power thing more than Sammy, who seemed to go out of his mind for a while there after his divorce from Swedish actress May Britt in 1967. After years of being kicked around, fighting for the right to sleep in the same hotel as white people, Sammy reveled in the peace-and-love inclusiveness of the revolution. "Doing His Own Thing," proclaimed a December 1969 Sands showroom ad that showed him in Nehru jacket and love beads, surrounded by psychedelic pop art.

The Vegas that remembered the old Sammy didn't know what to make of him. A bullnecked *Sun* pundit named Paul Price put the "love it or leave it" screws to him after Davis told a London paper, "America stinks and the whole world is in a mess, so I'm moving where people have decent values." But these were heady, insane times. The Manson killings were on the front page. The Osmond brothers were playing Caesars with Marty Allen. Bobby Darin—introduced to the Strip by George Burns in 1959—dared to call himself "Bob" and to wear blue jeans and scuffed boots onstage, flipping the peace sign and singing "anti-war and brutality to man songs," according to Ralph Petillo of *Panorama,* who pleaded for Bobby to come to his senses and "give us another 'Mack the Knife.'"

The whole world went crazy in '69. An ad for Sammy at the Sands reflects the *Laugh-In* era.

And what more can be said about this Forrest Duke column header from November '69: "There's a mod look and sound in both acts in the Flamingo Room. ... Al Martino, long a favorite with members of the Establishment because of his pleasant love songs, now has many of his songs newly arranged [by his conductor Al Pellegrini], which retains nostalgic value while bowing to the youngsters. Dick Shawn, a pioneer in the literal long-hair department, now has even longer tresses, and he kids the kids more devastatingly than ever, a mod device which brings yocks from groups of all ages."

But by the summer of 1970, the wheels were starting to come off the groovy train. That August, Sammy collapsed from pneumonia while filming a segment of the TV series *The Name of the Game* at Lake Mead. "I have to [slow down]," he told reporters, "or I'm not going to be around for long." He didn't slow down enough. A year and a month later, he was admitted to Sunrise Hospital in Las Vegas for what a hospital spokesman called "a misalignment of the liver caused by too much exertion." Not two months later, he was back onstage at the Sands.

Perhaps Sammy needed a vacation, but it was Sinatra who took one. After his hero's welcome at Caesars, Sinatra pitched another casino-floor fit in September 1970. The scenario was amazingly similar to the one at the Sands three years earlier: The casino refused to grant Sinatra more credit at the baccarat table. Sanford Waterman, one of Sinatra's Cal-Neva co-owners in the early '60s, was sent in to smooth Frank's feathers. Biographers now differ on the specifics, but all of them have Waterman pulling a gun on Sinatra to calm him down, and some have Sinatra saying, "I hope you like that gun because you may have to eat it." Local newspapers reported that Sinatra went for Waterman's throat. "My reports indicate Waterman still had finger marks on his throat where Sinatra grabbed him," District Attorney George Franklin said. "There seems to be reasonable grounds for making the assumption that Sinatra was the aggressor all the way."

The singer defended himself with a threat: "If the public officials who seek newspaper exposure by harassing me and other entertainers don't get off my back, it is of little moment to me if I ever play Las Vegas again. ... I have no intentions of going back—now or ever. I've suffered enough indignities."

Sheriff Ralph Lamb wasn't intimidated: "If he gives me any trouble, he's going to jail. I'm tired of him intimidating waiters, waitresses, starting fires and throwing pies. [Was this the Chairman of the Board or the Three Stooges?] ... I'm tired of him picking on the little people around here."

Frank decided he'd had enough. On March 23, 1971, at the age of 55, he announced he was retiring from show business for a period of "reflection, reading, self-examination."

On January 25, 1974, he stood on a Caesars Palace stage and told those attending a no-expense-spared gala that retirement had "seemed like a good idea at the time." But then, he said, "You wake up and find you've been replaced by Rodney Allen Rippy." The crack about the cute child star was directed to an audience that included Johnny Carson, Lucille Ball, Lorne Greene, Red Skelton, and Jack Benny. "My Way," recorded in 1969, had become something of a theme song for Sinatra, but he did not sing it on this night of renewed beginnings—Waterman was now out of the picture—choosing instead to go out on a high note with "I've Got the World on a String." Caesars ads proclaimed, "When the man sings, the whole world is in love."

Sinatra was back, but the Vegas he returned to was its ever-changing self. A few blocks away on that comeback night, Elvis Presley was opening a Las Vegas Hilton stand that was by now a twice-annual routine. Who was the real King now? *Sun* columnist

# Frank and Lefty

Nothing was more controversial throughout Sinatra's career than his friendship with the mob. His longtime affiliation with "the boys"—particularly mob boss Sam Giancana—cost him his friendship with President Kennedy and his casino license for the Cal-Neva Lodge in 1963.

But another friendship with a "goodfella" comes to humorous light in the wake of Nicholas Pileggi's 1995 book *Casino* and the Martin Scorsese movie of the same name. Both chronicled the drama surrounding bookmaker turned casino boss Frank "Lefty" Rosenthal and mob enforcer Tony Spilotro, played in the movie by Robert DeNiro and Joe Pesci, respectively.

In September 1977, Sinatra, his lawyer Mickey Rudin, and *Las Vegas Sun* publisher Hank Greenspun had combined their stock in an attempt to take over control of the Del Webb Corporation. When opponents brought up the Cal-Neva episode, Rudin fired off a letter complaining about the "cheap shot(s)" and claimed the entertainer threatened to "disassociate himself from the state of Nevada" if they did not stop.

Joe Delaney broke it down thusly: "If we are talking total attendance numbers, Elvis may have an edge [because of the Hilton's larger showroom capacity], but not if casino quality is taken into consideration. ... Ask any casino boss in town whether he would rather have the casino action with Elvis and two thousand people at the Hilton or Frank and one thousand at Caesars. ... It would be Sinatra, unanimously."

Dino was holding his own as well. While still a weekly presence on network TV, Martin signed a $200,000-per-week contract to begin working the 1,200-seat Celebrity Room at the MGM Grand Hotel. Like the International before it, the 2,100-room MGM was built by Kirk Kerkorian and stood for a time as the largest hotel in the world when Martin inaugurated it on December 5, 1973.

But a generational rift began to separate images of Frank, Dino, and Sammy. To their original fans, they behaved like icons—doing fundraisers, staging celebrity golf tournaments, and accepting honorary degrees. The little desert town that had served as their playground was becoming a city, and the three were generous in returning favors.

"This town made me and there ain't no doubt about it," Davis noted on December 16, 1976, at "The Greatest Birthday Party Ever Held," a $100-per-plate benefit for the United Negro College Fund, which was held at the Las Vegas Hilton in honor of his 51st birthday. Sinatra performed concerts to raise more than $5 million for the University of Nevada, Las Vegas, which in turn awarded him a doctorate "for his considerable work in humanitarian causes and efforts that have raised millions of dollars for charities"

But a scant three weeks earlier, Sinatra had appeared on the initial episode of *The Frank Rosenthal Show*—a local program Rosenthal used as proof to state gaming regulators that his presence in a casino consisted of something other than running it for the mob. The show was heavily promoted as the first in local television history to be televised live from a casino—the Stardust, the scene of the mob skim depicted in the book and movie.

Alas, only the studio audience saw the show. A tape machine broke down at the TV station shortly after the opening. Viewers saw a "One Moment Please" sign for the rest of the hour and missed the other stellar guests—Jill St. John, Robert Conrad—as well as Sinatra's plea for Las Vegans to protest the NCAA's two-year probation of the UNLV basketball team.

Early that year, Sinatra had lost his mother, Dolly, when a plane carrying her to his Caesars Palace opening crashed in the San Bernardino Mountains. That November, the Stardust hosted a six-hour, $500-per-plate tribute dinner and gala. Rosenthal was there, along with Allen Glick, the front man and token casino president played by Kevin Pollack in the movie.

at commencement ceremonies in May 1976.

But it's likely that many of those college graduates, now tuned to the ironic humor of the *Saturday Night Live* era, saw the aging swingers as dirty old men riding on drunken memories of their glory days. By the mid-'70s, the connotations of the word "Vegas" had changed as well. As rock grew from a revolution to a musical industry in itself, the city didn't fit into the new touring patterns that called for bands to play sports arenas. The gamblers hated rock anyway. Vegas became a city divided. On one side were the aging tuxedo acts; on the other, the middle-of-the-road pop stars—the Jacksons, the Carpenters, Donny and Marie—who didn't have enough rock credibility to worry about the stigma of playing a casino and who made the guys in gold chains and pinky rings feel hip and with it.

In this environment, Wayne Newton damn near makes sense. Along with beyond-belief magicians Siegfried and Roy, Newton is the rare homegrown Vegas act to become an international attraction. He did so by combining the Rat Pack-era saloon singer with Elvis' brand of sequined middle-aged rocker. "I was twenty-five or thirty years younger than the contemporaries who were doing the same kind of music," Newton says. "I was really a fish out of water, meaning a throwback to another generation."

Wayne started working the Fremont Hotel lounge downtown with his brother Jerry in 1959. A high-school dropout, he was too young to be in the casino and had to stand backstage or outside between shows. A Bobby Darin hand-me-down called "Danke Schoen" became Newton's breakthrough song in 1963, enabling him to record dozens of albums even if he rarely had an original hit of his own. The cute boy with the pinchable cheeks and high voice tickled the fancy of mid-America when he appeared on the Jackie Gleason or Lucy shows.

By the '70s, the high-school cuteness had morphed into a look that came to embody the quintessential Vegas lounge lizard: jet-black hair, Elvis sideburns, pencil-thin mustache, and—tapping into his partial American Indian roots—embroidered vests and a colossal belt buckle in the shape of a silver eagle. Wayne was the cultural bridge between Elvis and Frank. Sinatra dropped by the night Newton bought the Aladdin Hotel, while Elvis and his manager, "Colonel" Tom Parker, sensed a kindred patriotic country boy they could take under their wing. Newton's over-the-top shows would incorporate much of the melodrama of Presley's Vegas years: a spaceship descending to the stage for the "Also Spake Zarathustra" opening, a "curtain" of rain to make mush of that damned cake someone left out in "MacArthur Park."

# The autumn of my years

The 1980s began as a low point in Las Vegas history and ended with a boom that had no precedent. With Elvis dead, Sinatra, Sammy, and Dino were the only real names the city had to hang on to. It decided to make nice with them. After hearing character testimony from the likes of Gregory Peck and receiving a letter from President Ronald Reagan, the Nevada Gaming Commission erased the Cal-Neva smear of 1963 by granting Sinatra a gaming license to become an "entertainment consultant" at Caesars. "I'm not saying he's a saint, by any means," Board Chairman Richard Bunker said in early 1981. "But we have not found any substantial reason he should not be granted a gaming license."

Paul Anka notes: "I think that luster started to unravel around the eighties. He [Sinatra] was doing a lot of politicking, and I thought he had a lot more fun earlier." But then again, Sinatra was by now—finally—a happily married man. On July 11, 1976, he had tied the knot for the fourth time with Barbara Marx. "Las Vegas is very meaningful to me," she told the audience at a golf tournament gala after his death, "because this is where Frank and I did much of our courting. ... We saw more than just a few of those beautiful Las Vegas sunrises."

Though not as high-profile a newsmaker, Dean Martin had done astonishingly well at the MGM. Even after his TV show and movie career faded, he still pushed the

# Sinatra: Humanitarian and Lifesaver

Every sinner is also a saint. At least with Frank Sinatra, "the contradictory part of his personality was part of his mystique, part of his draw," noted entertainer Phyllis McGuire.

While Sinatra's bad-boy antics were celebrated, his good deeds were often less heralded. But in a small town like Las Vegas, his participation was all it took to launch the annual "Nite of Stars" benefit for St. Jude's Ranch for Children in 1966.

"When Frank said yes, everybody else wanted to come breathe the same air he did," Reverend Herbert Ward, the ranch's administrator, said of the event that became a boozy blowout for charity.

Despite the annual rollout of the Strip's top talent, the Boulder City haven for abused and neglected children suffered from administrative turnover and was $5,000 in the red by the time Ward faced the end of the 1971 fiscal year.

On a Sunday, Ward remembers, "I called the children together and we prayed, because that was the only thing I could think of to do." On the following Wednesday, a check mysteriously arrived from Sinatra for $5,000. The only note was something to the effect of, "Please do not publicize."

And some anonymous crapshooter may owe Sinatra his very life. In May 1969, Sinatra was playing blackjack in the Caesars Palace casino when the shooter doubled over in a seizure. Sinatra rushed to his aid and administered CPR until the arrival of staff doctor Joe Fink. Somewhere along the way, the entertainer had acquired "a good command of the basic procedure" and displayed it in front of the startled gamblers, Fink recalls.

showroom's 1,200-person occupancy limit between 1977 and 1981. His kidneys started acting up the next year, but it didn't keep him away from the "Miggum," as he fondly referred to the hotel. But when his son Dean Paul crashed an Air National Guard fighter jet in the San Bernardino Mountains in March 1987, the singer lost his zest for the good life.

Davis followed Frank to the Caesars Palace lineup in 1974. But Sammy was the rare performer to confess, in his autobiography *Why Me?:* "A performer like myself should play small rooms. Five-hundred seats." Nonetheless, he stayed at Caesars through 1982, when his bad habits began to get the best of him. The showman took his first extended break from the Strip, he later told the *Review-Journal's* Pete Mikla, to break a long-time drinking habit. "It was more a ritual than an alcoholic craving," he claimed. During his absence from the Strip, the singer fell at home and fractured three ribs in December 1983. "After all that drinking, I had to fall down when I was sober," he quipped. The fall caused him to miss a Rat Pack reunion planned for the opening of the Thomas & Mack Center, a sports arena on the UNLV campus. Diana Ross filled in.

Davis was back in Vegas working the Desert Inn with renewed energy in 1985, but was set back again by hip surgery in early 1986. "The hip just wore out over the years," he told Mikla. "Iron wears out, so I guess flesh and bones can wear out, too." A year later, he decided to ease the workload by teaming with Jerry Lewis at Bally's. "We're just about the last of the down-front performers," Lewis noted in October 1988, when the two taped the act for an HBO special. They combined their separate acts by performing a short opening routine that included testimonials about Lewis giving up smoking and Davis being on the wagon. "You didn't know you were at the Betty Ford Clinic tonight," Lewis said.

Only Frank adapted to the big sports arenas. In 1980, "[Theme from] New York, New York" was that rare new song that stood on its own yet sounded like one of the classics. The anthem became Sinatra's last major hit and gave people a reason to get fired up about seeing the 65-year-old legend again. Frank obliged—outside of Vegas, Reno, and Atlantic City—by touring like the rock stars did.

As far back as May 1969, *Sun* columnist Joe Delaney wrote the type of review that would characterize the rest of Sinatra's performing career. "As an instrument, his voice is all but gone," Delaney wrote. "He hits certain off-notes that would be considered unforgivable by someone else. But just like his attitude, even this song salesmanship sans 'voice' seems part and parcel of the complete Sinatra today. Perhaps that is why the autobiographical statements such as 'My Way,' 'Cycles,' and 'That's Life' were best received." If Delaney's assessment was premature considering how much longer Sinatra carried on, it never became less true. By the second half of the 1980s, Sinatra's vocal tones had become less important than his legend and his legacy. People wanted to see him—maybe for the first time, maybe for the last.

"He was doing sixty shows a year for Bally's [counting Las Vegas, Reno, and Atlantic City]," says Richard Sturm, who was entertainment director at the hotel when Sinatra joined Martin and Davis as part of the showroom lineup in late 1987. "There was certainly a new audience watching Sinatra. You could see tons of younger people really standing up and getting into it." At that time, Las Vegas had not yet started to reinvent itself and was still perceived by the outside world as a retirement home for has-beens. Sturm doesn't believe the perception held water. "People just don't fall into these rooms," he said. "They're very selective in what they see." The Rat Packers "were icons, people synonymous with Las Vegas, and people loved to see them."

Frank came to Bally's from the tiny Golden Nugget, where he had been working to further a business friendship, which had begun in Atlantic City, with budding casino mogul Steve Wynn. Sinatra's opening night at Bally's on October 29, 1987, came with a surprise. Just when he finished "Mack the Knife," Davis strolled out from stage left, then Martin from stage right. When Sinatra made a crack, Davis told him the dynamic had changed: "You ain't the leader anymore!" It was the last time the three would stand on a Las Vegas stage together.

But when Sinatra's management came up with the idea of all three hitting the arenas for a reunion tour, it seemed like just the ticket to make sure everyone's heirs would be a little better off. A month later, it was official. "It's unusual to be in this gear so early in the day," Sammy said when the tuxedoed trio greeted the press at Chasen's in Beverly Hills on December 1, 1987, to announce the tour.

"Don't believe it," Frank replied. "We've come home early in the day like this many times." The tour would reach those people who never made it to Vegas, he explained: "We thought we'd maybe get around the nation and let them see how bad we are." Sammy announced that he planned to do a medley of Prince tunes: "I'm opening with 'Purple Rain' since he's wearing my old outfits anyway."

Frank acknowledged, "We are being looked at by younger members of the audience. I don't do rock—I don't understand it. But maybe we can educate someone to a little better music."

True to their explanation, the tour would not include Vegas. But when it opened in the round at the Oakland Coliseum on March 18, 1988, fans essentially saw the three Las Vegas showroom acts combined into one. ("He'll do the trench coat, he does the drunk, and I play the little black Jew," Davis had told reporters.) Dino stumbled out to warble, "Drink to me only with thine eyes," before looking up to ask, "How long have I been on?" Sammy provided a dynamic contrast, still soulful as he scatted "I've Got You Under My Skin" to the beat of a snare drum. His tuxedo jacket came off to reveal a Hawaiian shirt, and as he began to sing "I've Got to Be Me," he walked to the upright piano and slipped a large ring on each finger. "You recognize me now?" he quipped.

Sinatra seemed at home in the center of the sports arena after performing that way for much of the '80s. Finally it came to the point where the magic, if any, would occur. The other two joined Sinatra onstage for some banter that seemed winningly familiar, albeit a bit labored. "You are still the chairman of the board," Davis proclaimed. "Yeah," Martin countered. "You're still the chairman, and we're still bored." They draped a blanket around Sinatra's shoulders and handed him "a golden-age cocktail" of Geritol and prune juice—"gets you going and keeps you going"—before all three goofed through "Side by Side," "All or Nothing at All," "Volare," and "The Oldest Established Permanent Floating Craps Game" from *Guys and Dolls*.

"Thank you for hanging in there," Davis told the crowd, and the sentiment went both ways.

It should have ended there. They should have gone out with style. Instead, their separate endings were sad and anticlimactic. Dino made only a few of the tour dates before dropping out, blaming the kidney ailment. (The gossip columnists blamed Frank for riding him too hard, and there may have been some truth to it: Frank told Larry King that Martin just wasn't used to working so hard.) Liza Minnelli stepped in to finish the tour, and Dino went back to Bally's. "Everything's perfect; I feel great," he told reporters during a quick photo opportunity arranged by his manager on opening night. "Frank sent me a kidney, but I don't know whose it was."

It was surprising that Sammy, being the youngest, was the first to go at age 64. And because he was the first, his death on May 16, 1990, hit the town the hardest. It was partly that he went so fast, after news of his throat cancer became public. But it was also because he'd been part of the town for so long, a member of the entertainment community who'd attended such "show kids" rituals as the Halloween Beaux Arts Ball as late as 1988. He was the guy who would send champagne to other acts on opening night, or invite groups of dancers out for Chinese food or for screening 35mm prints of movies in his hotel suite. Jerry Kurland, a journeyman tap dancer who performed in an act called the Dunhills, remembered Davis' salutation of "Howya doin', dancer?"— a means of acknowledging a fellow hoofer. "He cared for all the show kids, all of us who worked hard," Kurland said. In an unprecedented move of cooperation, the hotels on the Strip joined together to dim their lights for the fallen star.

Dino kept going—unfortunately. Perhaps it was a stubborn habit after 200 engagements and audiences collectively touted (by the hotel) as more than a million people, something that felt too familiar to quit. But he kept performing even when he was doubled up in pain, drawing a sigh of relief from the crowd when he would finally take a seat on a tall stool. A month after Sammy's death, Martin's old lines rang too true to laugh at: "If I'd known I was going to live this long, I'd have taken better care of myself," he'd say in a barely comprehensible voice. Struggling through unrecognizable versions of his famous hits, he grabbed at his chest, grimaced, and tried to blame his discomfort on a "bad hotdog." But people didn't head for the exits until he recalled the death of Dean Paul, looked skyward, and shouted, "Why, God? Why didn't you take me instead?"

The marquee at Bally's—which for years had welcomed tourists with Dino's name in customized cursive lettering—came down for good soon after. He lived the rest of his days quietly in California and died on Christmas Day, 1995, of acute respiratory failure. "Dean was my brother, not through blood, but through choice," Sinatra said in

A publicity photo for the aging lions' reunion tour in 1988 did a better job of conveying the spirit everyone expected than the shows themselves.

a nationally released statement. "Good times and bad, we were there for each other," he generously allowed, since Martin had been one of the few people who never put up with his crap.

Sinatra had a few more good years, or at least lucrative ones. People still paid top dollar to see him reading lyrics from a gigantic TelePrompTer and eventually losing his place all the same. He was the only one of the three to really notice the change the city would make at the end of the '80s. "What used to be the draw of the name of the performer is now the name of the hotel," notes Tony Orlando, the "Tie a Yellow Ribbon" singer who first played the Las Vegas Hilton lounge in 1970 and rode the entire showroom cycle before seeking greener pastures in Branson, Missouri. "What used to be Sinatra is now the Mirage, or the MGM, or whatever hotel is now the attraction. It's the environment you find yourself in, much like a theme park. ... They're not putting stars in now. They're putting cities in as the attraction: Monaco, Paris, Star Trek, the galaxy."

Sinatra had another word for it: papier-mâché. That's how Sonny King says the chairman described the changes in his town: "When he worked there, in his era, Las

Vegas was solid rock. And then he turned around and said, 'It's papier-mâché.'"

"That town grew up around him," says Paul Anka. "It kind of ran its course, and frankly he just stayed too long."

Some people liked to claim that in the Bally's era, Sinatra never wanted to even spend the night in Vegas, that his private plane flew him back to Palm Springs after every show. Not true, says Sturm: "He did at times go back, but he used to spend the majority of time at the hotel. He'd have dinner every night in one of the restaurants and tell stories."

In early 1992, Sinatra made the rare appearance in front of his hated enemies of the press to pose beside Steve and Eydie, Shirley MacLaine, and Paul Anka in a Desert Inn suite. The occasion? Announcing the hotel's return to a good-ol'-days star policy in its 550-seat showroom. "What?" Sinatra said, making a move for the door when informed of the capacity. "Let's go. I can put that many in my car."

By the time a typically bizarre list of celebrities—including Robert Stack, Spiro T. Agnew, and Teri Garr—showed up for his 77th birthday party in December 1992, there was a debate as to whether the chairman was embarrassing himself onstage and whether his friends should tell him to hang it up. "If I know this man, he must work," Anka said in July of 1993. "To tell him he can't work—it ain't gonna fly. His enjoyment is when he's onstage. That's his fix. That's his needle up the arm."

A flock of celebrities was again in town when Sinatra opened the new MGM Grand Hotel on New Year's Eve, 1993. Unfortunately, most of them were there to see Barbra Streisand. The $1,000-per-ticket concert from a superstar who rarely performed live was as big a world news event as the "Summit at the Sands" had been in 1960.

If nobody paid much attention to Sinatra, it was because nobody realized that he would sing in Vegas only one more time, on a weekend that concluded May 29, 1994, at the MGM. "People were forgiving of any problems he was having onstage," Sturm recalls. "I never had a complaint from anybody about those shows."

And so Frank Sinatra left Las Vegas the way he entered in 1951—without a big stir. No big retirement for him. Been there, done that. He never set foot in town again before his death, at home in California, on May 14, 1998. As far as Las Vegas was concerned, he went down swingin'.

> ❝ He [Sinatra] brought unmatched excitement to the Strip and defined the word 'swinger' for all times. With his little gang of merry men, he established forever a sense of free-floating fun and frolic that captured the imagination of the world. ❞
>
> Gregory Peck
> May 30, 1998

# The Beatles in Vegas

While the Strip had successfully intimidated Elvis and the Rat Pack still held sway in 1964, there was one force Vegas could not defeat: Beatlemania, the biggest musical happening since, well, Sinatra or Elvis.

"There's a revolution going on in this country—and *we're* the revolutionists," a *Review-Journal* letter writer named Chuck proclaimed in 1964. "What are we revolting against? People who are *old, old, old.*"

Chuck was protesting the paper's dismissive reaction to news that the Beatles would make Las Vegas the second stop on their now infamous 1964 tour of America. Announcing that the Fab Four would play the Las Vegas Convention Center on August 20 provoked a summer of anticipation and a generational war in which the city's youth took up arms (or at least pens) to protest the likes of *R-J* columnist Don Digilio calling the Beatles "fly-by-night entertainers."

Stan Irwin, the Sahara Hotel's entertainment impressario, booked the group less for his high rollers than for their children. Booking agents for the band "started at the Flamingo and went down the Strip" seeking offers, Irwin recalled in 1989. "I'm the only one who seemed to have known about the Beatles, so I bought them."

It's more likely the hotels considered them a "kids" act. It's doubtful the entertainment directors could have been completely ignorant, since the Beatles had already been on the *Ed Sullivan Show* and had charted several hits. Also, the first Beatles movie, *A Hard Day's Night,* was playing at the Huntridge Theater the week of their visit, and comedian Breck Wall was doing a parody of "the hairy quartet" in *Bottom's Up,* a sketch comedy revue at the Castaways.

When Irwin offered blocks of seats to each of the major resorts,

"they couldn't care less since they didn't know who the Beatles were," he said. But after 1,400 teens stood in line to get tickets on June 29, "they [the resorts] were calling back, frantically asking, 'Do you still have those tickets? Our best players' children want to see the Beatles.'"

The Fab Four flew into Las Vegas in the wee hours after their first concert in San Francisco. Hotel officials were congratulating themselves for pulling off a discrete landing—until the motorcade approached the Sahara to find it surrounded by fans, who had to be kept at bay by sheriff's deputies with bullhorns. The caravan pulled into the back shipping dock to slip the lads onto a freight elevator, and hotel employees "formed an arm-in-arm link, a fence of human beings," to hold back the crowd, Irwin recalled. "If any of us had fallen, we would have been stomped to death. It was absolutely frightening."

Showroom headliners the night of the Beatles concert included Liberace at the Riviera, Pat Boone at the Sahara, and Patti Page at the Sands.

Trivia

The Beatles remained sequestered in a hotel tower. They stayed in suite 4722, according to a newspaper account—probably accurate, since a *Sun* reporter and photographer documented the short hallway dash and barged in long enough to help Ringo Starr "work the telly" before getting the boot. Fans, in the meantime, were shooed away from elevators and stairwells below.

"The funniest thing," Irwin said, "is that the Beatles decided to take the date because they wanted to see Vegas. What they saw was the airport, the room at the Sahara, and the Convention Center Rotunda [the since demolished assembly center seen in backgrounds of *Viva Las Vegas*, which had played theaters that spring]." The Beatles headlined two concerts that included Larry Lee and the Leisures, the Insiders, the Righteous Brothers, and Jackie DeShannon. Ticket prices ranged from $2.20 to $5.50.

The Righteous Brothers' Bill Medley remembers the Beatles as a tough act to open for: Fans "screamed all the way through our show, [and] they were still screaming for the Beatles. ... It was an hour and a half they had to live through before they saw their guys. When you're talking about a thirteen- or fourteen-year-old, that's an eternity."

Photos of the event show the band on a simple stage rimmed by helmeted policemen. The front rows included a surprising number of men wearing jackets and ties—perhaps hotel high rollers who decided to go after all. But, says Nick Naff, the Sahara publicist who would later witness the comeback of Elvis, "there was an electricity in that room that I'd never experienced before in my life. ... It was actually so tense, I was afraid the minute they [the Beatles] hit the stage there was going to be a riot."

Most who were there remember that the screaming all but drowned out the pitiful sound system. The half-hour set included "Twist and Shout," "Can't Buy Me Love," "Long Tall Sally," and a nod to Vegas-style showtunes: "Till There Was You" from *The Music Man*. The *R-J's* Donald Warman determined the fans obviously cared "nothing about music in any form" and said the screaming robbed them of "an interesting and, in many ways, remarkable performance."

"I can remember one thing that was amazing," Medley recalls. "I wondered why they would turn the lights on when the Beatles would go on. It wasn't the lights going on. It was flashbulbs—so many going off at the same time it just lit the place constantly until they left."

After the show, the Beatles bantered with the press. When asked if they regarded themselves as musicians, John Lennon answered, "Well, we're in the union, so I s'pose you'd have to say that, in a way, we're musicians."

Then it was back to prison at the Sahara, where slot machines in their rooms helped keep the boys entertained. The next morning, they were off to Seattle and the *R-J* reported, "Las Vegas Survives Beatles—Barely." But, of course, Vegas would never be the same.

"We kind of watched that whole thing in five years go up in smoke," Medley noted of the Rat Pack scene. Not that Sinatra didn't hang on—25 years later, he was singing George Harrison's "Something" in the showroom at Bally's.

# THE ALL-NIGHT PARTY

The thick smoke. The clinking of glasses. Chatter and laughter. And tumult. Tumult? That's the word Keely Smith and other veteran lounge acts use to sum up the unique vibe of the lounge. "[Accordionist] Dick Contino is a good performer, but he doesn't tumult," the singing star and ex-wife of Louis Prima once explained. If booking the lounge were up to her, the lineup would include her former stage partner Sam Butera, as well as Freddie Bell and the Treniers—all heavyweights from the golden Vegas lounge era of the late '50s.

"My thinking is, if an entertainer like Sinatra is in the big room, if he's gonna get offstage and go in the lounge, he doesn't want to have to sit there and listen to a Vic Damone or a Jack Jones," Smith said back in 1992, when the Desert Inn was experimenting with name attractions in its "Starlight Theatre" (a pretentious '90s name for a lounge). "No matter how much he may like them, he doesn't want to have to sit at attention. He's gonna want to go in, have a couple of drinks, joke around with his friends, and have this music going. These people should be getting offstage in that big room and come in the lounge to have fun."

Back before Vegas needed roller coasters to show people a good time, the lounge provided the motion, if not the sickness. It was the place where the high and low rollers were separated only by a few tables, where the showroom headliner and the blackjack dealer met on equal ground. The place where the low-priced drinks and free music took the sting out of the casino's bite. And it was "the cheater's room," as one veteran of the Sinatra management camp called it, because "instead of the wife, it was where they met the girlfriend."

The main room, regardless of the headliner, was built around a formality. You paid your money to be dutifully impressed by a show, then you dutifully returned to the tables. The lounge, a stone's throw from the pit, was the rendezvous, the sober-up chuckwagon buffet at 5 a.m., or that one last drink before dawn.

"A lounge was happy," says Keely Smith.

"Lounges probably produced more revenue customers than the showrooms," adds comedian Pete Barbutti, who came to Las Vegas with a group called the Millionaires in January 1960. Because the showrooms offered dinner, "for three hours they didn't get another dime out of you." But in the lounge, "a three-hour period [offered] three different acts. The audience would turn over, plus it was not considered bad ethics to get up and walk out in the middle of a set to make a couple of lay-downs."

"In those days there were no nightclubs or sports bars where employees could go," says Freddie Bell. "They would all come into the lounge—showgirls, pit bosses. The five a.m. show would be packed. The Sands would serve Chinese food."

"Lounge" also became more than a place. It evolved into a musical form of its own, one that went from pre-rock-era tumult to later become the living embodiment of cheese: Who can't remember Bill Murray singing "Star Wars" on *Saturday Night Live?*

Both sides seem equally sublime now. In an era when pop music has had all the life squeezed out of it by marketing consultants, lounge resonates as the original definition of "interactive." You could shout out requests. You could joke with the act. It was the place with no wall between performer and audience, no pretense, and seemingly no script.

"A showroom act is A-B-C-D-E. ... You have to get those people back in the casinos," says Sonny King, the veteran entertainer whose contract with the Sands once called for him to work either the showroom or the lounge as needed. "The lounge shows, they didn't care how much you went over[time] or what you did after the first song— anything was ad-lib after that. ... The lounges were freedom, and the main showrooms were scholarly."

"I talk to the people one-on-one; I touch them, let them touch me. ... I talk to them as if they're in my living room," says Keely Smith. "That's what we call 'tumult.' It's having fun with them, having them answer you back. Having them call you Keely as opposed to Miss Smith. I like that warm friendliness."

The better the lounge act, the better you'd be duped into the illusion that a six-hour-per-night routine was really a spontaneous and freewheeling laboratory of entertainment. "There was always that feeling that, 'Oh, he might come and sit in your lap,'" says Claude Trenier, enduring front man for the pioneering R&B act the Treniers. "We always had fun. That's what I liked about the lounge." He laughs at the time his twin brother Cliff looked down from the stage to see that he had hit a six-spot on the keno board during one of the games he had bet before going onstage. "He didn't say nothin' to anybody. Boom! Right across the bar he went. The others were asking, 'Where's he going?' 'I don't know.'"

And you never knew who might show up, who might jump up onstage. "What was good about those days was the camaraderie between performers," says Trenier. "As soon as the [headliner] would finish his show in the main showroom, he'd head over to the lounge. Because it was a place to be seen."

Keely Smith: "When you'd walk in and see Harry James on the stage of the Flamingo, and he would see us and stop playing and he'd wave—and we'd wave—and everybody in the room would know Louis and Keely are there."

Louis Prima was the undisputed king of the lounge. With saxophone second banana Sam Butera and Smith—his wife from the time of his 1954 arrival in Vegas until 1961—Prima did more than anyone except Sinatra to fuel Vegas' image as a wild all-night party. Prima didn't invent the lounge anymore than Sinatra invented the showroom; he was just in the right place at the right time. But it was Prima who became the quintessential lounge act and put the Sahara's Casbar on the cocktail napkin of history as "The Wildest Show in Vegas."

Before Prima and Smith came to town in late 1954, the Strip had toyed with the lounge concept for nearly 10 years. Claude Trenier remembers working the Flamingo in the late 1940s, before the hotel even had a lounge. The freewheeling Treniers made their Vegas debut on a showroom co-bill with comedian Myron Cohen. "We just liked to play—we would have played for nothing," Claude Trenier says. Since the group had so little stage time each night opening for Cohen, they improvised: "They had a free buffet in those days [outside the showroom], and we'd set up [and play] out by the buffet."

But the casino was not yet sure how to react. The group would start playing and a crowd would begin to gather, so the pit bosses would yell, "Cut it off!" "We were cleaning out the casino," Trenier recalls with a chuckle. "We'd wait about a half-hour, start up again, then cut it again when it got too crowded. ... The casino wanted 'em at the tables." That, he says, "was more or less the forerunner of lounge."

As the Strip began to get more crowded, however, each hotel needed a hook. Bill Miller, entertainment promoter for the Last Frontier and the New Frontier, shared a theory with Trenier that still holds true: "The key to a hotel here in Vegas is, first, you've got to get something to draw people in. Second, you've got to make them stay there. Once they walk out that door, you don't have a shot at them. That's when they found out the lounges would stop the people."

Or babysit them. "When we first started in the lounge, the big gamblers used to seat their wives in the lounge and leave them," Smith notes. "And they were okay; they knew they wouldn't be touched, that nobody would try to pick them up. It gave the gambler the freedom he needed to go gamble."

# Music and mayhem

The first real lounge act, as it's come to be defined, was the Mary Kaye Trio. The name hasn't lingered like that of some Vegas legends, but longtime natives and veteran performers all give the trio credit for launching the lounge as a late-night gathering point and forum of improvisation. Their admirers included Judy Garland, Marlene Dietrich, and Spike Jones. Sammy Davis Jr. was playing congas onstage with them that night in November 1954, before he caught a late ride to Los Angeles and lost his eye in a highway car accident.

Norman Kaye and his sister Mary were of Hawaiian descent, but they grew up in St. Louis, Missouri, in a musical family. Norman had an operatic voice; Mary was a formidable guitarist, as well as a talented singer. The earliest group was known as the Mary Kaaihue Trio, a spin-off of their father's band, Johnny Kaaihue's Royal Hawaiians. In 1946, Norman was discharged from the Army and joined Mary and comedian Frank Ross as the replacement for the original third partner, who reported for active duty about the same time.

The trio first played Vegas the following year in the Last Frontier's "Horn Room"— so named because of the antlers and big-game trophies mounted over the bar. (Ross was quick to call it "the horniest room in town.") They were back on the Strip to work the El Rancho Vegas in the summer of 1952, and by the time of their return to the Last Frontier the next summer, they were riding on the momentum of TV appearances and a successful stint at Hollywood's Mocambo club.

This time the trio was booked into the Last Frontier's Ramona (dining) Room. When their engagement ended, Mary remembers Eddie Fox—a former dancer then serving as the hotel's entertainment director—suggesting, "Let's try the kids in the lounge." When the act began to pack the Gay '90s Bar, Fox told them, "You might as well move here." They ended up working the midnight-to-dawn shift for 22 weeks that year.

The trio's return the following summer did not go ignored. *Las Vegas Sun* columnist Ralph Pearl reported in June 1954: "Requests [for the group] have poured in from persons in all walks of life, with the show folks topping the list." Betty Hutton, Phil Silvers, the Andrews Sisters, Red Buttons, Milton Berle, and Red Skelton were now counted among the fans of the Mary Kaye Trio.

Norman remembers that chorus girls from neighboring hotels "would bring the whole line in," and "with the girls came the boys." The trio employed a versatile arsenal to keep the regulars entertained. "We never did the same act twice," Mary says. "We could put any song anywhere. They came back night after night, because they never knew what we were going to do, and we didn't either." By July 4, Pearl was describing a lounge that was overflowing at 4:30 a.m. with people who would "whistle, stamp their feet, and applaud like mad while spending their money with a reckless abandon."

"Our music was real music," Norman says of the trio that, by 1957, had a recording career with its own versions of "Mad About the Boy," "My Funny Valentine," and "Lonesome Road." Mary's progressive guitar playing and their complex vocal harmonies—often compared to the Hi-Lo's—gave the trio the ability to tackle almost any song. But the real secret weapon turned out to be Ross' comedy. When Norman was onstage singing a dramatic song like "Ebb Tide," Frank would make a big show of stepping down to the bar, mixing a drink, and tossing it down before the end of the song.

"Frank Ross was probably the inventor of what they call lounge comedy today," says Pete Barbutti. "Shecky Greene, Don Rickles, everybody who followed—they all learned it from Frank Ross. He's the guy who started that whole concept of tumult comedy, of not having routines and jokes. Someone would get up and go to another table, and he would refer to it: 'What are you doing over there? You should be over there.'"

Even the gents who eventually became known as the Rat Pack took a cue from Ross. "They used to sit and watch the lounge shows, and started to incorporate that spontaneity in the main-room set," says Nevada Lieutenant Governor and former entertainer Lorraine Hunt. She and her husband Blackie are both former lounge performers; his group, the Characters, alternated with the Mary Kaye Trio at the Sahara during the Rat Pack's 1960 "Summit at the Sands." Lorraine recalls how Ross "used to do a bit where he'd jump down and grab a big glass and start pouring in everything from every bottle along the bar. Then he'd find somebody at the bar to drink it."

The Mary Kaye Trio soon had all the hotels rethinking their lounges, booking larger and louder outfits to play small stages that had been designed for organists or piano trios. Most stages were tiny spaces raised above and situated behind the actual bars.

During their 1954 stint at the Last Frontier, the Mary Kaye Trio—siblings Mary and Norman with comedian Frank Ross (left)—pioneered the Vegas lounge as not just a place, but a freewheeling entertainment style.

"We did a lot of choreography, and we kicked over the bottles in the first show," Freddie Bell recalls.

The Flamingo Stage Bar rimmed its 120-foot circular bar with eight speakers, advertising "stereophonic sound" for show bands such as Three Dons & Ginny or the Playboys. Sedate string quartets were replaced by "the midnight to dawn beat" of the "wild" Bill Davis Trio or "television's zing zang zanies," the Kirby Stone Quartet. "The name of the game was liquor," notes Sonny King. "You get those people a little tipsy, and they'll go out and gamble. The bosses were wise enough to entertain this thought. They got better and better with the names in the lounges."

The pump was primed, and all it took was a little shuffle rhythm and New Orleans showmanship for things to break wide open. Enter Louis Prima.

# The wildest show in town

Las Vegas was actually a comeback for Prima, who was almost 44 the first time he set foot in town. The New Orleans native had written the standard "Sing, Sing, Sing" for Benny Goodman, which paved the way for him to form his own big band in the '40s. When the gravelly voiced bandleader hired Keely Smith as a singer in 1948, she was only 16 to his 34. They married four years later.

Prima's arrival in Vegas was not a stroke of genius, but of desperation. "Louis and I were flat broke," Keely Smith recalls. "I was pregnant and we didn't have a job." Prima and his fourth wife had attempted to breed racehorses on farm property they'd bought in Louisiana with an eye toward retirement. However, she says, "The horses took all our money, and by the time the big-band era went out and we got rid of the horses, we were broke."

Prima placed a desperation call to Bill Miller—who booked the Sahara, as well as the Last Frontier—because he used to work Miller's Riviera nightclub in New Jersey. "Louis called Bill, and he told him the truth," Smith recalls. "He said, 'Bill, we're broke and we really need a job.' Bill said, 'Okay, come on to Las Vegas and I'll put you in the lounge for two weeks.'"

The Primas and their band drove cross-country in three cars and arrived in time to discover that Cab Calloway was finishing his stint in the same lounge where they were starting theirs. That discovery almost cost them the job. Because the segregated casinos allowed black performers to work but not to socialize on the Strip, Prima was shocked to hear that his old friend wasn't allowed to sit and have a drink with him. "Louis tried to reach Bill Miller on the phone, who—thank God—was on his way driving to Mexico," Smith recalls. "Louis Prima was going to cancel our two weeks because of that. And here we were broke. I mean broke!"

Instead, the two weeks that began on November 24, 1954, were extended through the holiday season—traditionally the city's slowest time. Before leaving New Orleans, Prima had seen saxophonist Sam Butera and his band, the Night Trainers—who had recorded a single, "Easy Rockin'"—packing a club back home. Prima told Butera that if his fortunes changed, he would be calling. Before Christmas, he was calling. Butera joined the band on December 26 and, says Smith, "It just took off like a rocket."

Butera adds, "We thought with the sound entering the casino, it would make the gamblers start groovin' and betting and forgetting about what they were losing. And that's the way it worked."

Butera says he originally wanted to be a be-bop jazz saxophonist. But, he explains, "I had a family and it was hard to support them. In order for me to make some money, I had to change my style completely." He started listening to Fats Domino and other rock 'n' roll legends, and rearranging Prima's stock big-band arrangements to fit the "honkin' wild style" he was hearing in French Quarter nightclubs.

Local newspaper ads reveal the quick rise of Prima and the larger lounge scene. On the band's first weekend in town, it was billed in tiny print as "Louis Prima & His All-Star Quintet, featuring Keely Smith," tucked into the corner of an ad for the showroom act—"Arthur Godfrey's pals," the Vagabonds. By January 8, 1955, Prima's name anchored its own two-column print ad, which also billed three trios for "continuous musical entertainment" from 4 p.m. to 6 a.m. By the following May, the ad sported Prima's photo, and he was alternating with bigger names like Billy Ward's Dominoes (featuring a young Jackie Wilson). The band was now known as the Witnesses, and Prima's finger-popping tumult achieved its longtime billing of "The Wildest Show in Vegas."

When the Last Frontier decided to jettison its cowboy duds for a space-age look in the summer of 1955, the rechristened and heavily remodeled New Frontier included a new home for the Mary Kaye Trio: the "out of this world" Cloud 9 lounge, adorned with

CONTINUOUS MUSICAL ENTERTAINMENT

from 4 P.M. to 6 A.M.

LOUIS PRIMA

AND HIS ALL-STAR QUINTET

Also

Kay Martin Trio

Sando Deems Trio          Werner Trio

in the casbar . . .     HOTEL SAHARA

Louis Prima's accidental success in Las Vegas is reflected by this modest newspaper ad, which ran a scant six weeks after his first engagement at the Sahara in November 1954.

# Hey Boy! Hey Girl!

The swing revival of the late '90s and, with it, the resurgent interest in Louis Prima finally brought to light a nearly forgotten curiosity: the only movie Prima and Keely Smith ever made.

In early 2000, the American Movie Classics cable network aired the 1959 obscurity, *Hey Boy! Hey Girl!*—which has never been released on video—in tandem with a new documentary about Prima. The movie revealed itself to be typical of other low-budget double features from Columbia Pictures (which also drafted the Treniers for rock 'n' roll musicals): a song-driven vehicle that existed mostly to showcase its musical stars, and the thinnest of plots to drive it along.

Still, the movie lived up to its curiosity in ways that were mostly unintentional when it was made. Obviously, it offers a rare chance to see Prima, Smith, and Sam Butera and the Witnesses at the height of their Vegas popularity, doing large portions of their act in the musical segments. Beyond that, the feature is an odd contribution to the history of Vegas movies in that it really isn't one—despite the fact that it was mostly made there.

Newspaper reports stated that nine out of 11 shooting days were spent in Las Vegas in late October and early November 1958, mostly in and around the New Frontier. And yet, the dialogue makes no reference to Las Vegas, and the movie doesn't show any of the usual establishing shots of downtown neon or marquees along the Strip.

Judging by the squeaky clean plot, the movie was an attempt to introduce Louis and Keely to middle America. A friendly priest (James Gregory) steers the couple down the road to romance after Keely recruits the entertainer to play a fund-raising bazaar for her parish's youth camp. Perhaps a more neutral setting was seen as helpful in downplaying the legend of "The Wildest Show in Vegas."

But the movie may have been a little confusing to matinee audiences unfamiliar with the Primas or their schizophrenic town. The opening sequence shows Prima singing "Oh Marie" in the hotel's Venus Room and, a few minutes later, Smith coming into the hotel lobby from outside. (Freeze-frame the scene, and you see cars whizzing by on the Strip in the background.) But then the story shifts jarringly to the modest houses of an ordinary residential neighborhood. Familiar mountains in the background offer the only hint that the brief exteriors of the church and the house used as Smith's dwelling are in Las Vegas. (Best guess for the neighborhood? The downtown area south of the old Las Vegas High School.)

There's humor in watching the business-minded Prima, stilted even when playing himself, become a crusader for a kids camp while under the spell of the young do-gooder. (Oddly, Smith's character is named Dorothy Spencer, while Prima and Butera answer to their real names.) She becomes his new "girl singer" and eventually the recipient of the sexy Italian's passion—limited in the movie to a quick smooch after walking her home. Nonetheless, in some of their scenes, the couple's natural chemistry together compensates for the novice acting.

But small details, largely outside the formula screenplay, hedge even closer to reality: Prima's slick suits and the body language that reminds everyone he's "the Chief"; the couple's age difference, which the spoken script can't decide how to acknowledge; the banter among Butera and the band members, particularly when they're recruited to go on a hike up Mount Charleston to show Dorothy's kid brother Buzz that they're really swell guys.

The mountain and Mount Charleston Lodge apparently weren't closely enough associated with Las Vegas back then to blow its cover—both are identified by name. The gang discovers that the lodge has been repossessed by the city, and Prima has the idea to acquire it as a youth camp by selling $35,000 worth of raffle tickets. The most tellingly Vegas scene in the movie has the Venus Room's maître d' checking his reservations list and shaking his head at a couple until they contribute to a donations bowl.

murals of celestial bodies. If you happened to be in town the first week of June that year, your lounge-hopping choices would have included the Treniers in the Starlite Lounge of the new Riviera Hotel and jump-swing king Louis Jordan and his Tympany Five at the Sands.

The *Las Vegas Sun's* "On the Town" columnist Alan Jarlson wasn't so sure he liked the sudden developments. "It's impossible to hear the tinkle of glasses—much less the conversation of your partner—ordinarily so familiar with the tête-à-tête for which a cocktail lounge should be designed," he wrote. "All is muffled by the din caused by entertainers who insist on rivaling their vocal chords and instruments with an atomic explosion."

Everyone else seemed to favor the explosion.

"Lounge" was 40 years away from having its own designation in record stores, but it was clear that something special was taking form in these small rooms. Prima's sidemen would later say that the lounge helped him read people: If he could see the audience, he could tell what it wanted. That, along with being a natural-born showman, enabled Prima to inject the repetitive schedule of the lounge with a sense of spontaneity, making the crowd feel as if it was seeing something different each night.

"Everything we did, we found onstage—including all the lines that Sam used to throw," Smith says. A little-known singer when they came to Vegas, Smith saw her fame grow as she found her place in the stage show. The couple played upon their age and physical differences—the brash Italian lurching, gyrating, and mugging, while his thin wife in the Dutch-boy haircut kept her distance and looked on calmly, either in amusement or in horror. It was an interplay lifted almost exactly by Sonny and Cher for their TV show in the '70s.

"The deadpan happened because we did five, forty-five-minute shows, and I was up there like a half-hour each show before I even opened my mouth," Smith says. "I didn't know what to do with myself. So I used to just fold my arms, cross my legs, and lean up against the piano. And I watched everything that went on in the room, and the casino, too. And then when Louis would come and pull on my skirt, he would be disrupting what I was watching, and I'd look down at him like, 'Don't bother me.'"

The sets, on the other hand, fell into an exact formula. "He was a master at lining the show up," Smith says of her ex-husband. "He would feature himself in the first three songs, then he'd feature the trombone player, then Rolly Dee [DiIorio, who died in April 1997] the bass player, or sometimes the drummer. Then Sam, then me, then he and I would close the show together."

Freddie Bell adds, "Nobody could pace an audience like Louis. He was the best at pacing the crowd. He had a feel for an audience. I've never seen anybody better. He made everybody around him look good, had a tremendous way of showing off his people." The small band structure that had been an economic necessity conveniently left more open space for each sideman to shine. Film footage of the band onstage shows antics such as Prima vamping to "Oh Marie," with Butera parroting every vocal

Keely Smith adopted a deadpan stage presence to counteract the manic antics of husband Louis Prima and saxaphone sidekick Sam Butera. The Sahara act was "The Wildest Show in Vegas" by 1956.

phrase with a saxophone retort until Prima finally gets the better of him. "What happened?" Prima asks. "You can't play in Italian?"

"You will never see another lounge like the Sahara," says Sonny King, who worked there from 1955 through 1958, even while he toured with Jimmy Durante as a second banana. (He remembers once doing two shows with Durante at the Desert Inn, then racing over to the Sahara for his sets there.) "In the corner they had a barbecue pit. You'd eat sausages and peppers on Italian bread, steak sandwiches—in the lounge. I think the fire laws came in and took it out."

Musically, however, every night was "a challenge," King says. "I proclaimed that if you could go and do a good show in that type of environment, then you could work in the hellhole of Calcutta." With three bartenders working in front of the stage, he adds, "you really had to perform and capture their [the audience's] attention. It was a good time, and it was a terrible time in those years, at that stage of the game."

# They rock, they roll, they swing

The Sahara's success echoed up and down the Strip. Rival acts such as Mickey Katz were billed as "those madcap zanies in a riot of hilarity." Prima's influence is obvious in *Shakin' Up Vegas,* a live album recorded at the Stardust by Tony Pastor and his "Singin' Swingin' Pastors." Another copycat act was the Goofers, which later would include Rolly Dee. Collectively, the freewheeling attitudes introduced the spirit of rock 'n' roll to the Strip. In those brief years before the electric guitar took over the genre, lounge music was sometimes even called rock 'n' roll.

The success of Freddie Bell and the Treniers defies the usual perception that Vegas was alien to rock 'n' roll. That would be true in the '60s, once the Beatles redefined it. But Bell and the Treniers were early arrivals on the lounge scene, and both were in the movies that gave the infant music its name: Bell in the 1956 Bill Haley vehicle, *Rock Around the Clock,* and the Treniers in its 1957 sequel, *Don't Knock the Rock* (ad line: "For every cat and 'gator from the poles to the equator!"). Sam Katzman, the producer of both movies, was a regular Vegas visitor who rubbed shoulders with both acts, either in the lounges or in the race parlors, where they shared a mutual love of the ponies.

The Treniers—the plural surname of twin brothers Claude and Cliff (short for Heathcliff)—had been combining the words "rock" and "roll" to describe their sound since their beginnings in the late '40s. A promoter at the Blue Note jazz club in Chicago couldn't determine what to make of their sound and decided to bill them as "the rocking, rolling Treniers," based on the lilting background vocals, "We're gonna rock, we're gonna roll."

"Rock and roll hadn't got big yet," Claude Trenier says. "It was really rhythm and blues … mostly triplets. The white kids would listen to it because their parents didn't want them to listen to it." By 1952, however, the Treniers were neck and neck with Bill Haley—their neighbor in a Wildwood, New Jersey, club—in promoting the phrase in song titles such as "Rockin' Is Our Business" and "It Rocks! It Rolls! It Swings!"

The twins, with a band that included their lifelong saxophone sidekick, Don Hill, dropped out of Alabama State College—where they fronted the AlBama State Collegians—to play a 1941 gig in Columbus, Georgia. Claude Trenier remembers the logic: "What are we gonna be when we get out? Musicians. Well, we got a chance." But only after dropping out did they realize that the instruments belonged to the school: "We didn't have no foot pedal, no drumsticks. One of the guys went out and pulled some limbs off a tree [to use as drumsticks]. The promoter said, 'I'm not payin' for that shit!'"

But the band persevered until World War II temporarily separated the crew. Claude—who enjoyed being a singer more than a bandleader anyway—eventually joined Jimmie Lunceford's band as lead vocalist. It worked out so well that Lunceford kept him even after learning that the singer couldn't read music: "I fooled him for months, because while the band was rehearsing, I was listening to the melody. I had a great ear." The band scored a hit record, "That Someone Must Be You," with Claude as lead vocalist in 1944. When the draft board called up Claude, twin brother Cliff stepped in as a replacement.

After the war, Lunceford said he couldn't afford both brothers, that they would have to work out between themselves which one would stay. The brothers agreed, but first persuaded Lunceford to let them try out a gimmick they'd been contemplating, at

# Esquivel: Space-Station Vegas

When Bar-None Records released a compilation CD called *Space Age Bachelor Pad Music* in 1994, the title gave solid form to a gradually coalescing retro movement. "Space age" and/or "bachelor" suddenly became buzzwords to classify forgotten albums that had collected dust on the bottom shelves of thrift shops and used record stores.

The CD's composer, an all-but-forgotten Mexican bandleader named Juan Garcia Esquivel, was newly hailed as a genius by the likes of *The Simpsons* creator Matt Groening. Jaded young hipsters, who thought they had heard everything, marveled at the exaggerated separation of the "living stereo" that had tweaked the tweeters of hi-fi nuts with the essential gear in the late '50s.

The *New Sounds in Stereo* created by Esquivel!—emphasis added by RCA, his original record label—ventured to the outer frontiers of recording techniques to deliver amazing contrasts in sounds. Swanky Latin rhythms suddenly exploded into astral choirs or orchestral bursts, punctuated by out-of-this-world sound effects that still startle even in the synthesized age. It was the soundtrack of tastefully excessive living, even if the swinger image came mostly by implication. The dapper bandleader was sometimes seen as a bespectacled face on the back of the albums, but sci-fi paintings of luscious lunar nymphs dominated the covers.

Imagine what it would be like, then, to step into a time machine and out of the Stardust Hotel's *Lido de Paris* floorshow to walk up on the man himself—not only live, but in the lounge! Esquivel's new converts may not realize that he was a longtime Vegas fixture, anchoring the Stardust's lounge lineup from early 1963 to 1971.

Esquivel broke his hip in Mexico in 1993. The injury left him bedridden in his brother's house, able to enjoy his resurgence only by long-distance telephone calls from admirers. On Memorial Day weekend of 1997, the 79-year-old composer was happy to recall his days in Las Vegas in a slow and sometimes weak, but still cogent voice. (Esquivel since passed away.)

"I foresaw that the big bands were going to end, so I was preparing a small show," he said of the strategy that brought him to Vegas. "I presented the show [and] talked to the audience. I explained to them the reason why I was with a smaller group, because it was impossible to have such a large group as I had. Just imagine lodging and plane tickets for thirty people."

Musically, the reduced forces compelled the bandleader to be even more inventive. He came up with devices such as "boo-booms," his name for 24 bongos, chromatically tuned. "They could reach two octaves, and you could play melody," he said. "The drummer was very talented, and he had them set in such a way that they were compact."

Along with instrumental creativity, the ensemble had, well … visual appeal. Always one with an eye for the ladies (he was married four times), Esquivel determined that his slimmed-down ensemble would consist of six musicians and four female singers. When he first landed the Stardust gig, he auditioned 147 women to fill the four spots.

"Every girl was a different nationality—Japan, France, Switzerland, Italy," he said. "Four different nationalities and four different styles. If it was necessary, they would sing in English, but [each performed] one song of her own country. … The girl from Switzerland would yodel."

A yodeling babe had to surprise lounge-goers, particularly since the bandleader would position the ladies to the side of the stage when each show opened, as though they were going to sing only chorus vocals.

"I had dressed them so smartly," he recalled. "They were just so attractive, the audience was fascinated. They had such a display of talent. They were dressed in such a way that at one point, they tore their dresses with the Velcro material and they would show their legs. … Not to be nude, of course, but they would show enough to attract the boys."

The show was billed as "The Sights and Sounds of Esquivel," and the girls weren't the only sights. Predating Pink Floyd and Genesis by several years, Esquivel rigged up a light show in which, he said, "the lights were combined with the show, in combination with the chords. The guy who ran the lights was a musician, and he would combine them, small and big lights."

Show-goers would pour out of the *Lido de Paris* showroom to stumble onto this sound and light spectacular. "The idea was to have such an interesting group that the people leaving the show were attracted," he recalled. "The people leaving the show were supposed to gamble. [Our show] was kind of a compromise, because you had to be good enough to attract [some of] them, but not so good as to attract all of them. I used to have fights with the pit bosses: 'Juan, we want you to be good, but not *as* good.'"

Esquivel played piano and served as the emcee for the sets. "I was funny," he said, recalling part of his routine: "Good evening, ladies and gentlemen. My name's

Esquivel. The name is difficult to pronounce." If someone asked him to repeat the name, he would rattle off "all the names" he had in Spanish. "I am Juan Garcia Carlos ..." etc., etc., adding a list of family names before the kicker: "But you can call me Esqui!" Introducing each girl individually, he would say something like: "This little delicate fragile flower, so gorgeous, is Nana. Nana Sumi. She was made in Japan."

The bandleader used to keep 16 tuxedos backstage, because he would end up soaking wet at the end of each set. When each night's shows wrapped, he rehearsed the band at 7 a.m. before everyone went home. "Even at that time, still the tables were busy," he recalls. "We had to be busy. We had to be presenting completely new shows. There was such competition."

Audiences usually didn't know him as a ground-breaking recording artist; during Esquivel's first two years on the Strip, the Stardust advertised its *Lido de Paris* show almost exclusively. But headliners on the Strip considered him a peer. "[Frank Sinatra] used to go every time he was in town to see my show," Esquivel recalled. "He brought with him famous stars: Yul Brynner, Barbra Streisand. I knew [Sinatra] was there, because I used to receive a napkin with, 'Juan, please play "Bye Bye Blues."' I knew that was Frank."

Sinatra "could be very mean with the people he didn't like, but he was very generous," dropping $50 tips when he came to the lounge. "He was very humble," Esquivel adds. When introduced to huge ovations, Frank would stand up and "start applauding to the audience. Instead of taking bows, he would applaud to the audience. It was a nice gesture on his part."

Esquivel's good memories of Las Vegas include a night when a power outage silenced all the electronically amplified equipment. "Someone put some candlesticks on my piano and I continued playing," he said. Years of dashing back and forth between Reno and Las Vegas lounges finally ended for Esquivel when the Stardust closed the *Lido* show for an overhaul and used the downtime to remodel the lounge area into a race and sports book—which would prove a deadly rival for floor space in casinos for years to come.

Vegas would miss the tear-away dresses and exotic percussion solos, and subsequent lounge acts could have used a smidgen of Esquivel's imagination. As he put it: "You'd better be creative. Otherwise, you're just another guy."

a show at the Apollo Theater in New York: One Trenier walked off one side of the stage in the middle of a song, and the other one stepped onstage from the opposite side, picking up where the first twin had left off. "Man, we stopped the show cold," Claude recalls. "We went upstairs and took off our uniforms, and Lunceford came upstairs and said, 'Put those uniforms back on. They're still screaming for you.'"

The Treniers spun off as their own entity after Claude decided to stay in Los Angeles and began working multiple nightclub dates. He called his brother and announced, "Heathcliff, money's growin' on trees!"

Cliff joined Claude on the West Coast, and the twins started doing the switch routine they had done with Lunceford. It never failed to please: "We had a lot of people swearin' off drinkin'," Claude jokes, though one time the police saw him running in the alley behind the Melody Club and pulled him into a squad car—leaving a puzzled Cliff stranded onstage.

While the Treniers played the El Rancho and Last Frontier, casino executives started noticing their drawing power. Though Los Angeles would remain their home base, by 1955 they were spending much of their year in Las Vegas.

The sound that evolved from their kinetic, sometimes improvised, stage show also opened the door for them as recording artists. At the Riptide nightclub in Wildwood, said Claude, "We could be playing 'Am I Blue' or anything, and the crowd would be chanting, 'Go! Go! Go!'" When a record company expressed interest in the "Go!" song, they were forced to confess they didn't have one. "We were just singing that because the crowd would be singing it." But off the cuff they improvised two verses, then let Hill riff on the saxophone. The record executive loved it. "We decided we'd better go write some words," Claude said, adding that the 1951 song was "the first one that got up to the Top Ten for us."

Freddie Bell carved out some early rock history the next year when he cut a toned-down version of the Willie Mae "Big Mama" Thornton song, "Hound Dog," in his native Philadelphia. The song, he says, was "just a regional record." But it was a big region that included New York, Philadelphia, and Cleveland, and Bell says the song was No. 1 for 16 weeks on *American Bandstand* in the show's pre-Dick Clark days.

Like the Treniers, Bell didn't consider himself a rock 'n' roll singer until Katzman's movies four years later. "I never was really a rock 'n' roller; I was thrust into it by Columbia Pictures," he says. "I had always been a nightclub performer. ... We had the red outfits with little bellboy caps and brass buttons. We were more of a nightclub act than a rock 'n' roll band." The difference was obvious by the time Elvis Presley came to Las Vegas in April 1956. Bell and his Bellboys were "rock," at least in their ability to get 500 Vegas kids dancing on Fremont Street when the band serenaded them from a flatbed truck to celebrate the opening of *Rock Around the Clock* at the Fremont Theater. But when he went back to the Sands lounge, Bell still fit in. Elvis, on the other hand, "looked strange to us," says Bell. "We were not used to the sideburns and heavy hair. He didn't dress the way Vegas people did."

Twin brothers Claude (far left) and Cliff Trenier (second from right) showed the Strip how to rock 'n' roll when their group became Las Vegas regulars in the mid-'50s. Pictured performing at the Sahara in 1968, the Treniers kept rolling even after Cliff's death in 1983.

Bell had realized just how much Vegas was a world of its own three years earlier, when Sands entertainment impresario Jack Entratter hired him as a blind booking. Bell had never been to Vegas and didn't know much about it.

"I called Jack Entratter at the Sands and said, 'I'm here.'"

"Who are you?" asked Entratter.

"I'm the act."

"What act?"

"The lounge act. How do I get to the hotel?"

"Take a cab."

"Where do I stay?"

"Find a room."

"I drove to the Sands and it said 'Frank Sinatra' [on the marquee]," Bell recalls. "I told the band opening night, 'Don't unpack. They're throwin' us outta here.' When I saw the layout of the stage, the bottles in front of us ... I swear the first night I thought I was gone. ... The lounge was only twenty-eight feet away from the roulette table. A rock 'n' roll, screaming dancing band was unheard of in Las Vegas."

But Entratter and Sands owner (of record) Jake Freedman believed in the Bellboys and became their defenders against the protests of the pit bosses. "Entratter saw the potential of the lounge business," Bell says. "We were lucky that we stopped people from leaving the hotel, or else we were out of there." Fancying themselves a white version of the Treniers, the Bellboys covered the Treniers' songs in their shows, which happened to fall during a long stretch when the Treniers were working elsewhere. When they turned up in town again, Entratter checked them out and came back to report, "Hey, Freddie, I just saw these schvartzes up the street doing your act."

Being in good standing with the owner didn't guarantee the lounge acts respect throughout the casino. "If the casino had a game going, you were expendable," says Bell. "As small as the Sands was, you would automatically get a note [ordering the band to quit playing], especially if somebody complained." Whatever audience was gathered in the lounge was inconsequential if someone was losing $100,000 at the crap table—not uncommon in the roaring '50s. "Vegas was a dice town," Bell says.

Sam Butera remembers it similarly: "The pit bosses [were] coming to Louis and telling him, 'You have to be quiet; you have to turn the sound down.' Louis would get very perturbed, because what we were trying to get across is energy: Make these people happy and make 'em want to stay there and enjoy themselves. It got to such a point that Louis said one night, 'Pack up your things. We're going home.' That's the way Louis Prima was. He wouldn't take seconds from nobody, not if he thought he was right. He had to prove a point. Sure enough, we didn't work the next night. Then they came to Louis and said, 'There's no people in the lounge.' They came and begged him to come back to work."

Freddie Bell wasn't so lucky. Eventually, the Sands pit bosses were able to have a volume control installed in the casino pit, so they could turn the lounge PA system off themselves. One night, Bell and the Bellboys took to the stage and lip-synched for the better part of a half-hour, as though they'd already been turned down. Entratter was at the bar laughing hysterically, and since the former Copacabana club bouncer had protected Bell—affectionately referring to him as "Little Dago"—the singer figured it was okay. When the set ended, Entratter told Bell: "That's the funniest thing I ever saw. You're fired." Fired, at least, once the band finished the number of weeks left in its contract.

Bell was ready for a break anyway. His drinking and gambling were wiping out his salary. At the end of 1958, Bell swore he would move away from Vegas. "I was going on the road to earn money to come back to Vegas and pay my bills."

But by then, the lounges had become too lucrative to repress. They had taken on such a life of their own that no one really cared if rock 'n' roll, as defined by the electric guitar, had now passed them by. In fact, Sahara boss Milton Prell made it clear to his entertainment director, Stan Irwin, that he didn't want rock bands in his lounge. Bell, in the meantime, decided the rock fad was leaving him behind and changed his act to what he thought was a more commercial style, with more standards and some comedy. Irwin caught up to him in New Orleans and loved the new Freddie. He hired Bell for a two-week run in 1959 that lasted 11 years. For years, Prima and Don Rickles rotated as headliners in the Sahara lounge—which had expanded from about 160 to around 240 seats—with Bell working as Rickles' usual lead-in act.

Freddie Bell and his Bellboys—playing the Sands in 1953—were branded as rock 'n' rollers, but they really followed more of a nightclub tradition that adapted easily to the booming Vegas lounges.

Rickles' three sets began at 2 a.m. and ended as people were having breakfast from the chuckwagon that rolled into the lounge. "I always figured it was going to be murder, but actually [the crowds] were good," the comedian recalls. "But it was a tough way to go. It was three shows a night in those days. But you were young and full of piss and vinegar, so who cared? If I did it today, they'd have paramedics in the wings."

"We outdrew the showroom," Bell says. "There was a line waiting outside to come in the lounge. We walked out to a full room every show." Patrons had to "buy" their way in from three captains—"Ali Baba and the two thieves," Bell called them. "The sunken bar in front of the stage was where everybody wanted to sit to be picked on by Rickles." The captains would hold those seats, "waiting for big money to show up," even if it meant Bell playing to an empty front row.

## Packing 'em in

The lounges had become almost as important as the main showrooms, and the lounge performers almost as well-paid as the headliners. A main-room act was lucky to be booked for two to six weeks each year, but the top lounge acts worked year-round. At their peak, the Treniers were making $15,000 per week. "It was a bidding war in those days; now they bid the other direction," Claude Trenier says with a laugh. Instead of becoming a fixture at one lounge, the group worked them all: the Royal Nevada, Thunderbird, Mint, and Silver Slipper. "If you're gonna leave a five-thousand-a-week job, you've got to get more." The Treniers' manager, Seymore Heller (who also represented Liberace), taught them another trick: "Ask for twenty-five dollars more per week for every week you're held over. You know they ain't gonna let you go if you're doin' business." One extended engagement in their early days saw their salary go from $300 to $1,250 per week.

The Treniers and other black acts experienced the schizophrenic personality of a Vegas segregated by Jim Crow laws from 1947 to 1960. "We would go in and do our show in the lounge and then go sit out by the swimming pool to wait for the next show," Claude recalls. And no black performer, from Nat King Cole to Sammy Davis Jr., was allowed to stay in the hotel where he worked. Most were relegated to a shabby boarding house on what was then called "the West Side" (an area now just northwest of downtown). Eventually the Treniers spread enough good will that they were able to stay at a Strip motel; the owner and his wife were fans.

(Because Vegas was a young city, its racism was less deep-seated than that of the South. The segregation was more a concession to gamblers from the prejudiced states. The growing clout of the entertainers had much to do with ending segregation abruptly in 1960. Three years prior, Harry Belafonte had negotiated a written contract with the Riviera that guaranteed him the headliner's suite. Billy Eckstine had more direct methods, according to Claude Trenier. When a dice-table stick man informed him, "We don't let niggers play here," Eckstine cold-cocked him.)

By day, the lounge acts would golf together or hang out at the apartment complex where many of them lived, northwest of Sahara Boulevard and the Strip (now a rundown area known as Meadows Village, or as "the Naked City," which owed its name to the large number of showgirls who also lived there and sunbathed in the nude). "At night when you got off, you went to see the other acts," Freddie Bell says. "There was no competitiveness. Today, it's dog-eat-dog. The acts would kill each other to get the job. In those days everyone was on the way up. The town was building, and we were all growing with the town. It was like family. Performers were a family. One night I had Sammy Davis on drums, Nat King Cole on piano, Jerry Costanza—a great conga player— the Ritz Brothers, and Martin and Lewis onstage at the same time."

In 1959, Sonny King moved from the Sahara to the Sands, where he would be a regular for the next 13 years. His style was more in the standards tradition than like the shuffle or R&B acts. That, plus his father-and-son-like relationship with Durante, made him a favorite of Sinatra's. The chairman used to tell him, "You look like a truck driver and sing like a fairy."

King was often the lounge act during the Rat Pack's fabled showroom stays. He remembers the maître d' keeping people lined up outside the lounge by putting "reserved" signs on every table until it came time to collect lucrative tips for seating. "People would lose precious sleep because they knew the boys would come in," King says. Even locals who had to work the next day "wanted to see Frank and Dean. They didn't want to see them always on the big stage. They wanted to see them in the lounge because it was off the cuff."

Sonny King had his own following in the lounges while working as a second banana to his mentor, Jimmy Durante, in the big room.

King recalls that he would get things started by singing a song such as, "You're Nobody Until Somebody Loves You." From his seat, Sinatra would shout out, "Whoever you are, on my worst day I did a better job on that song than you did." And then King would respond, "Well, whoever you are, why don't you come up and prove it." And then Dean would laugh at Frank's rendition, and Frank would say, "You think you can do it better?"

"It took maybe a half-hour for all of them to sing one song," King says. "And then they would break a straw hat, or pour a drink on each other. ... On my birthday, Sinatra ran a party for me and threw the cake in my face." One night, King adds, bandleader Vido Musso was so blitzed, "he didn't realize that they were cutting his tuxedo pants to the size of bermuda shorts. I turned around and said, 'Vido, what happened to your pants?' He was so drunk, he looked down and said, 'Those damned dry cleaners! They shrunk my pants!' The next day, Frank got him a whole new wardrobe. But anything for a laugh. If Frank ripped the shirt on you, the next day you got a dozen shirts."

The stories that came from the lounges fueled Vegas' "Sin City" reputation. *Time* magazine called Prima's show "doggedly vulgar." The Treniers delighted audiences with a little ditty called "The Suitcase Song":

> I saw her snatch ... her suitcase from the window.
> I kissed her as(s) ... she departed for the station
> To see her brother Jack off ... on the train.

The Treniers also recorded a "race" or "party" single called "Poon-Tang!"—an old

Southern expression for the female genitalia. Like the comedy records of their frequent lounge partner Redd Foxx, the single was kept under the counter at record stores. As a publicity gimmick, the Treniers printed labels that read "Extra Fancy Lower Alabama Poontang" and wrapped them around sealed (but empty) tin cans. "We must have given out a thousand," Claude says. "Those things cost like two fifty apiece." They used to tell people: "There's poontang in it, so wherever you open it, be in an open space. 'Cause sometimes poontang spoils. And when it spoils—ooo-eeh!"

In truth, however, the lounges sported a variety of sounds, particularly as their drawing power increased. Bandleader Harry James settled in town and became a permanent fixture in the Flamingo's Driftwood lounge, often sharing the billing with Della Reese. Bandleaders such as Gene Krupa and Artie Shaw were commonplace. Country acts, including Bob Wills and Ray Price, played the Golden Nugget downtown, while Patsy Cline played Del Webb's Mint in December 1962, just three months before her death. (She was astonished by the money—$1,000 per day—but crushed to discover that she was playing all-night sets in a cramped lounge instead of a glamorous showroom.)

A teen-age Wayne Newton dropped out of high school in 1959 and began playing the Fremont lounge with his brother Jerry. The next year, Pete Barbutti made an inauspicious debut at the New Frontier's Cloud 9 lounge. As a solo act, he would become known to late-night talk show audiences as the comic pianist who made a cigar holder out of a toilet plunger head that was suctioned to the side of his grand piano. But he first came to town in January 1960 as part of a group called the Millionaires.

Employees who heard the group rehearsing its first day predicted big things for the musicians. But they were the support act for headliner Frances Faye, a performer with an ego as big as her piano. "She came in in a wheelchair," Barbutti recalls, because "she had fallen at one of the hotels and it was helping her lawsuit." She quickly informed the group that it could not move any of the music stands or equipment for her nine-piece band, even though it was a common courtesy to shift things around onstage. "We had to set up behind the other risers, and you couldn't see us. It was horrible. ... People were getting up and leaving because they thought we were a recording."

Entertainment Director Bill Miller was contacted during his vacation in Florida and informed: "You've got to come back and fire this group. They're chasing people out." The night Miller returned, Barbutti says, "we didn't know he was in the audience, but we knew we were a horrible bomb. We just wanted to finish the gig and get out of the town. We hated the town." But then Faye came off the stage and rolled by Barbutti in her wheelchair. "She grabbed me by the sleeve and, without any eye contact at all, said: 'The keys on my piano are a little sticky. Get some soda water and wash them off.'

"I just flipped, man. I jumped on top of her grand piano and I just went off," denouncing her and the hotel. But the audience started to laugh. So Barbutti called

A publicity photo for the Goofers taken at the Sahara in late 1959 sums up the manic, anything-goes atmosphere of Vegas lounges in the '50s.

the trombone player to come stand on top of the piano with him. Then the guitar player. Finally, even the drummer. "We did a show from the top of her piano, jam-crammed together. The audience loved us. Bill Miller was in the audience, and he signed us up for months."

Two years later, Barbutti went solo and eventually was contracted by the Sahara to work as either a lounge attraction or showroom substitute, as needed. "At the Sahara, there was a bartender who was there for over a quarter of a century named Ramsey," the comedian recalls. "He was a guy who never smiled. [Because] he was between you and the audience, it became a thing where I'd tell a joke and then run to the other end of the stage to Ramsey and pull him over and tell him the joke. He never smiled, so that became a joke in itself."

Working a Las Vegas lounge, Barbutti notes, "you have maybe seventy-five cities represented in your audience and maybe a hundred employment scenarios. ... They're not polarized. Your dimensions are widened. That's what always made Vegas the best place for a comic to work. It was more demanding, because when you were working Cleveland, you were the only game in town. But here, there were nine other guys working on the Strip. You had to work harder; you had to be doing new things because you'd get the same people coming back. It was more challenging, but the audiences were better."

But it couldn't go on forever.

# To better days

"Sometimes you can burn yourself out," says Mary Kaye. Her trio was the first of the major lounge acts to hang it up when they staged a celebrity-filled final performance at the Tropicana in 1966. Norman had moved into a real-estate career; he was the contractor for Harry James' house on the Desert Inn Golf Course. Ross, who died in 1995, went on to become a booking agent. He promoted the famous tennis match between Bobby Riggs and Billy Jean King in 1974.

The great partnership of Louis Prima and Keely Smith came to an end in late 1961 when their marriage fell apart. Though he was the life of the party onstage, Prima away from the spotlight was almost uniformly described as a cold, distrusting person with few friends. In New Orleans, he was known for voicing the words "union scale" when hiring musicians, but tapping two fingers to his chest to signal that he really was offering half that. As soon as a business meeting ended, he made copious notes of

## Guess Who?

You never knew just whom you might have been watching in a Vegas lounge.

Many fans know that Kenny Rogers belongs with Wayne Newton on the short list of lounge cats who became big concert acts, and that he established himself as a post-New Edition solo act by working the Golden Nugget lounge circa 1977. But Rogers worked Vegas even in the early '60s as part of the Bobby Doyle Three, which backed up the Kirby Stone Four in the Thunderbird lounge. (With me so far?)

"I played bass, and we did a lot of vocal things," Rogers recalled. "But I never sang the songs. The guy who was the piano player [Doyle] was a much better singer than I was."

The trio frequently shared the T-bird lounge with R&B dance act Teddy Randazzo in 1964. One of Randazzo's sidemen, Kenny Rankin, went on to a respectable career as a cabaret jazz singer. "We had the only dance floor in a lounge on the Strip," Rankin noted. "When the shows broke, this was the big hang."

Speaking of jazz, keyboard great Joe Sample played the New Frontier with an everything said in the meeting. "He didn't trust anybody—he had been taken advantage of so many times," Smith says. "We never had anything to do with the musicians. ... He always used to tell me, 'Babe, keep 'em over here. Don't let 'em in.'" Prima's offstage contact with his band was limited to open houses on Christmas and the Fourth of July.

It was about the time the Primas were testing the waters in the main showrooms—playing the Desert Inn in early 1960—that Louis began to cheat on her, Smith claimed. "I think he went through male menopause," she said. "I don't think Louis would have given up his career or his home if he could have controlled it. I'm just sorry I wasn't old enough to have figured out how to handle it and weathered the storm for a few years. But I couldn't. It hurt too much."

The two were divorced October 3, 1961, on grounds of mental cruelty. Just before their marriage broke up, Prima put $15,000 down on a $65,000 house on the Desert Inn Golf Course. "The only thing I got was [the] unfinished house," Smith says. "Everybody assumed I walked out of this divorce with a lot of money, but I walked out broke." Her confidence as a performer also was shattered, and it would be some time before she emerged as a solo artist. She married for the second of three times in 1965, to Nashville record producer Jimmy Bowen.

"I never knew how big we were until after we divorced," she says. Prima was afraid of plane travel, which limited the group's options outside of Vegas. "I was very happy.

R&B group called the Hollywood Nighthawks only once before deciding that playing piano in a Vegas lounge was not what he wanted to do with his life. "It must have been nineteen sixty; I was twenty-one years old," Sample recalled. "I realized that wasn't my cup of tea." He went back to Los Angeles to record three songs in a one-take rehearsal that landed the Jazz Crusaders their first record deal.

But the most schizophrenic lounge act of all had to be Dick Dale, "King of the Surf Guitar," who says he retired his Fender twang to lead a 17-piece big band at the Golden Nugget and other lounges during the '70s.

"I used to do songs like 'Danny Boy' and 'I Left My Heart in San Francisco,'" Dale recalled in 1995. "They loved my trumpet. I would get on the drums and do drum solos. They would never allow drum solos, because it would bother the people on the blackjack tables. But I did 'em the way Gene Krupa did 'em. They would tap their toes. When I did do the rock 'n' roll kind of stuff, it was kind of subdued. If I did a surf song like 'Let's Go Trippin','' it was very easy," he said.

## All Agree!
### IT'S TREMENDOUS ENTERTAINMENT!
### THE MOST EXCITING STAGE SHOW IN TOWN!

**Extra!**
3rd Show
Friday
2:15 a.m.
It's Swingin'

**Two Great Shows Nightly!**
DINNER SHOW 8:15 P.M. — LATE SHOW 11:45 P.M.

By 1960, the
Primas were
ready to jump
from the
lounges to the
big showroom
stage at the
Desert Inn.
But the
partnership
and marriage
both ended by
late 1961.

# LOUIS & KEELY
# PRIMA SMITH

### with SAM BUTERA and THE WITNESSES

★ Donn Arden Production
★ Carlton Hayes and
   His Orchestra

Wilbur Clark's
**DESERT INN**
**& COUNTRY CLUB**
LAS VEGAS, NEVADA

FOR RESERVATIONS CALL DUdley 2-6000

I was married to a man I adored. I had two wonderful children." Granted, not many housewives in the '60s worked from midnight to 6 a.m. But even that "wasn't abnormal to me," Smith says. "I'd sleep till noon. I'd get up and spend all day with my kids, then I'd take a nap and go to work at midnight. I was up onstage with my husband and people I liked. What was there for me to stop and think about?"

Prima introduced his new "girl singer," a 21-year-old former receptionist named Gia Maione, in the summer of 1962. In January 1963, columnist Forrest Duke reported that the bandleader had "bought her a sports car and whisked her off to Reno"—on her way to becoming the fifth Mrs. Prima. A month later, the couple slipped out after a Lake Tahoe gig and tied the knot 20 miles away, in the tiny town of Minden, Nevada. But Gia would never quite escape the shadow of Keely, and Prima's act was losing its "wildness" in the face of British rock 'n' roll.

Louis Prima's one remaining mark on pop culture would be as the voice of King Louie in Disney's 1967 animated feature *The Jungle Book,* doing a memorable duet with his Las Vegas showroom buddy Phil Harris on "I Wanna Be Just Like You." On October 17, 1975, Prima underwent surgery at Cedars-Sinai Medical Center in Los Angeles to remove a brain tumor and lapsed into a coma. Four months later, he was transferred to a nursing home in his native New Orleans, where he remained in a coma for nearly three years. He died on August 24, 1978, at the age of 66. Butera kept the act going even before Prima died, which angered Gia enough to sue him over using the name "The Witnesses." Butera changed the name to "The Wildest."

By the late '60s, the Vegas lounges were being attacked from within and without. Musical culture was changing with the Woodstock generation, and lounge bands eventually had to either get out or get groovy. At first the winds of change seemed to blow past Vegas. With rare exceptions, such as Juan Esquivel (whose cheeky hit "Mini Skirt" is kept alive today by lounge revivalists Combustible Edison), a look at the lounge lineups during that lovin' Summer of '69 reveals a city largely unfazed: Shecky Greene anchoring the big lounge at the Riviera, Harry James and the Doodletown Pipers at the Frontier, Righteous Brother Bill Medley at the Sands.

By the next summer, however, the Legitimate Theater at the new International Hotel was hosting its 200th performance of *Hair.* Pat Moreno's *Artists and Models Revue* at the Thunderbird offered the chance to "Rock Under an Orange-Colored Sky." The Mob was playing "Up, Up, and Away" and "A Taste of Honey" at the Tropicana's formerly jazz-heavy Blue Room. And a group called—whoa!—Magic Grass was working Nero's Nook at Caesars.

The late '60s were the golden years for at least one act, the Checkmates. The R&B outfit headed by Sonny Charles and Sweet Louie (Marvin Smith) held its own against acts such as Ike and Tina Turner (who borrowed the Checkmates' arrangement of "Proud Mary") and enjoyed its only hit song as recording artists, "Black Pearl," at the height of the group's lounge popularity in 1969.

Sonny and Louie grew up as boyhood friends in Fort Wayne, Indiana. They served

# Exotica!

Today it's the people from exotic locales who seem fascinated with Vegas, from the influx of new residents from Hawaii to the busloads of camera-snapping Chinese on the Strip to the Japanese whales who bet thousands per hand in the baccarat rooms. But for years, it was the other way around.

The Strip's fixation with all things exotic began in the early '50s and continued well into the '70s. Yma Sumac, whose eerie vocals were among the flood of lounge/exotica recordings reissued in the '90s, played the El Rancho Vegas in January 1952. By November of that year, show-goers had their choice among *Dancers of Bali* at the Thunderbird, the *Sans Souci Revue*—featuring Miguelito Valdez and his Music of the Americas Orchestra—at the Flamingo, and "a stirring United Nations Revusical" at the Desert Inn, featuring Ming and Ling ("those Chinese hillbillies") and the most exotic beast of all, a young Buddy Hackett.

The fascination with all things Hawaiian, Tahitian, and Cuban, and with just about anything involving a bongo drum, probably owed its appeal to servicemen who'd experienced a taste of the South Pacific before settling down to life in the suburbs.

A sampling of the island winds as they blew through the Nevada desert:

✳ Suave *Ocean's Eleven* hipster Cesar Romero hosted the *Havana Mardi Gras* at the Dunes in June 1957, with "50 Torrid Latin Temptresses!" That same year, the Dunes lounge offered Josephine Premice and her Afro-Cuban Calypsonians: "Wild! Savage! Electric!"

✳ The Kim Sisters' publicity bio claimed that the three girls—Sue, Mia, and Aija—sang for American troops during the Korean War in exchange for "food and goods they used to sustain the entire Kim family." A talent agent brought them to America, where they became overnight sensations after appearing on the *Ed Sullivan Show*.

The "terribly frightened Korean girls," as columnist Ralph Pearl recalled, ended up as part of the Thunderbird's *China Doll Revue* in 1959 ("20 of the most beautiful Oriental showgirls ever assembled on any stage ...") and soon settled into the lounge rotation at the Stardust, where they would be "draped in mink coats and expensive perfumes" (Pearl again), sharing the stage with Senior Esquivel for years to come.

✳ Of similar longevity were "Hawaiian charmer" Nalani Kele and her *Polynesian Revue,* also in the Stardust lounge throughout the '60s. The Polynesian production was among the first to break away from the Prima-style shuffle act and instead to offer a mini-production show featuring costumes and choreography. Kele married Shecky Greene in 1972, but this odd Vegas showbiz matchup did not last.

✳ Martin Denny was advertised merely as being "at the second piano" at the El Rancho Vegas in July 1951. But a few years later, the $10 million Hawaiian Village in

Waikiki signed Denny and a newly organized quartet to play in the new resort's lounge. Denny's combo soon became a must-see, and in December 1956, the group recorded its winning mix of martini music, bird calls, and bamboo sticks for the now classic *Exotica* album. "At the Shell Bar, and later in the lounge of Las Vegas' Royal Nevada, you could hear a martini drop when the group swung into one of its delightful compositions," noted the album's original liner notes.

"Mr. Cherry Pink"

Perez Prado!

El Rey del Mambo    the King of the Mambo

IN THE SHOWCASE LOUNGE

Tropicana

Till 5:00 A.M.

Perez Prado brought a little bit of mambo to the Tropicana in the late '50s.

Denny ventured to the mainland to play both the Royal Nevada and the Flamingo in 1957, then returned to convert the Sands into his own "Quiet Village" in November 1962, accompanied by what columnist Forrest Duke called "three lovely WOW!-type torso-tossers."

✳ Arthur Lyman, the vibraphonist who left Denny's band for a solo career in 1957, brought his own bird calls to the Tropicana's Showcase Lounge in November of 1964.

✳ And Les Baxter, who wrote the hit single "Quiet Village" and much of the rest of Denny's *Exotica* album, was billed as the "King of Exotic Music" when he and his Vocal Chorus played the Thunderbird in July 1952.

✳ Perez Prado, the Cuban "King of Mambo," worked into the mid-'60s in the Tropicana's Showcase Lounge after his hit, "Cherry Pink and Apple Blossom White," put him on the U.S. map in 1955. In the summer of 1999, another Prado composition— "Mambo No. 5"—was reworked into "Mambo No. 5 (A Little Bit of …)," a huge hit for Lou Bega.

✳ Steve Parker, a producer who was arguably more famous as one of Shirley MacLaine's husbands, promised "75 Ravishing Island Queens!" in his *Philippines Festival* at the Dunes in November 1961.

✳ Not to be outdone, the incomparable Don Ho and a cast of 80 threw "the biggest party ever held in Las Vegas" at the new International Hotel in November 1969. The revue promised "the 20 most beautiful Tahitian dancers in the world."

✳ For those who couldn't wait until sundown, the Flamingo hosted the afternoon show *Geisha 70*, starring Izumi and "a stage full of topless Oriental showgirls," that same year.

in the Army together under the late '50s "buddy system," touring in the entertainment division of the Army's Special Services. Afterward, the civilian version of the Checkmates set its sights on Las Vegas.

The trouble was, Charles recalls, "you had to have an act to play Las Vegas lounges." The quintet learned one: "We had the little broomstick with the pony's head on it. I'm talking real corny. But it worked for those days, because everybody did that stuff. Everybody wore wigs and hats and that kind of thing."

Fortunately, the Pussycat A Go Go came along in the summer of 1964 to serve as the city's first non-gaming rock 'n' roll club, occupying now vacant land south of the Desert Inn. The club allowed the band to be "high-energy without the comedy," Louie notes. Unlike the casino lounges, the Pussycat had a dance floor. "I think that was the thing that made it fun," Charles says. "Those who wanted to dance could, and for those who didn't, we were like the show band. ... Our beat was always constant, but we would do our shows around it."

The two made the transition to hotels such as the Sands and Caesars Palace. With jazz singer Nancy Wilson, they even recorded a *Live in Las Vegas* album that met with modest success. "But the tempos were all show tempos," Charles realized,

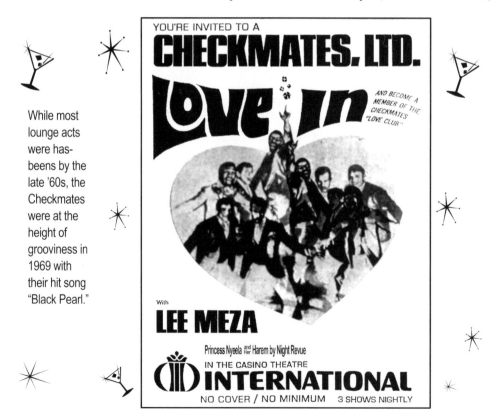

While most lounge acts were has-beens by the late '60s, the Checkmates were at the height of grooviness in 1969 with their hit song "Black Pearl."

and they turned to legendary producer Phil Spector to help them make a proper recording. "I don't care if you're a show band; we're making a record," Spector told the group during the sessions that yielded "Black Pearl," a Top 10 single.

In 1968, Freddie Bell saw the casino ownership shifting to corporate control and decided to retire to Newport Beach, California. His plan was to open a supper club that would enable him and his performer wife, Roberta Linn—with whom he had recorded the 1964 album, *The Bells Are Swinging*—to settle down and raise their children. But the 300-seat showroom arrived at the end of an era. Bell went broke in four years, and his marriage fell apart in the process.

He was trying to get voice-over work in Los Angeles when a musician from the old days told him to get back to Vegas—and to get back into rock 'n' roll. Bell spent three months making $600 a week fronting a band called Action Faction, which included three go-go dancing girls in G-strings who couldn't sing a note. "God, they were bad," he says. Stan Irwin urged him to form his own rock band, so he got "five outlandish people together" to proclaim, "Freddie's Got a Brand New Bag," changing the words to the James Brown hit. "I wore the bells; I wore all the outfits, trying to be what was happening at that time," he says. "But for me it didn't work. It was this totally rock, Woodstock kind of band, and here I was a Louis Prima kind of act. It didn't mesh."

> " We've shut down the factories—the lounges. Most of the showrooms, most of the nightclubs throughout the country are closed. So where do these people learn to do that? "
>
> Wayne Newton
> 1996

However bad the damage done by shifts in pop music, it was compounded by the attitudes toward the lounge within the hotels themselves. Gradually, they shifted from "headline" to "jukebox" acts, cover bands re-creating the Top 40 with an emphasis on the dance floor.

Sam Butera states: "What really annoys me is your people that are coming up today. They call themselves musicians. They're not musicians. They get a record and they copy it and they see who can copy it the best. They don't know how to entertain; they never spent any time trying to learn. It's just a lost art.

"I used to go and hang out after I got through work. Where am I gonna go hang? I'll go home and go to bed. I used to go look for a session. [When Musicians Local 369 was headquartered next to the Tropicana Hotel, the hall was famous for late-night jam sessions.] Session? Forget about it. You got no musicians in this town."

It's hard to say who inspired the "lounge lizard" stereotype as parodied by Bill Murray or Bud E. Luv. It could have been any number of performers trying to hang on to the "down-front" tuxedo school of cabaret performing in the rock era, even if

# Diamond Dave: The Eternal Gigolo

Until the "lounge" revival in the '90s, knowledge of Louis Prima to people under 40 was limited to either the voice of Shaggy Bear Baloo in *The Jungle Book* or shaggy rock wailer David Lee Roth's remake of "Just A Gigolo/I Ain't Got Nobody."

The latter was an unlikely hit for an unlikely singer in 1985, particularly since Roth copied Prima and Butera's arrangement exactly, rather than trying to rock out with it.

Sam Butera's approval seemed to vacillate depending on the night. Sometimes from the stage he would denounce Roth as a "goniff" (thief). Other times, when he was performing with Keely Smith, the two would settle for gently reminding the crowd, "We did not steal this song from David Lee Roth. He stole it from us."

"I discovered Louis Prima being played over a sound system in an out-of-the-way bar in Huntsville, Alabama, probably fifteen years ago," Roth recalled. "I carried [his tapes] around in my suitcase for years. It was something that I always listened to as a means of 'vacation' [from rock]."

Van Halen fans are squarely of two camps when it comes to the classic, hard-rock band: Dave Roth or his replacement, Sammy Hagar. While "Sammy People" like their rock anthems more sincerely melodramatic, "Dave People" are more disposed to what he calls the "classic show" school of shtick and patter. "I'm honored to be part of that circle," he said. "That's traditional and classic."

"Gigolo," he noted, merely updated a show business continuum that ran from the days of Al Jolson through Van Halen's extroverted brand of heavy metal. "That is the tradition of a toast

David Lee Roth was a little too far ahead of the retro-swing trend when he ditched the spandex and heavy metal hair in favor of a jumpin' jive look in 1994. The act fizzled and he was soon howling again.

and a tear," Roth said. "What makes that tune work? It's essentially a sad lyric. Why is everybody celebrating when that chorus hits? That's that old-world philosophy."

And so at least a few fans were rooting for him when Roth decided to become a Vegas showroom star himself in 1994. Drafting Edgar Winter to lead a large stage band and assembling some colorful costumes, choreography, and dancing girls, Roth set out to "create something new" on the Strip. "It's not about duplicating a time period; it's not about becoming 'Vegas,'" he said. "If we're going to access anything from the past, let it be an attitude … a certain ability to laugh and improvise."

All fine words—Roth is very good at words—but the act stiffed miserably and was abandoned after a couple of engagements. Booking agents should have realized the basic, insurmountable dilemma: Those who would have "got" Dave's show stayed away. Having already dismissed him as a loudmouthed ass, they probably never stopped to consider his potential for this type of thing. On the other hand, those '80s metalheads who remained loyal (mostly biker-looking chicks with lots of eye makeup and tattoos) were completely perplexed by Dave's new cabaret leanings and just wanted to "Jump." A toast and a tear, Dave!

Though David Lee Roth aligned himself closely with Louis Prima, another testosterone-oozing, chest-thumping, peroxide-blonde rock 'n' roll screamer—Motley Crüe's Vince Neil—ended up with the golf-course home Prima was building at the time he and Keely Smith divorced.

Neil moved to Vegas in 1995, seeking a break from the Sunset Strip glam-rock scene after the cancer death of his 4-year-old daughter. "I looked up at Spanish Trail and Summerlin, and those are bitchin' houses," he said of the newer, gated golf-course compounds.

*Trivia*

But when he saw the former Keely Smith residence, he was smitten: "I thought, 'Fuck, this is *cool*. It feels like Old Vegas.' That's what I really dug about it. … Any house that had a waterfall in the living room going into a koi pond, I figure that's the house for me, man."

they'd never had the legitimacy of their own recording career, à la Prima or Buddy Greco.

Dondino, who performed for more than 10 years at the Four Queens Hotel downtown, embodied the stereotype down to the giant medallion of a butterfly—he says that one once led him out of a forest when he was lost—nestled into his well-displayed chest hair. By the time he left town in early 1993, Dondino (Domizo Melchiorre) was perhaps the last dependable source for shopworn gambling jokes and lounge-lizard anthems such as "Volare" or "Tiny Bubbles." Even so, the man took pride in his work. "When I get out on a stage, it's not a lounge; it's a showroom," he said during his Four Queens heyday. "It's my palace. I don't care if I work—excuse my expression—a toilet. The customer is in a showroom at my show."

Many of the veteran loungemen—including the Treniers, Sonny King, and the Checkmates—forged gamely into the '90s. Butera and Smith reteamed for three years at the Desert Inn. But even if the material itself hadn't changed, allowing for moments of warm nostalgia, everything around it had. Claude Trenier recalled the last time that Frank Sinatra jumped onstage with him, in Atlantic City in the early '80s. "He called down and said, 'Tell the Treniers to hold up the show. Barbara wants to see it.' We waited for him." When Frank finally arrived, the Treniers led into "(Theme From) New York, New York" by joking about Sinatra's recent designation as an African tribesman. As the tune began to build, Sinatra announced, "They're playing my song," and walked up onstage. "The people looked [into the lounge] and saw Sinatra onstage, and they came like a cattle call," Trenier remembers. "Security guards were going nuts. They said, 'Get him off! Get him off! He's clearin' out the casino!' I said, 'You tell him to get off!'"

# Keeping lounge alive

One performer was able to keep the dance floor burning and the spirit of the Vegas lounge alive well to the end of the 20th century, proving that Top 40 cover tunes could be mixed with improvisational theater. His name? Cook E. Jarr.

Jarr is the one lounge act so irresistible that he could lure filthy rich showroom magician David Copperfield and his supermodel girlfriend, Claudia Schiffer, to a squalid little lounge inside the seedy Continental Hotel. He's the act that irony-based comedians Dennis Miller and George Carlin like to check out in their free time. And small wonder: How often can you see a jet-black hairstyle resembling that of horror movie hostess Elvira topping off leopard prints, leotards, hip boots, and sometimes, if you're lucky, a codpiece?

But with Cook—"not 'Cookie'; 'E' is the middle initial"—the audience is laughing with him, not at him. Putting his own unique spin on such Top 40 novelties as Tone Loc's "Funky Cold Medina" and M.C. Hammer's "2 Legit 2 Quit" doesn't stop the Jarr from reaching back to more classic show business by imitating Sammy Davis Jr. or Tom Jones (another admirer and sometimes drinking buddy). Nor does it stop him

Wearing heavy gold jewelry, tights, and sometimes even a codpiece, Cook E. Jarr carried the wacky spirit of lounge into the '90s.

from dispensing valuable advice onstage about everything from sports betting—he claims to gamble $300,000 a year at the sports books—to boiling the perfect pasta.

Cook E. Jarr was one of Vegas' first Atlantic City imports. Though he tested the Las Vegas waters with a June 1970 stint at Caesars Palace, he did not arrive to stay until 1982, after making a splash in the East Coast resort city.

The South Philadelphia native, once known as Anthony Pettine, says his stage name came from two sources. The first was a lounge singer named Tony Carr, who was popular in the Wildwood, New Jersey, resorts where Pettine spent his summers growing up. In fact, the two were often mistaken for one another: "You know us Italians; we all combed our hair the same way." The second source was Philadelphia Phillies second baseman Cookie Rojas. "I started thinking, what would it be like to have a name like that?" recalls Jarr. "I started turning it over. Tony Carr. Cookie Jarr." If the name seems strange now, back then it was like, "You gotta take the boy to the hospital—something's wrong with him," he says with a laugh. Although he wanted a name that would be easy to remember, he admits, "I think I went a little bit overboard."

Nonetheless, it was the name that went on his first single, "Please Be My Baby," which was purchased largely by factory workers at the Boeing plant where the aspiring singer was employed, building helicopters for Vietnam. His outgoing charm made him popular enough for his co-workers to elect him president of their union. But he was also well-liked by the "white shirts," which posed a dilemma: "The company said, 'What do you want to be a union president for? We'll make you a supervisor.' I said, 'Look, I need some time to think about all this.'"

Management didn't know that Pettine had already decided he would rather spend his days as Cook E. Jarr. "When I saw the Beatles, I said, 'I ain't workin' no more.'" Not that he totally dug the Beatles. It was more like, "What the fuck is this? They're doing old Chuck Berry songs and I'm workin'?"

So he decided to take a leave of absence and spend the summer of 1967 in Wildwood, where he hastily assembled a band to back him on tunes such as "The Land of 1,000 Dances" and Mitch Ryder's "Detroit Medley." An agent caught the act and asked the musicians if they'd be interested in working Atlantic City for $1,000 per week.

There was no need to mention that Atlantic City clubs were mob-controlled, or that ground-floor entertainers just provided distraction for second-floor gambling. What the agent didn't mention was that the mobs were feuding. When a car bomb blew out the back wall of a stage where the Jarr would have been performing later that night, he pleaded with the agent to get him out of the contract and headed back to Wildwood.

In 1969, RCA records released *Pledging My Love,* the first album by Cook E. Jarr & The Krums. The character on the album cover was draped in what people would now identify as a Prince look. "Only there was no Prince at the time," Jarr notes. "I would go to the drapery stores and buy material." He used to wear boots under bell-bottoms, capes, and big collars, "but always tight, tight pants, man. That's why the women would always show up, to check out the bulge." And that's just good business. "I'm serious. The tighter the pants, I always found I made more money," he says. "So then when baggy pants came in, I decided I'd give 'em a shot. Forget it. The money dropped off. The tighter the pants, the more money."

The Jarr and his nine-piece band landed a gig to fill in for the high-energy Checkmates a few times a year at Caesars Palace. Nero's Nook "was really a mini-theater, but they called it a lounge," Jarr noted. The name act playing the lounge during that engagement was O.C. Smith, who'd had his only serious hit two years prior with "Little Green Apples." Trouble was, Smith worked with an acoustic jazz trio of piano, bass, and congas. The Jarr, on the other hand, "came out smokin'" to a James Brown tune, doing what Michael Jackson made famous as "the Moonwalk"—"only we used to call it 'the Slop.'"

After a couple of nights of having to go onstage after the amped-up act, Smith "didn't want to follow us anymore," the Jarr recalls. He was presented with new set times—9:30 p.m. and 3:30 a.m. "My jaw was slammed," he says. "My intent wasn't to upstage the guy." He was outraged about getting the graveyard shift—after all, he adds, "It wasn't nineteen sixty-one anymore"—and he swore off Vegas after completing the gig.

It wasn't until June 2, 1982, that Jarr would return, after becoming a local sensation in the now legal gambling corridor of Atlantic City. Unbeknownst to him, the prospective buyers of the Brighton Hotel had caught his entire act: the cape, top hat, and cane; the champagne bottle stuffed down his pants when he was imitating Tom Jones; everything. They later told him, "We had such a great feeling, we decided, 'Let's buy this dump.'" They later bought the Sands in Las Vegas and sent Jarr there for two weeks to try to generate some excitement in the faded hotel. This time, he never went back. He trusted a family member to sell his house on the East Coast.

After all these years, Cook E. Jarr's followers will find him whether he's playing on or off the Strip. In his bejeweled hands, the tradition of butchering tunes from all genres with equal gusto—which can be Bill Murray-painful in lesser hands—rises to the level of art. "You gotta stay current," he says. "Everybody wants to hear the good stuff—the good new stuff. I do the rap stuff, but only if it's in the Top Ten. ... Tunes such as [Young M.C.'s] 'Bust A Move,' they're almost comical dance tunes that cross all the boundaries." But, in the old tradition, he works without a set list. "If I see cowboys walking by, I do fifteen minutes of country music. ... Anybody can deal with 'Achy Breaky Heart.'" Besides, he says, "You kind of scare away some of the people you don't want—the gangsters."

When it comes to crowning the next lounge king or queen, no heir apparent is on the horizon. The late '90s swing revival brought a resurgence in Prima's and Louis Jordan's jump-swing sound. But no one younger than Jarr—who in recent years has become the star of Harrah's outdoor Carnaval Court lounge—has emerged to do the full-blown "act" that combines music, comedy, and chatter. But, of course, everything goes in circles, and there's something indefatigable about lounge lizards. Perhaps the Jarr-man sums up the unsinkable spirit of lounge when he says, "If you never made it, you're never a has-been."

Or, in the words of Keely Smith: "I just think the lounge made us work harder. ... It kept our feet on the ground. When you're flying all over the country with first-class treatment in the best hotels, it's kind of hard to keep your feet on the ground. If you're in Las Vegas working midnight till six in the morning, and your best friends are cab drivers and hookers and waitresses, you're pretty normal."

# Vegas Rediscovered

In 1988, a punk rocker named Michael Cudahy moved his band Christmas to Las Vegas. "We had been obsessed with the music and the whole world it promised for a long time. ... It was like a weird calling," he recalled a few years later.

What he found disappointed him: "There were about three good lounge acts, and the rest were bad country bands or drum machines with a guy singing."

Cudahy came to a corny realization that reminded him of a certain movie. "It was like a *Wizard of Oz* thing," he said. "You're not going to find what you're looking for by going somewhere else. It's either in you, or it's not."

Cudahy determined that it was. He adopted the moniker "The Millionaire" and changed the name of his band to Combustible Edison. Because (even more remarkably) the band recorded on Sup Pop—the Seattle label that pushed grunge into the mainstream—Combustible Edison's *I, Swinger* album helped solidify a movement that came to be known variously as neo-lounge or "the Cocktail Nation."

"Eventually you realize there's enough chaos, depravity, and barbarism in the world," said the punker-turned-Millionaire. "There's a big void for something soothing and sensual."

The movement closely paralleled the early '90s return of swing (which eventually eclipsed it and nearly rendered it moot), reaching as far as to discover the music of Juan Esquivel and buried treasures such as Los Angeles' Dresden Room—where the aging hipster piano duo, Marty and Elayne, found themselves singing duets with celebrities and later making a cameo appearance in the movie *Swingers*. However, news of hot hangouts like "Mr. Phats Royal Martini Club" inside Johnny Depp's Viper Room on Sunset Boulevard was slow to filter back to Vegas, and the impact was minimal.

"[A friend] said, 'Keely, you would not believe what goes on there,'" a perplexed Keely Smith recalled in 1996. "He named me a girl from television, Christina Applegate. I don't know who she is, but evidently she's a star. He said that she goes in there on Thursday nights and does Keely Smith. They know all the Louis and Keely records."

Joe Sehee, a.k.a. Joey Cheezhee, introduced Las Vegas to the neo-lounge world when he convinced Bob Stupak to let him do his lounge-on-roller-skates act in the Vegas World Showroom in 1990. But with the exception of Sehee's friends—usually imported

Michael Cudahy (right) didn't find the Vegas of his dreams in 1988, so he tried to revive the lounge scene by adopting the moniker "The Millionaire" and changing the name of his band from Christmas to Combustible Edison.

on charter buses—most Vegas pilgrims expecting to find the Holy Land of Hipness went home disappointed. The larger retro movement hit the rest of the country just when Vegas had shed the cocoon of both its small-town ways and its storied past, embracing its first modern-rock radio station and L.A.-sanctioned hangouts such as the Hard Rock Hotel.

The Millionaire understood. Las Vegas was "the butt of so many jokes" for so long, he theorized, that "it's just not ready to get back to it." But he was not so naive as to look back on Vegas history through the oblique haze of a martini glass. The lounge scene idealized by Combustible Edison "probably never was," Cudahy concedes. "The image of Las Vegas is probably a lot like [that of] the Old West. It's probably a little bit of fact and a lot of mythology."

# Comedy on the Rocks

The jokes changed over the years, but the truth never did. Vegas has always been good for a laugh. For musicians, post-1960s Las Vegas began to pose that nagging question of credibility. Showrooms were fine for the Carpenters, Barry Manilow, or Donny and Marie. But Led Zeppelin? Yeah, right. Comedy knew no such prejudice or class distinctions. "Funny is funny," as Buddy Hackett would say, be it baggy-pants burlesque or cutting-edge monologue. The showroom door was open to all, and all have passed through it.

To some, Vegas was a way station: Woody Allen playing Caesars Palace in November 1966, or Richard Pryor co-billed with Pat Collins, "The Hip Hypnotist," at the Aladdin the following September. Others stayed as long as they wanted: Buddy Hackett's tenure from 1952 to 1996 rivals Frank Sinatra's. The open-door policy held true in the late '90s, when stand-up comics—Drew Carey, Tim Allen, Jerry Seinfeld, and Rosie O'Donnell among them—rose from the franchised comedy clubs, struck gold in TV land, then returned to a fat paycheck in the main rooms.

However, in a book called *Cult Vegas,* the focus must remain on the handful of nightclub comics whose showroom careers spanned decades, and who defined a distinctly Vegas ethic through their dangerous reputations and a boozy brand of humor. Three men in particular stayed in action from the '50s into the '90s, and it's safe to say that Las Vegas would not brandish its wicked legend without them: Buddy Hackett, Shecky Greene, and Don Rickles.

But the history of bad-boy comedy in Vegas must begin with a pioneer who came a generation earlier: Joe E. Lewis. Born in 1902, Lewis was already in his 50s when Vegas began to soar. His age and background bridged the vaudeville era to a new generation of stand-ups. Before he headed to the Big Casino in 1971, Joe E. pointed the way from the team comedy that marked the earliest days on the Strip—Abbott and Costello, the Ritz Brothers, Olsen and Johnson (who are buried in Las Vegas)—to the monologue as a less theatrical and more interactive forum. Joe E. also taught fans to celebrate their vices. "It's post time!" he'd proclaim in his gravelly voice, raising a glass to his twin passions: ponies and poison.

Those who know Lewis mostly through his movie biography, *The Joker Is Wild,* regret that his fame came before comedy albums and HBO specials. Frank Sinatra, one of Joe's biggest fans and boosters, blended so much of his own life and self-image into his portrayal of Lewis that his personality overshadowed the ostensible subject of the film.

Lewis' relative obscurity—a career confined to the nightclub stage—enabled Dean Martin and countless other public inebriates to appropriate his shit-faced shtick for a wider viewing audience. Most people don't even realize they're quoting Joe when they say things like, "You know you're not drunk if you can sleep on the floor without holding on."

Sinatra's blurred portrayal also ignored Lewis' song parodies, which were part of his act from the days of his 1933 breakthrough "hit," "Sam, You Made the Pants Too Long" (taken from the hymn, "Lord, You Made the Night Too Long"). Song parodies to the tunes of topical hits such as "Autumn Leaves," "The Great Pretender," and "My Way" were staples of his act.

"Joe E. Lewis never drew multitudes of people," says lounge star and friend Freddie Bell. "He was not a big draw like the big acts. But his customers were heavy gamblers." El Rancho owner Beldon Katleman loved Lewis, too. "[Katleman] didn't have to pay him, because Joe lost everything gambling," Bell explains. Joe's mid-'50s salary of $6,500 per week—modest compared to the money that began to fly to stars like Liberace—was sure to find its way back to the casino cage. Eleven years after the El Rancho burned in 1960, Joe quipped to his longtime "wiseguy" buddy Swifty Morgan that the money raised in a charity tribute dinner would go to pay off his marker at the casino.

When Lewis played the El Rancho in April 1951, he was still part of the unfocused parade of supper club headliners—the Ink Spots, Lena Horne, and somebody named Harry Richman ("America's Foremost Entertainer," ads proclaimed)—to march through the first hotel on the California highway. Casino Darwinism eventually thinned the herd to those acts who best appealed to gamblers, and Joe began coming back more often.

Putting strippers on the bill added solid beauty-and-the-beast contrast from the earliest days, if Lewis' 1951 opening act—Ming Chu, "internationally known Oriental dancer"—was any indication. Burlesque star Lili St. Cyr debuted at the El Rancho that same year as a separate headliner, but she and Joe were eventually matched in a frequent, popular co-bill of booze and broads; her choreographed musical routines provided the perfect classical prelude to his roadhouse jokes and songs. Joe was a product of vaudeville and burlesque tradition himself, and he had no problem sharing the marquee with billings such as 1959's *La Nouvelle Eve*—"Paris' naughtiest revue."

*The Joker Is Wild* suggests that Lewis had the voice to be a nightclub singer on the level of Sinatra. However, Art Cohn's 1955 book of the same name—the source material for the movie—reveals that comedy was woven into even his earliest days as half of the vaudeville team called "The Dardanella Boys" in 1925. But the pivotal incident in Lewis' life was spelled out in the book much as depicted in the movie: Lewis had become a popular draw on Chicago's speakeasy circuit when he defied Al Capone's top "soldier," Machine Gun Jack McGurn—later blamed for the St. Valentine's Day Massacre—to work a rival's club.

News sources differed on the year—the Associated Press said 1929; United Press International claimed it was 1927—as well as on the place, an alley versus Lewis' hotel room. Cohn's book says the incident occurred in the earlier year and in Lewis' hotel room; three hoods knocked on his door and, when he answered, attacked and savagely beat him. They fractured his skull with a pistol butt, slashed his throat from one side of his jawbone to the other, and punctured his vocal chords. Lewis crawled out to the elevator, found help, and eventually recovered, but his speaking voice was reduced to the bullfrog rasp that became his trademark.

In honing his comic instincts and song parodies, Joe discovered that his own hard-knock life and sinful pursuits could also provide grist for his comedic mill. Foster Brooks and other Lewis successors would try to distinguish the drunk stuff from their offstage personas. Not Lewis. He made only humorous attempts to pretend that the straight shots of Scotch onstage and the obsessing over racing forms were

Tom Douglas presents

# JOE E. LEWIS

AUSTIN MACK at the piano

3 SHOWS NITELY — 8:15 — 12 MIDNIGHT . . .

*A special exciting celebrity show at 2:30 a.m. Sunday thru Friday. JOE E. joins the 2:30 a.m. celebrity show every Saturday night.

# Lili St. Cyr

GEORGE · · ELAINE
TAPPS · · DUNN

DICK RICE AND HIS ORCHESTRA

AND A SPECIAL 2:30 AYEM SHOW !

EL RANCHO VEGAS

RESERVATIONS    DU 2-1300    EMILIO — Maitre D'

Though Lewis paved the way for a new generation of comedians, his vaudeville past was perfectly compatible with the striptease talents of Lili St. Cyr. The two were co-billed at the El Rancho Vegas through most of the '50s.

merely acts. Vegas was a small town, and people knew that Joe E. walked the walk like he talked the talk.

"Lewis is not only a great casino-crowd draw, but often puts on his best shows right at the dice tables," observed Katherine Best and Katherine Hillyer, authors of the 1955 book, *Las Vegas, Playtown U.S.A.* "Not too many entertainers dare go near the tables, [but] Lewis, Jimmy Durante, and the Ritz Brothers fight the dice right alongside the nonentity customers to the general hilarity of everybody." Everybody, that was, except Joe. "You can have the time of your life being miserable," he used to say of a Vegas vacation.

"He never drank during the day," says Freddie Bell. "He played gin. But he would make up for it at night. I tried to drink like him, which almost killed me." (This, despite the fact that Lewis battled diabetes and had part of his stomach removed in 1955 because of ulcers.)

"One night," recalls Bell, "I went to see him at the El Rancho, and he says, 'Let's go to the Thunderbird.' I didn't have any money. He says, 'Don't worry; everything's on me.' Well, he loses thirteen grand. I lose four grand. I think everything's on Joe. The next day, the casino boss from the Thunderbird says, 'What are you going to do about this marker?' So I go back to Joe and I say, 'Joey, last night when we went to the T-bird and gambled, you said everything was on you and I ended up losing four thousand.' He says, 'Was I with you last night?' He didn't even remember who he was with that night. I knew I was screwed."

In 1957, Sinatra lobbied hard for a Las Vegas world premiere of *The Joker Is Wild*. On August 23, 1957, his wish came true. Sinatra wore a jockey cap and held the reins of a horse, on which the tuxedoed comedian rode down Fremont Street to the doors of the El Portal Theater. Cary Grant, Lauren Bacall, and Carol Channing were in the audience. "If I'd have known you people were gonna eulogize me, I'd have done the right thing and died," Lewis told the crowd.

The movie was oddly sober and grim, with Sinatra's devotion to the comedian perhaps betraying his darker fears of the common ground they shared. Though the movie paints alcoholism as the ruin of relationships, it ends with an optimistic, "I can quit when I want to" attitude that suggests a bit of denial on the part of the filmmakers and the crooner.

Sinatra remained loyal to his fading mentor, who had moved to the Flamingo after the El Rancho closed and eventually to the Sands, where he and Sinatra shared the stage of the Copa Room in March 1965. Later that summer, the Sands built a new "show lounge" to accommodate Joe and other name acts. (On opening night, Sands greeter Jackie Heller told the crowd, "Joe E. is going to be late because he ran into his dad." Then Joe walked on with the punch line: "My Old Grand-Dad.")

It had to be one of Sinatra's toughest punishments to stay away from the Riviera on the night of September 13, 1970, when he was scheduled to co-host a testimonial dinner for Lewis in the Riviera showroom. Based on jokes reportedly told at the

For once, Joe E. Lewis got to ride a horse—instead of losing money on them—when Frank Sinatra led him down Fremont Street to the El Portal Theater for the August 23, 1957, world premiere of *The Joker Is Wild.*

bash—co-host Dean Martin said to "give [Frank] credit, or he'll bust up the joint"—it's likely the chairman was either boycotting the Strip or thought he had to keep a low profile after throwing a tantrum over casino credit and scuffling with a Caesars Palace executive and the local constabulary.

More than 1,300 other friends and fans packed into the Versailles Room to honor Lewis, who was by then a ghost of his former self after suffering a stroke. Tony Martin sang new lyrics to "It's Magic," written for the occasion by Sammy Cahn. George Burns, Jack Benny, Joan Rivers, Jimmy Durante, and Marty Allen all offered verbal salutes.

Then, as columnist Forrest Duke wrote, "The tears began to flow—from everybody on the dais and just about everyone in the audience—because it was Joe E.'s turn. He tried to complete his takeoff on 'My Way,' but not many of the funny lines ('I know I drank a lot, threw up on every highway/I was a souse, but not a louse, I did it my way') were audible." But when Joe E. proclaimed, "It's post time!" the audience rose and applauded loudly. It was one of his final public appearances. Joe returned to his native New York City, fell into a diabetic coma, and died a few days later on June 4, 1971.

# Flied lice and dirty jokes

One man paying tribute to Lewis that night at the Riviera had been working the Strip for almost as long. Buddy Hackett rose for a serious salute to Joe, but began by repeating with mock shame some of the choice profanities heard that evening. "I'm sorry I started it," he told the crowd.

If Hackett didn't invent the dirty joke, he at least made himself famous for telling it on the Strip. His act was shocking by the standards of those days and especially effective coming from a rotund cartoon character of a man—5 feet 6 inches, with a bulbous nose and funny voice—who could so easily step back into the sunlight world of *The Music Man* or Disney's *The Love Bug*. (Hackett filmed the 1969 Disney comedy during the week in Burbank, then headed to Vegas for 2:30 a.m. weekend shows in the Sahara's Congo Room.)

"My comedy comes from me," Hackett said of his inimitable mix of Catskills-era one-liners, spontaneous crowd banter, and locker-room jokes, which he told giggling with the contagious zeal of a seventh grader. "[A good comedian] doesn't consciously put it together. He studies. He learns."

Hackett had learned plenty by the time he first played the Desert Inn in November 1952. Born as Leonard Hacker in 1924, he recalled getting his first laugh from his family as a boy. Tagging along as an apprentice when his upholsterer father had jobs in the Catskills mountain resorts, Hackett was able to observe entertainers at work. By the time he was 17, he was working as a bellhop and making his own inroads into Catskills show business as a party entertainer. Before much more time had passed, he was earning a solid living in the clubs around New York state. "There was enough work for a guy starting out just in Brooklyn that he didn't have to go anywhere else," Hackett said. "There were forty or fifty clubs just in Brooklyn."

Hackett's first Las Vegas offer came in 1952, when his agent told Desert Inn operator Moe Dalitz, "I've got a funny kid for your show." Hackett claims he told Dalitz, "I can't work for two thousand a week."

"You're brand-new," Dalitz replied. "How much you want?"

"No, no, you don't understand. That's too much money. I don't know how to be funny for two grand. Listen, Mr. Dalitz, I can't do that."

"How much you want?"

"Four hundred a week."

"Seventeen fifty a week and not a penny less!" Dalitz said.

Billed as "A Fast Man With a Laugh," Hackett joined the *International Revue*—

"Saluting our friends across the sea with a stirring United Nations revusical"—for a three-week run that began at the hotel on November 4, 1952.

What constituted an "International Revue"?

"There was a flat of a boat, and you walked out like you were coming off a gangplank," Hackett recalled of the Desert Inn's modest staging. "There was a line of girls that did three spots. The whole show ran one hour and fifteen minutes, with four acts and three line numbers." Hackett shared the spotlight with "Ming & Ling" ("Those Chinese Hillbillies") and a monkey act.

The comedian made it back to Las Vegas a year later, sandwiching his evenings as the El Rancho Vegas opening act for Gordon MacRae around the November filming of *Fireman Save My Child*—a comedy originally intended for Abbott and Costello that wound up teaming Hackett with Spike Jones. By this visit, Hackett had scored a hit novelty record with his show-closing routine, "The Chinese Waiter," a riff on a misunderstood waiter in a restaurant frequented by Jews.

When he returned to the El Rancho Vegas in November 1955, his weekly salary was now up to $3,600. But home base was still in the Catskills, where he lived large

As a Sahara Hotel partner, top Vegas headliner, and all-around fun guy, Buddy Hackett ruled the roost in the '70s.

in the Concorde Hotel and drove a white Corvette convertible with red leather seats. Eventually, he was lured to the Pulitzer Prize-winning play *Lunatics and Lovers* and a 1956 sit-com, *Stanley,* with Carol Burnett and Paul Lynde, which aired live from New York. Still, Hackett says he "loved being part of the beginning" of the Strip. He went on to become the rare performer to appear there through four decades.

When the mush-mouthed comedian made it to the Sands for a 1958 co-bill with Julius LaRosa, he still worked in the crowd-pleasing set pieces, such as send-ups of Mickey Spillane potboilers and the Chinese waiter routine: "Flied lice! Flied lice! Whassamatta? You no speak English?" But he also was venturing into a more autobiographical niche with routines about early gigs in basement dives or the horrors of being at a drive-in movie without a car.

By 1963, Hackett had settled into regular gigs at the Sahara Hotel, which would become his longtime home base on the Strip. But Broadway would interrupt one more time. In the 1964 musical *I Had a Ball,* he improvised much of his role as a Coney Island carnival barker. Opening night was a critical dud, he said, "except there was one good line in one review because my Uncle Lou was one of the typesetters at the *Herald Tribune."* At the end of the next night's show, Hackett informed the audience, "The critics have taste in their ass," and sat down to talk, tell stories, and do little bits of his comedy act.

"A year went by and the show was still running," he recalled. The cast "all had jobs because I was doin' that thing at the end. ... I'm stayin' in that show, 'cause it's all these kids' jobs." But at the end of a year, the cast didn't seem so appreciative. One night he yelled at them for making too much noise in the downstairs dressing rooms while he was still onstage, and they threatened to file a complaint with the Actors Equity Union. Rather than fight, Hackett quit: "I said, 'I don't wanna be in no more shows. I'm goin' to Las Vegas.' And that was it. I went to Las Vegas."

As he honed in on the casino crowds, his comedy became less stagey and more nightclubby, more circuitous and less structured. He would start with a lengthy joke or personal anecdote. Something in that story would remind him of another one. Or the anecdote would provoke a conversation with the audience. Later—sometimes much later, when you least expected it—he'd hit you with the end of the first joke. Often he would have seven or eight stories going at once.

"Ever sit home with a remote control and change channels?" Hackett noted in 1992. "I'm trying to be the remote unit. ... At first I didn't know I was doing that. I only figured that out about a year ago." In the early years, comedians were expected to adhere to a certain formula: an opening song, a little mimicry, the one-liners, and a song-and-dance finish. "Over the years I started to get rid of all that," he said. "I started to just walk out onstage, and I would start in the middle of the sentence: 'And another thing ...' People would turn to each other: 'What was the first thing?' I would just talk until I couldn't talk no more. Sometimes I finished with a song; sometimes I didn't. I gave up bands and all that, because I hated rehearsing."

As the '60s progressed, the off-color stories became Hackett's other trademark. His oft-repeated rationalization: "If it's funny, it isn't dirty. If it's dirty, it isn't funny." Or, "The only really dirty word is 'kill.'" While Joe E. Lewis' burlesque variety of stand-up had been suggestive, he drew the line at profanity onstage. Hackett pushed the envelope, not only saying the words himself, but coaxing them out of matronly ringsiders. By 1968, "Adults Only" signs were posted outside the showroom to warn those who might confuse his film image with the nightclub show.

The dirtiness was "a rebellion," in the opinion of Buddy's contemporary, Shecky Greene: "He was getting tired of doing those [standard] things. I think it had a lot to do with when Lenny Bruce got big. Lenny and he were very close friends, and I think he took on that thing thinking he could do it."

By today's standards, the act would be considered relatively tame. "I've seen things on TV that make me look like a Boy Scout," Hackett said in 1989. Comedian Pete Barbutti notes that the shock value of the day overshadowed the admirable craft that went into the routines: "He put the [off-color stuff] into such context that you couldn't help but say, 'Son of a gun, the guy is right.' It's brilliant the way he introduced the words into the show and then managed to work around them."

Hackett never repented. "No doubt about it. Bob Hope went a lot further than Buddy Hackett," he said. "But he didn't do it wrong, and I didn't do it wrong."

Hackett was the rare performer who also became a corporate executive in a Las Vegas hotel. Thanks to his personal friendship with contractor and Sahara owner Del Webb, Hackett was named the Sahara's vice president of entertainment. "I didn't sit in an office; I just went to corporate meetings and offered my suggestions," he explained. "Then I worked with the nominal head of entertainment about what our plan should be. I tried to keep [the Congo Room] a great comedy room. We had very few headliners that weren't comedians. We had Rowan and Martin, Johnny [Carson], Jack Benny ..."

Always a dollars-and-cents guy who used the word "work" instead of "performing" or "entertaining," Hackett was proud of being a "hotel man."

"I may not be the best comedian in the world, but I've always been a good businessman," he said. "I was always proud to be that, even more than being the best comedian on earth. Every comedian is the best comedian on earth one night." Even when he returned to the Desert Inn in 1992 to perform on Monday and Tuesday nights, Hackett was keenly attuned to his crowd counts. "I don't want to sell out ninety percent. ... I want to get the extra eighty people," he said. When asked why—since he was working for a straight salary rather than a door split—he sputtered as though it was too obvious to bother explaining. "I want the casino to show that other difference in money."

Hackett never became an official Las Vegas resident, but lived in a hotel-owned golf-course house when he was in town. And he maintains that, unlike Lewis, he never fell in with the city's assorted vices. "I worked and I played golf," he said. "I never was on the Strip except to go to work. After work I'd go home, to my little house. I never hung out. My life was very uneventful, very quiet. All my energy was right onstage. And between shows I never left the dressing room.

"In twenty-two years at the Sahara, I never once had dinner in the House of Lords [steak house]," he added. "Rickles had the stamina and the ability to do the first show, go down and have a big dinner with wine and cocktails. ... I'd go to my dressing room at seven p.m. and stay there until two-thirty a.m. without eating a thing. I couldn't work with anything in me. I ate my last food at two-thirty in the afternoon and my next food at two-thirty in the morning."

# No spray wax

If Hackett faced his obsessions backstage, Shecky Greene wishes he hadn't been so public with his. Greene's wild-man reputation in the '60s outdid Joe E. Lewis' gentleman drunk of the '50s. One of the many sad ironies of Greene's career, notes longtime friend and fellow comedian Pete Barbutti, is that the legend of his antics sometimes outsteps his achievements onstage. "Shecky never knew how talented he was—and until this day has no idea," Barbutti says. "He thinks he was funny. He has no idea how brilliant he was."

Greene debuted on the Strip two years after Hackett, at the Last Frontier in 1954. "That was almost the last frontier for my life," he said. "I started drinking very badly

## A Night on the Town

Many tales are told about the good old days of Vegas. This is one of them. It's recounted by Pete Barbutti, with the precision and detail of a story told many times.

According to Barbutti, whenever Shecky Greene decided to go on the wagon, he would phase into it with a big solo drinking binge to brace himself for the coming dry spell. One such night circa 1973 or 1974, he was getting the job done at a Paradise Road restaurant called Villa D'Este (now Piero's), when Buddy Hackett tracked him down and joined him, setting his handgun on the table—Hackett had a permit to carry a concealed weapon—to the mutual discomfort and annoyance of Greene, the waiter, and the restaurant management.

"Halfway through the conversation," Barbutti says, "Buddy got mean with Shecky because Shecky had fired his gardener, a Latino guy who hadn't showed up to do his lawn for six weeks. Buddy found out about this somehow and said, 'You're a rat bastard for firing the guy, because the guy needed some dental work and now he can't get it done.'

and gambling very badly. I was the kind of person that everyone wanted in Vegas. For all the success I've had there, I paid for it."

He was born Sheldon Greenfield in 1926, but when his brother started calling him "Shecky" at age 3—no one is sure why—the name stuck. Greene says he grew up an "all-American boy," drinking neither in college nor during almost three years in the Navy. But even at age 20, he was already seeing a psychiatrist for what would become a lifelong struggle against depression.

Greene had almost given up on an early stab at show business and was about to return to school in Chicago when he accepted a job at the Preview Lounge in New Orleans. His act caught fire. But so did the place. "I never thought I'd leave there, but we burned down," he said.

He moved to Reno, where he married his first wife, a blackjack dealer whom he blames for starting him down the path to infamy: "She was a gambler and drinker, and I became a gambler and drinker."

An agent lined up Greene's first Las Vegas gig at the Last Frontier. The comedian had second thoughts about the job and turned it down, but his wife called the agent and reinstated the gig behind Shecky's back because she wanted to see Vegas. Greene debuted at the Last Frontier on December 6, 1954, as an opening act for Dorothy Shay, the "Park Avenue Hillbillie" (as ads spelled it).

"This turned into an argument. Shecky picked up his money and threw down his last drink and said, 'C'mon.' So they walked across Paradise to the Hilton. Shecky made a lay-down of like five hundred [dollars] and threw the dice and won five hundred, and he let it ride and won again. He picked up the money and toked each one of the dealers twenty-five bucks. Then he cashed in and took the money and stuffed it in Buddy's pocket and said, 'Here. Go tell the gardener to go get his teeth filled. Now let me alone. I want to get drunk alone.'"

They were walking back across Paradise Road when, as Shecky recounted to Barbutti, "Buddy called me a waldo." And what did that mean? "I have no idea what it means," Greene said, "but apparently it is not the thing to call me when I have been drinking."

"He hit Buddy and knocked him out," Barbutti says. "Left him in the middle of Paradise Road. Cars were driving around him like an island. Shecky went back, but he couldn't wake Buddy up, so he took the keys to his Mercedes and his gun, went over behind the Villa, and buried them in the desert. Shecky got a cab and went home. About two hours later, Buddy called him—'I can't find the keys or my gun.' So Shecky got up, got dressed, went back down, and the two of them were on their hands and knees in the desert, looking for the gun and the keys."

He made an instant convert of *Las Vegas Sun* columnist Ralph Pearl, who wrote: "Here's a guy who looks more like a left tackle on a reform school football team than a comic. However, he's a comic. That I'll vouch for, as will the capacity first-night audiences who refused to let him off the stage. ... Look for big things from Shecky Greene, a guy who works so hard even his sweat sweats."

Pearl's instincts were dead-on, since Greene was held over for the Last Frontier's next two headliners. Not that he understood the significance of that at the time. "When you're drinking and gambling, you don't know what is a big deal," he recalled.

Greene became a permanent fixture in Las Vegas, moving to the Riviera lounge in 1957 and to the Tropicana in 1959. The Trop had been struggling financially, and after a showroom gig, Greene asked Casino Manager Kel Houssels if he could work in the lounge. "But they didn't have a lounge; they had a bar," Greene said. "He [Houssels] wouldn't let me change the room. Both of us were very stubborn." So the comedian proposed, "I'll put a board over the bar and I'll work off the board." The board-on-a-bar was as right for the act as he'd suspected, but his business sense lagged behind his comedic instincts: Greene declined an offer of five points in the hotel. "Give me five hundred more on my salary," he demanded.

The comedian kept the Tropicana on the map during one of the Strip's periods of stagnation. The big players who packed the lounge made up for losses in the struggling main showroom until the hotel imported the *Folies Bergere* revue later in 1959. The lounge was Greene's venue anyway—the perfect vehicle for a manic, freewheeling, and semi-improvised brand of stand-up.

Jokes quoted from Greene's Last Frontier days read like stock one-liners: "I went to a very exclusive school. They had bars on the windows so nobody could sneak in. ... I was a real honor student: 'Yes, Your Honor. No, Your Honor.'"

But at the Trop, locals knew they were in for a more spontaneous stream of humor, just as they knew all three sets each night—10:15 p.m., 12:15 a.m., and 2 a.m.—would be different. "It's difficult to explain to anyone who hasn't seen Shecky Greene perform just what he does, how he does it, and why he is so successful doing it," columnist Forrest Duke wrote in 1962, trying to convey how the comedian combined storytelling, music, physical gags, and insult humor.

As one who also worked the lounges, Pete Barbutti can more easily explain lounge comedy, where inspiration was born of necessity. "You're forced to create material because you're working seven days a week, two shows a night," he says. "You get sick of hearing yourself say the same thing, so you start going in new directions. You get barometers, see certain things that work.

"What you do is you learn the mechanics of it," Barbutti notes. "The formula is three guys walking down the street—it's not two or four. ... It requires a certain formula for the joke to play out. You learn those mechanics, and then you simply apply them to something that happened to you that day: You went into the restaurant to order something and the waitress said this to you. So [retelling it in the act], you went to three different restaurants. The first one [waitress] said this. The second one said this. ... After you do that eight or nine times, all of a sudden, instead of being a thirty-second joke, it becomes a five-minute routine about waitresses."

And no one understood the formula better than Shecky Greene. "Shecky's talent was more of a gift; Buddy's was studying the art form," Barbutti notes. "Everything Buddy does is absolutely critically analyzed, dissected, and put back together again. Shecky was never analytical about it." His genius was more the ability to take a subject with no apparent humor value, such as the aria from *Madame Butterfly,* and turn it into a six-minute routine. All his bits were embellished with mimicry and dead-on impressions of show-biz contemporaries: Danny Thomas, Harry Belafonte, even Buddy Hackett.

"I was a dialectitian, a storyteller. I would elongate things," Greene explained. "If I told a joke, it would be a twenty-minute story. I would do the characters. That was my style of humor. That's why in television, they never could write for that." Old jokes became long jokes. Extended riffs on one idea, such as "caca on the moon"— the notion that the Apollo astronauts left more behind than footprints and a flag— became eight-minute signature pieces.

By early 1963, Shecky Greene's antics in the Tropicana's lounge made him a bigger draw than many showroom stars.

Though he hated the label, Greene became known as a "Vegas" or "lounge" comic because of the way he worked a gambling crowd. "My whole act was about Las Vegas—gambling, drinking," he said. "That's what that particular group of people at that time could relate to. ... I would take everything that was happening around us, or everything that had happened the night before or that day," and use it in the act. He also worked within an ice-cube's throw of the crowd, feeding off "that personal thing that people feel in a nightclub, that you could not touch in the movies."

Greene left the Tropicana in April 1963 after finding out that the Mary Kaye Trio was getting $10,000 per week to work the lounge, while he was getting only $6,000. "I went to Mr. Houssels, who I really loved, and asked him why. He said, 'There's three of them and only one of you.' So I said, 'Now there's only three of them because my contract's over.'"

He moved to the Riviera for the duration of the '60s, where he got his $10,000 and—this time—two points in the hotel as well. At the Riv, Greene was a must-see, with a reputation for dousing himself with whiskey or doing whatever else it took to bleed a laugh out of his audience. But these were the years when the research and development for his material began to overwhelm the act itself. "A lot of people would come in to see if I was drunk on the stage: 'You gotta come see this guy, because he does crazy things.'" And he did. "I used to do back flips and all that shit. It doesn't make you any funnier, but you think you're working harder that way."

Alcohol didn't just free Greene's inhibitions. Because of his manic-depressive personality, the booze was "mood-altering," his friend Barbutti noted. "It would not just make him drunk or mean. It would turn him into a different individual." Greene became like Jekyll and Hyde, and his friends, Barbutti said, would come to recognize "the look we all know as 'the animal'—the tie is off, shoulders broader than normal, hunched over, hair falling in his face."

But the Riviera also was a struggling property, and management had to put up with his excesses. In June 1964, Greene took a "leave of absence" from the hotel, which replaced one of his summer stints with a revue after a rift with management made the papers. On January 6, 1965, Greene was arrested when hotel officials claimed that the comedian "became offensive in the lounge and began picking on and insulting other guests," according to news reports at the time.

As the booking officer wrote "drunk" on the police form, Greene reportedly shouted, "I resent that!" and responded to questions by saying, "You want me to do my whole act?" The next day, the Riv took his name off the marquee—for the first, but not the last, time.

"I'd come back to work, and they'd be taking my name off the sign," Greene recalled. "I'd say, 'What happened?' 'You were fired.' 'Oh, I guess I'll go home.' And then they'd call me to come back."

Greene hated Riviera boss Ed Torres and told staffers to keep Torres out of the lounge while he was working. Management nonetheless insisted on wheeling out a giant cake one night to celebrate Torres' birthday, so Shecky took it upon himself to smash the cake into his own face. Another night, he decided the casino play was too loud and distracting to his act, so he marched out to a crap table and scattered a stack of $100 black chips across the room. Each time the Riviera fired him, and each time his long-term value to the hotel prevailed.

Shecky Greene—the quintessential Vegas comic—in a publicity photo.

Sometime during the first year after Caesars Palace opened in August 1966, Greene staked his biggest claim to Las Vegas infamy: He drove his car into the fountain in front of the new jewel of the Strip. (In the early years, the fountain divided a driveway and was bordered only by a standard curb, though Greene says he also took out a signpost en route.) Alas, part of the story is apocryphal. When the police waded into the fountain and opened the car door, legend has it that the comedian instructed, "No spray wax." It was a Buddy Hackett line, which both comedians used in retelling the tale. Greene remembers saying instead the more mundane "I guess I'm arrested" to the police officer, who was surprised to see him alive and well.

"I had incidents that are frightening," Greene recalled years later. "Sometimes I sleep now and I jump up from nightmares of the days that I was drinking and driving my car drunk.

"At the beginning of my drinking and escapades and arrests and all of that bullshit, that's funny," he said of some of the now legendary days. "But then," he noted, "it gets to the point where it's not funny. You become an asshole; you become an idiot. The respect for your talent completely has dissipated, and now they look at you as a complete fuckin' moron."

# A nice guy

The spotlight is probing the stage but can't find its target. Suddenly, Don Rickles breaks into the showroom from the side exit, one big prune-faced ball of piss-off. "Jeez, I'm workin' a home!" he says, machine-gunning the crowd. "Look at the old broads here."

Making his way from the audience to the stage, he riles himself up further as he chews out the band's conductor for the sorry crowd: "Bust my ass up here for a lousy hundred grand." Then he talks his way through his signature song, "I'm a Nice Guy," while pacing the stage and peppering the front rows between verses: "Sit up, goddamn it!" "Who picks out your clothes? Ray Charles?"

But no one takes umbrage. In fact, people have been lining up for 40 years to be insulted. You'd have to be some kind of hockey puck to take offense at Don Rickles, "The Mouth That Roared."

Rickles came to town in 1959 already vested with a reputation for insult humor. The comedian owed much of his early success to the enthusiastic support of Frank Sinatra, who would lead victims to Rickles' lion's den, the Slate Brothers nightclub in Hollywood. The room held only about 125 people, but "every celebrity in the world used to go there," Rickles recalls. "Sinatra was my hero and my benefactor. When Frank laughed, the world laughed." And in the late '50s, Sinatra was laughing at the balding Jewish pit bull of a comedian.

"In those days, my act was making fun of celebrities and talking," Rickles said. "I didn't do anything, really. I didn't have really an act. Oh, one or two things that were set, but I mostly ad-libbed." Then, even more than now, movie stars were treated like royalty, and to be ridiculed by the manic comedian was a rare treat indeed. "It caught on like crazy," Rickles said. "They used to stand in line around the block. It was unbelievable."

Sinatra could have brought Rickles to Vegas. But his act wasn't the kind that worked in a big showroom, and the Sands lounge wasn't big enough to seat the guaranteed crowd. Instead, Sahara entertainment impresario Stan Irwin saw Rickles in Hollywood and determined that he would be perfect to hold down the Casbar Lounge between the sets of popular Louis Prima. The 32-year-old comedian made his Las Vegas debut in

Don Rickles had already established his reputation as a comic pit bull in Hollywood before his Las Vegas debut at the Sahara in May 1959.

OPENING TONIGHT

HOTEL SAHARA PRESENTS

STILL ANOTHER EXCITING *Casbar* FIRST!'

DON RICKLES

The Emperor DON RICKLES Wants to See You

VIDO MUSSO
SALMAS BROTHERS

ART ENGLER SEXTET
THE SABRES
SANDO DEEMS

CASBAR THEATRE
hotel SAHARA

# Foster Brooks: So Real He Hiccups

Disneyland had "Great Moments With Abraham Lincoln." Vegas shared a few drinks with a Foster Brooks robot.

The MGM Grand Hotel opened in late 1993 and rewrote the rule book for how quickly a hotel could remodel itself. After ousting the management that had adorned the place with goofy cartoon mascots, giant plastic french fries, and creepy *Wizard of Oz* wax figures, the newly proclaimed "City of Entertainment" set out to refashion itself as a class act. But there was one tragic casualty, the one certifiable amazement in the whole 5,000-room hotel: an animatronic Foster Brooks, a comedian once known as the "Lovable Lush," which hiccupped and mumbled its way through 20 minutes of recorded material in the Betty Boop Lounge.

The silicone-covered pneumatic monument to a faded mid-level comedian took nearly $150,000 and 825 man-hours to perfect. Bartenders swore that real-life drunks would mistake the robot for the real McCoy, a part-time Las Vegan who once ventured into the MGM to see the thing for himself. "I look like an old man, which is what I am," Brooks said, a little unnerved after taking in the robot for the first time. "It's better than I'll look when I'm dead, I guess." At least he had the satisfaction of outliving the odd tribute.

Brooks bought his house near the Sahara Country Club in the late '70s, when he claims to have been the highest-paid opening act on the Strip. He pulled down as much as $40,000 per week warming up crowds for the likes of Robert Goulet, Juliet Prowse, and Buck Owens. Success came to Brooks relatively late in life—in 1970, to be exact—after years as a broadcaster in Louisville, Kentucky.

An act born of "wondering what those people would think if I made 'em think I'd been at the bar too long" caught the attention of Perry Como, who first brought the comedian to the International Hotel (now the Las Vegas Hilton). Eventually, Brooks became a regular on the weekly television roasts hosted by fellow chronic inebriate Dean Martin from the original MGM Grand Hotel (now Bally's).

In 1994, when Brooks was troubled by gout and walked with a cane, the 80-something comedian insisted that he hadn't touched alcohol in nearly 30 years. His everyday voice was closer to the slurry speech of his routine than many realized. "Some people think I'm really tight up there [onstage]," he said, even though "I sober up at the end [of his routine] and sing or do a poem."

May 1959. His reputation preceded him, judging by a publicity release that claimed he risked "a belt in the mouth every time he opened it."

To punch him out would have meant walking the plank. "I used to work over a bar," Rickles said. "They had a plank, and I used to cross over onto the bar and work on this tiny little stage." He did three sets a night, at 12:15 a.m., 2:30 a.m., and 4:15 a.m. During that crucial first month, Jimmy Durante, Marlene Dietrich, and Joe E. Lewis were among the willing victims who helped Rickles secure a permanent place in Vegas. Best of all, "The Insultin' Sultan" cracked the stoic facade of Sahara owner Milton Prell, ensuring that the seven-week run would be the first of many.

"I'm known to draw high rollers. The sharp group always comes to see me. I've always had that luck," the native New Yorker says. "This kind of excitement, this [casino] kind of atmosphere, is a Don Rickles thing." His "streetsy" style of humor, he adds, is "well-suited for this kind of town."

"The Merchant of Venom" worked the Casbar through 1967 (by 1964, he and Prima were booked for different stints instead of rotating the same night). His Las Vegas exposure opened the door to larger nightclub settings. "As far as my being a big star, it was after the Sahara that I got to what they call the class clubs," Rickles says. However, the true sign that he'd arrived was a bathrobe monogrammed with a nickname—"The Rhino"—that allowed him into the Rat Pack's after-five club in the Sands steam room.

It was an honor for a star to be picked on by Rickles: In 1961, columnist Ralph Pearl reported an unnamed movie star getting pissed off when Rickles failed to spot him. But it was Rickles' badge of honor to be humbled by the hand of Frank.

"I was with this girl, and she asked me, 'Do you know Frank Sinatra?' In those days I was single and looking to be lucky, so I said, 'Of course I do.' She said, 'Oh my God, if I could meet him ...' I said, 'It's done.'"

Sinatra was holding court in the Sands lounge, "sitting with a million people, and I walked up and said, 'Frank, it would really help me if you'd come over and say hello.' And he said, 'You got it, kid.' I said, 'But don't come right away. Wait a few minutes.'

"So I'm romancing this girl, and all of a sudden Frank Sinatra walks over and says, 'Hi, Don. And how are you, dear?' I said, 'Frank, can't you see I'm with a girl? I don't need you to bother me now.' The whole room heard it. Everything stopped. That's when [Frank] had the security guards pick me up and throw me out. Everybody got hysterical laughing. ... Yeah, it's a true story."

Rickles may be the only headliner who can claim to have performed on the Strip every year since 1959. The act is almost always the same; Rickles estimates there's about a 5 percent variation each show, depending on the crowd. The onstage band has been downsized over the years, but it still opens with his theme song, "The Matador."

He always manages to find an Italian in the audience. ("I know you're Italian— nothing matches.") And he never fails to locate a Jew and a Japanese or Chinese victim. ("We need the Orientals so the Jews have a place to eat on Sunday.") If he can't see a black guy, he invents one. "That was Johnny Carson's great line," Rickles recalls. "When

I would make up that there's a black guy in the back, Carson would say, 'Show me where the black guy is.'

"They're so busy watching me, hopefully, that they don't have time to look for a Japanese guy," Rickles adds. "When I worked in the lounge, [the captains] used to try to put funny people in front. That's before I was known. And it worked. But I never solicited that." As time went on, it didn't matter who was in the audience.

Rickles' act differed from Hackett's and Greene's in that Rickles always admits to playing a part: "I'm just a guy, a normal guy. I'm a very basic guy. It's two different lives. When I get out there

Rickles: The Mouth That Roared ... The Insultin' Sultan ... The Merchant of Venom—but a nice guy.

onstage, or when I'm at a big party with celebrities, I become that character that I do onstage." Audiences can feel the artifice of it. By the end of the show, when he puts a Band-Aid on the act with sentiments like "Never forget your mother" or "Pray for the day the bigots disappear," it's hardly necessary. Just using an arcane word like "bigot" wraps the act in a cloak of antiquity.

At least Rickles has been able to maintain his act, with varying degrees of interest, year after year. "Vegas is my roots; I wouldn't be coming if they didn't want me here," he noted in 1998. "If you look at the crowd, it's the high roller, the guy with the ring, the wife with the jewelry and the fur coat. You don't see that [in Las Vegas] anymore. But I bring in those kind of people."

## Neuroses and psychoses

Greene and Hackett also appealed to the old-Vegas crowd, but they were sidelined at times by their physical and emotional problems. Hackett—a man who once walked onstage in Atlantic City wearing only a large, strategically situated medallion—developed stage fright when he was 60 years old. "A lady psychiatrist named Claire Weekes wrote a book," he said. "She described those terrible fears: The actor, who never was afraid to go on, later in life develops stage fright because he wants to be better than he's ever been. Or he remembers some spectacular night that may or may not have been his best. But he remembers it. And he is competing to repeat it." The theory "makes so much sense," he mused in 1992.

Hackett's phobia cut back his work schedule as the '90s began. But then, seeking a regular familiar gig to confront his anxieties, he cut a deal to play Monday and Tuesday night shows at the Desert Inn in 1992. "When I go out here, sometimes I'm half-drunk," he said at the time. "This past weekend, I didn't drink at all. My stomach was so nervous, I couldn't take a drink. [But] sometimes I'm feeling good enough, I'll have two or three drinks. When I finish the show, I won't even know I've been on. 'I've done two hours? That's wonderful.'"

Ever autobiographical, Hackett, at 67, regaled audiences with an aging man's health woes. The opening line, "This guy finds a spot on his forehead, so he goes to see a doctor," became a launching point to talk about anything, from his urinary-tract problems to his sexual initiation in World War II. Some stories are seldom told, he

# H-e-e-e-re's Johnny!

Johnny Carson ran the most Vegas show on TV. And Vegas returned the favor.

*The Tonight Show* gave Buddy Hackett and other Vegas icons the closest thing to a showroom that the small screen could offer: an intimate, risqué, and seemingly improvised forum mixing bawdy humor and slapstick pie fights as smoothly as a martini. In exchange, Hackett and his friends at Del Webb rolled out the red carpet for Johnny at the Sahara whenever the great one could spare a weekend.

Carson first brought his nightclub act to the Sahara on July 7, 1964, only a year and a half after taking over *The Tonight Show* from Jack Paar. The show still originated in New York, and the monologue was not yet a nightly institution—most local newscasts covered up the 11:15 p.m. opening segment until the start time was changed in 1965. But Johnny was still a hit on the Strip. "He demonstrates what led him to video success—smooth stand-up comedy, expert ad-libbing, accurate impressions, and hilarious visual situation humor," columnist Forrest Duke wrote. "If Carson could spare the time, he'd be a blockbuster addition to the nightclub circuit."

Three years later, Duke proclaimed, "Johnny Carson and Frank Sinatra have the most powerful marquee names on the Las Vegas Strip." Often appearing for only one week each summer, "The Great Carsoni" was a tough ticket indeed.

The summer of '67 found Johnny tossing off his trademark one-liners drawn from the headlines ("Keno: the biggest swindle since Russia sold Nasser tanks with no reverse gear"). He also fielded notecard-submitted audience questions to show his quick-witted ad-libbing abilities.

Like he did on *The Tonight Show*—but unlike today's showroom sets by TV explained, because they are "locked up" in his head: "It don't come out, because if I force it out, it is not funny. It has to slide out."

In time, Hackett's mercurial temper and free-form approach made for longer lags between punch lines. *Las Vegas Review-Journal* reviewer Michael Paskevich reported an ugly scene from a Desert Inn show in June 1995: "'When I'm talking, button up!' he [Hackett] shouted at a fan who made the mistake of whistling out her support. ... His blunt sexual inquiries of a woman in the front row eventually prompted her male companion to utter an 'Aw, c'mon' in the hope that Hackett would move on to other prey.

"Big mistake. Hackett turned on the guy, bent down, and started with 'I'm going to rip your head off,' before pulling the microphone away to continue his obscenity-

---

successor Jay Leno—Carson veered from conventional stand-up to performance routines such as "Deputy John," the hung-over TV morning cartoon host; President Lyndon Johnson being interviewed by a wedding caterer; and Edward R. Murrow reading *The Three Little Pigs*.

In September 1971, Buddy Hackett received an opening-night birthday present from Johnny right in the middle of his act: a huge wrapped box containing sultry Joey Heatherton.

By August 1974, Carson's act included autobiographical bits about his sex life and a six-year-old routine about his adventures at the Mayo Clinic. "Deputy John," however, had gone by the wayside—too hard on Johnny's injured back.

He performed at the Sahara for 16 years, fading out after 1980 because Del Webb sold the hotel to more tight-budgeted operators. But Johnny remained a corporate citizen. His Carson Broadcasting Company owned the local TV station KVVU until 1985. And in 1980, he briefly thought his name was going on the Aladdin Hotel, until he found out that his bid to buy the place lost out to Wayne Newton. Newton's famous libel suit against NBC claimed that Carson was behind the network's reports about the singer and organized crime. (Newton won the suit, but the judgment was later overturned.) For years, Carson also owned a house in Las Vegas, off Eastern Avenue.

..heerrres Johnny!

WITH DOC SEVERINSEN BUD and CECE ROBINSON

SAHARA! congo room

laced tirade heard easily from 30 feet away. 'I'm just making friends here,' he declared, drawing big laughs from the folks who hadn't heard just how serious Hackett was during his nasty barrage."

On the surface, things started looking better for Shecky Greene in the early '70s. He married lounge singer Nalani Kele—the second of three wives—in December 1972 and began working the glitzy new MGM Grand Hotel in 1973. But, he says, "I used to finish a show and people would be standing up cheering, and I'd get off and cry. Because I was in a depression." The severe anxiety and depression eventually sidelined him. "I'd always have a panic attack before I got onstage. Always. I'd work through it. But some of them I couldn't work through after a while."

He remembers going to his bosses and saying, "I've got to quit show business and get out of Vegas. I have a very bad illness." And they'd say, "No, you're not an alcoholic." Why not? "Because," says Greene, "I was putting asses on the seats. As soon as those asses were not on the seats, [it was] 'Yeah, you're a drunk; you're a piece of shit.' That's when I knew my time was short-lived, when I heard the bosses say, 'Next?' That's the world's worst word."

By 1979, Greene had moved down from the MGM Grand's 1,200-seat Celebrity Room to the 600-seat Copa Room at the fading Sands. He worked there periodically until 1983, insisting even then, "I still care about this town." He could have handled the smaller crowds—the cozier room was his forte—but the manic energy was dwindling. "When I got on the stage and the energy was not there, that's when I knew it was over. Physical went with me as much as mental."

Greene soon left Las Vegas and moved to California, where he credits therapy and the antidepressant Zoloft for stabilizing his addictions and vicious mood swings. In December 1996, he recommended the drug to a well-dressed audience of well-wishers at the banquet for the 13th annual Governor's Conference on Nevada Travel and Tourism at Caesars Palace. "I say this because so many people are affected and there is help," he told them. "They won't become comedians if they take these pills, although I did have my act up for sale."

# One of the guys

Greene wasn't the only comic who called the city home: Barbutti, Pat Cooper, and the late Totie Fields and Redd Foxx were among those who could pull down enough steady work in Las Vegas to call it home. Of them, Fields was the rare female to crack the comedic boys' club and was just starting to spread her reputation beyond Las Vegas when cancer cut her career short in the mid-'70s.

Born Sophie Feldman, Fields started out as a singer. She met her comedian husband, George Johnston, in Boston in the mid-'50s. Soon, her comic bits between songs were getting a better reaction than the tunes themselves. Johnston became her onstage conductor and offstage manager and gag writer. Totie delved into what would become a long-running school of "fat humor." Not quite 5 feet tall and pushing

190 pounds, she sat onstage in a nightie and milked the most out of jokes such as, "I've been on a diet for two weeks, and all I lost was two weeks."

Like Greene, Barbutti, and other lounge comics who had no "outside" visibility as Hackett did with his movies, Fields benefited from exposure on talk shows such as those hosted by Mike Douglas, Merv Griffith, and Joey Bishop. They were the only real forums

Las Vegas comedy was still a man's world until Totie Fields made her presence known.

to introduce Vegas lounge stars to a wider audience. By 1968, Fields had built up name recognition as a full-time attraction in the Riviera's Starlite Theatre, the show lounge that Greene had made synonymous with comedy. By March 1971, she'd earned four weeks in the Riv's main room, climbing onto a grand piano for a musical ode to Paul Newman. (Ever wondered where Rosie O'Donnell got her Tom Cruise shtick?)

"She really was getting bigger," Greene says. "She was good. She knew how to play an audience." Fields was a tough cookie, carrying her weight (so to speak) in a man's world. "When you went into her dressing room, you had to put both hands over your crotch. That was a ball-breakin' lady," Greene adds. Buddy Hackett was even less fond of her. One night he felt compelled to whip out a pistol and blow her photo off the dressing-room wall at the Sahara.

And yet, Barbutti remembers her once telling him on a local TV show that there was a delicate balance to playing the boys' game without becoming one of the boys. "That femininity thing was part of the intrigue," he remembers her saying. "Once you crossed over and you became one of the guys, there was no longer anything unique about the fact that you were a woman."

But Fields' toughness could not overcome a string of health problems that began in April 1976, when minor surgery on an eyelid resulted in phlebitis in her left leg, which had to be amputated. She battled back, losing more than 70 pounds during her seven months in a hospital bed. For her comeback at the Sahara in April 1977, she weighed in at a trim 118 pounds, walking onstage with a cane. Her physical therapy? "My therapist put a sale rack on each side of the room and said to go shop," she told the crowd. "But the one thing that upset me was buying the leg. What do you do? Wait until after Christmas to see if they have a leg on sale?" She rang maximum drama out of her closing number: "I'll take anything Totie Fields can land on, brother; just as long as I've got a leg to stand on, I've got everything. ..."

The next October, a cancerous tumor was removed from her breast. On August 2, 1978, the city learned that Totie Fields had died of an apparent heart attack at age 48, the day before she was to open another stint at the Sahara.

# From riches to rags

As the story goes, an onlooker was watching Redd Foxx play blackjack one night and asked him why he was hitting an 18.

"'Cause I'm tryin' to get twenty-one, dummy!" Foxx retorted.

There's no way of knowing whether this anecdote is true or just should be, but it does sum up the riches-to-rags story that followed the *Sanford and Son* career of the gravel-voiced comedian in Las Vegas until his death in 1991. It's not that Foxx was a compulsive gambler. It's just that he had a certain, uh, logic to his finances that plagued him to the end.

The man born John Elroy Sanford on December 9, 1922, rarely enjoyed the prestige of other Vegas-based comics of long tenure, even though he employed the same off-color approach onstage and had the same zest for Vegas vice away from it. Racy "party" records of his routines, sold under the counter in the '50s, gave him a notoriety just right for Vegas when he debuted as a warm-up act for Dinah Washington before she died in late 1963. He then started working the fabulous Samoa Room at the Castaways in 1964.

"Las Vegas is based on gambling, drinking, and women. That's the big three. So if you approve of those things and don't like my language, what the hell are you doing there in the first place?" Foxx once rationalized to journalist Pete Mikla.

Not long after the International Hotel (now the Las Vegas Hilton) opened in 1969, Foxx rotated sets with the likes of B.B. King and Ike and Tina Turner in the Casino Theatre, a 400-seat "lounge" that was more like a good-sized supper club. Foxx thought he was at the height of his career. But then producer Norman Lear tapped him for *Sanford and Son*, an instant hit when it debuted in early 1972. Two years later, Foxx was known in every living room. But he missed his old work habits.

"I had a year and a half at the Hilton, doing just two, forty-five-minute shows a night for six nights, ten thousand dollars a week," he told one reporter. "I got off at two a.m. and didn't have to do anything until eleven the next night. After that kind of freedom for thirty-six years as a nightclub act, I can't adjust" to the rigors of prime time.

Redd Foxx was not a happy camper on November 28, 1989, when the IRS came calling at his Las Vegas home, seizing cars, furniture, and even the jewelry he was wearing to pay off a tax bill in excess of $1 million.

By 1976, NBC was tired of arguing with its star and allowed ABC to lure him away for an ill-fated variety show. Even during his TV days, Foxx kept coming back to work Vegas. But once the TV work ended, the money at places like the Silverbird—where his 2:30 a.m. weekend sets were billed as "Triple XXX Rated"—didn't keep up with the lifestyle he'd grown accustomed to. He filed for Chapter 11 bankruptcy in 1983.

By 1989, Foxx's tax debt had swelled to more than $1 million. That November, 15 IRS agents raided the house on Eastern Avenue where Foxx had lived for 22 years. They emptied the house, seizing nearly all its contents plus more than $12,000 in cash, and confiscated eight vehicles. The official list of items seized included eight pistols, three rifles, two shotguns, $670 in Sam's Town chips, wooden elephants from Thailand, a bass fiddle, an Indian chief headdress, and four hubcaps. Some of his belongings, including an inscribed gold watch given to him by Elvis Presley, were auctioned that summer. Court documents revealed a long history of bad business deals and a disregard for the tax man.

Foxx kept working—"for the government"—forfeiting most of the $15,000 to $20,000 he made each week at the Sahara and Hacienda hotels. He "four-walled," or worked for the ticket revenue, and paid his stable of opening acts, including Slappy White—his comedy team partner in the late '40s—and his nominal manager, Prince

Spencer, who was once one of the tap-dancing Four Step Brothers. Spencer invariably would be called back to the stage by Foxx for a climactic tap routine, rivaled only by Redd's famously emphatic closing bit, "You gotta wash yo' ass."

"[Because I] came up on the streets, that's the kind of humor I had to go for. I didn't have any professional writers," he once explained. But that didn't mean he approved of younger comics using words that he "wouldn't dare say" in his lifetime onstage. "But they say I'm the cause of it ... because of my party records. My first fifteen or twenty albums never had a dirty word on them, always double-entendre. Now you find seventeen-letter words and twenty-two-letter words."

But nothing in the Sam Kinison-Andrew Dice Clay era of the late '80s quite rivaled sitting in the broken-down Hacienda Hotel showroom, watching Redd tell jokes while sipping from a ceramic mug shaped like a breast. The Fred G. Sanford New and Used Store near his home at Eastern Avenue and Russell Road became a tour stop second only to the Liberace Museum for those seeking out the weirder side of Vegas.

In July 1991, Foxx cruised up to a wedding chapel in a red limousine and, with Slappy White as his best man, married his fourth wife, 40-year-old Ka Ha Cho. The long run at the Hacienda ended that month; Foxx was headed back for the big time, starring with Della Reese (who once sang for Harry James in the Flamingo's Driftwood Lounge) in a new sit-com, *The Royal Family.*

The show got off to a promising start. But on October 11, 1991, Foxx collapsed while rehearsing at Paramount Studios and died of "the big one"—a heart attack—at age 68. More than 1,000 people attended his Las Vegas funeral, including Mike Tyson, Flip Wilson, and LaWanda "Aunt Esther" Page.

# The rock 'n' roll comic

By the early '80s, Vegas had hit an entertainment dry spell. Aging headliners were demanding more money than hotels wanted to pay. Small, often amateurish drag and nudie revues were thrown together to fill the smaller rooms. There was one ray of hope, however, in a 1984 experiment: Mitzi Shore's Comedy Store at the Dunes Hotel.

Early career performances by the likes of Roseanne Barr, Louie Anderson, and Andrew Dice Clay at least enabled the Strip to remain current in one entertainment genre. At various points since the Comedy Store opened, the Strip has had as many as five franchised clubs. So far, Budd Friedman's Improv has survived the longest.

Touring stand-ups performing short, defined acts—many of them glorified auditions for sit-com or movie work—have largely replaced the boozy lounge comedy of the '60s. But there was at least one exception. Las Vegas was instrumental in the career of Sam Kinison, one of the brightest comedy names of the '80s and one whose self-destructive behavior fit into the city's bittersweet legacy of comedy borne of excess.

The cartoonishly larger-than-life "rock 'n' roll comic" was a failed Pentecostal

Although nearly every comedian has played Vegas, not every act has been successful. Case in point: The Three Stooges were replaced after one night when they opened on a variety bill at the Flamingo in October 1953.

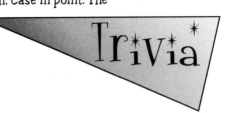

preacher raised in Oklahoma and Texas, who embraced the decadence of the spandex and leather heavy-metal scene in Los Angeles. Kinison partied with bands like Motley Crüe, borrowing some of their "bad-boy" aura to help him rise above the ranks of the more interchangeable comics working the Comedy Store on Sunset Strip. By 1988, he was one of the few comedians popular enough to record a comedy album, resurrecting a dated, nearly dead vehicle. As a payback to Comedy Store maven Shore, Kinison and his own rat pack—including, for the first time in Las Vegas, Mitzi's son Pauly Shore—took over the Dunes for a memorable three-week run in April 1988.

Kinison's comedy pals—"guys who have been on the bench for nine or ten years, guys who were good but didn't get the break I did"—were reveling in their new-found fortunes as "The Outlaws of Comedy." Carl LaBove, Kinison's manic second banana and best friend since their teething days in Houston, did high kicks in the backstage wings on opening night, just feeding off the energy as the pack waited (like usual) for its leader to descend from his hotel suite. "I feel the ghost of Elvis!" LaBove proclaimed to amuse the backstage crew.

"All those guys wish they were us right now," Mitchell Walters, a veteran stand-up, said later that night as he looked out the window of his Dunes suite to see the names of Jackie Mason and Red Buttons on the Bally's marquee across the Strip. "I mean, I love those guys. I think they're great, but they've been doing the same act for thirty years. They stayed in their mold. They didn't get a chance to branch out."

And Kinison was clearly on to something fresh, whipping his primarily blue-collar male crowds into an evangelical frenzy with profane tirades about the evil women who broke their poor hearts. He built the rants to a fevered pitch, and at the climactic moment would summon back to the stage one of his coattail holders, ceremoniously bearing a real live touch-tone phone (this was pre-cellular). Picking one lucky man out of the audience, Kinison would dial the number of "the woman who ripped his heart out and stomped on it," and actually phone her (or her answering machine) right from the stage. "You bitch! You whore! How do you live with yourself?" he would bellow in a primal rant.

"By the time the show's over, they're ready to get up a lynch mob and go after her," Kinison proudly observed backstage one night, explaining that it was all audience catharsis. "They're vicariously living out their frustrations through me."

A year later, Kinison was working to Memorial Day crowds in a Bally's convention hall that seated more than 2,000, while Sinatra was singing in the regular showroom. It was a career peak Kinison would never see again. Visibly loaded, escorted onstage by two gorgeous twins in G-strings to the tune of "Welcome to the Jungle," Kinison elicited big laughs by talking about screwing his girlfriend (one of the twins) while looking out the window of his suite, exploding in orgasm at the sight of his and Sinatra's names sharing space on the giant marquee. The rock 'n' roll rat pack now lifted the curtain at the climax of each show to reveal a band of celebrity drunks, such as Billy Idol, joining in on "Wild Thing" and "Under My Thumb."

But Kinison's excesses took their toll. Returning for New Year's Eve of 1989, Kinison binged for two days, then crashed just prior to his show. His handlers ushered him to the stage shortly before midnight, but the comedian could barely complete the New Year's countdown. Some hecklers in front marched out and demanded refunds, causing a ruckus in the lobby. Though he finished two shows after that, Kinison ended up giving back $42,000 from his paycheck to cover the midnight show's losses.

When Kinison returned the following May, it was damage control time. "It [the New Year's midnight show] was probably the worst show of my life; hopefully this is a makeup show," he said in an afternoon interview that was interrupted by a phone call from mentor Rodney Dangerfield. "Are you proud of me?" Kinison asked Dangerfield. "I haven't done any shit in eighty-one days. No coke, no booze in eighty-one days." After the call, Kinison said his doctor had assured him that "if I just take care of myself now, I won't have any liver or heart problems. He said, basically, I would get away with all the craziness and insanity that I pulled off."

Bally's, however, hedged its bet by courting another "hard-rock comic," Andrew Dice Clay. "The Diceman" was riding high on a controversial comedy album and misogynistic cable TV special. Clay was a contemporary of Kinison's in the Sunset Strip Comedy Store days and was sent home from the Dunes' Comedy Store during its trial run in 1984—either because he was "too dirty," as he would later claim, or because he wasn't "ready," as Shore remembered. Either way, Clay narrowed his array of impressions down to one leather-jacketed Brooklyn tough guy dubbed the "Hoodlum of Humor," and later struck pay dirt by adding profanity and outlandish sexism to the mix with street-corner musings about broads: "If they would just come out and say, 'Treat me like the pig that I am!'"

Feminist backlash was at a peak when Bally's rolled out the red carpet for a defensive Diceman before his hotel debut in August 1990. "I think there are more important issues in the world than a comic that curses," he said at a news conference. "Don't they realize I'm just a moron? They think there's some kind of hidden meaning, when it's a goof."

While Bally's let rock concert promoter Barry Fey take the risk of bringing in

Kinison, the hotel was quick to offer Clay a reported $1 million, 18-month contract to perform in its showroom. Kinison was frustrated by the fading interest in the L.A. "glitter-rock" scene to which he'd once hitched his wagon, but equally rejected in his attempts to branch out. He decided to go on the offensive, with Clay as his target. Kinison returned to the Dunes, setting up shop directly across the street from Clay's show in May 1991, and launched a verbal assault on the Diceman, accusing Clay of lifting parts of his act, if not his whole rock 'n' roll persona.

The days of "arena comedy" were over for Kinison. But his later dates in smaller venues like the Sands ballroom suggest that, given time, he probably could have reinvented himself. He thought his style would outlast the shock era and was trying to vary his act, to see if his audiences would grow with him into a deeper level of political or social humor.

He never had the chance to find out. Kinison married longtime on-again, off-again companion Malika Souiri in a Las Vegas wedding chapel on April 5, 1992. On April 9, the two were driving from Los Angeles to Laughlin, Nevada, for Kinison's first gig after a short honeymoon in Hawaii. On a two-lane highway near the California-Arizona state line, a pickup truck carrying two teen-age boys swerved into the wrong lane and hit the couple's Trans-Am head-on. Though he seemed to have few external injuries, Kinison died within minutes. Carl LaBove was following in a car behind them. He claims Kinison's last words seemed to be a conversation with God: "Why? Why now?"

# The last laugh

May 19, 1996, was a sad scene backstage in Buddy Hackett's dressing room. It was his last night at the Desert Inn for the foreseeable future; at that point the door was still open for a return, but Hackett later suffered a heart attack and announced he would never perform again. Maître d' John Lopez led the showroom captains into the dressing room to thank Hackett for his four years of bringing back the old-style gamblers. Trying to cheer up a visibly melancholy Hackett, Lopez told the comedian that new names, such as Dennis Miller, pack the showroom. But the minute the show is over, Lopez said, "they [members of the audience] hit the bathroom and the door, and bang—they're out of there."

"Even if the gamblers show up, they think they brought 'em in," Hackett said of the hotel management, who "weren't even born" the first time he played the hotel in 1952.

Today, Kinison's fellow "outlaws" have scattered, playing the small franchised clubs. The Diceman carries on, still offering the same basic act at Bally's during male-oriented weekends like the Super Bowl. But his name no more stands out—let alone provokes outrage—than that of Louie Anderson, George Carlin, or any other comedy star on the Strip. Rosie O'Donnell commanded an $80 ticket at Caesars Palace when she broke away from taping her afternoon TV show for housewives.

Drew Carey taped an HBO special in which he adopted a "Mr. Vegas" lounge persona, but the jury is out on his long-term drawing power.

There will always be young talents, such as Chris Rock, who will make a name for themselves in the showrooms if the love of performing can keep them away from bad movies and sit-coms. But in modern-day Vegas, the comedians have become just so much of the theme park scenery. The laughs still tinkle, but the danger has melted.

# Drawn Out in Vegas

Let's face it. The stories behind most of today's comedy stars aren't that interesting. They spend years schlepping around the club circuit, smoking dope with other comics, hitting on patrons, and staying up late bitching about who stole what joke—until one day they get that lucky TV breakthrough and the other comics start bitching about them.

Drew Carey was as lucky as any of them when he landed his ABC sit-com in 1995. But the comedian with the unflappably down-to-earth Joe Average image once revealed the tough times of four misspent years in Vegas—long before the city knew such a thing as comedy clubs.

"The lowest, most depressing days I ever had were in Las Vegas," he allowed. "Las Vegas was the last place I tried to kill myself."

After an unsuccessful attempt at college, the Cleveland native became a nomad in the late '70s, ending up in Las Vegas several times over a four-year period. "All my life I've been really restless and wanted to do other stuff than what I was doing," Carey said. "I was never really happy or knew what I wanted to do exactly, so I would just go from town to town, job to job, hoping that would be the thing I could have fun with."

His Las Vegas résumé included a stint as a bank teller and a stretch at a Denny's restaurant on the Strip. He remembers taking the No. 6 Strip bus to get to work, hoarding coupons for cheap buffets, and living in a weekly motel on Fremont Street.

"There were bloodstains on the walls and hookers in and out of the place all the time," he said. "And the cockroaches—oh man, I could never get rid of the cockroaches. They were everywhere."

His lowest moment? "I had to go give plasma one time because I was so broke," Carey says. "[The facility] had this so-called doctor that gave you an exam before you could give plasma. He was like a shaky old alcoholic. It was one of the lowest days of my life."

But some inner strength must have redeemed him: "I never got desperate enough to go to Mr. Sy's [Casino of Fun]." The casino later became infamous when owner Seymour Husney pleaded guilty to a charge of crime against nature with a minor in a 1978 child-sex-for-hire case. Even before the scandal, the place was so seedy, with food so intimidating, recalls Carey, that "of all the things I did—giving plasma and everything—I had too much pride to go to Mr. Sy's."

After taking a non-lethal dose of sleeping pills in Las Vegas, Carey headed back to his beloved Cleveland and, eventually, into the Marine Corps Reserves.

He came out in 1986 with his trademark buzz cut and black plastic glasses—and with enough confidence to try his luck at comedy. He remembered the Vegas days, when he would nurse a beer just out of cover-charge range at the Sahara lounge to hear sets by Pete Barbutti, the Unknown Comic, and the late Wayland Flowers.

When he comes back to Las Vegas now, Carey says, "it's some of the happiest times." On one of his first trips back as a paid comedy club attraction, he revisited the seedy motel and other haunts. "I was so thankful and happy. It's like God gave me a second chance after all the bad times I had there."

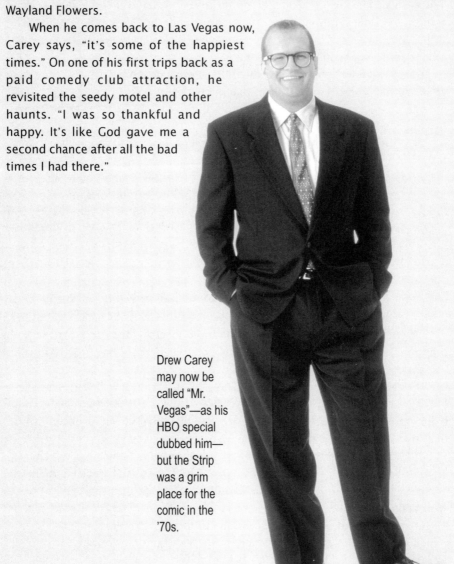

Drew Carey may now be called "Mr. Vegas"—as his HBO special dubbed him—but the Strip was a grim place for the comic in the '70s.

# THE COMEBACK KID

On July 20, 1969, man took his first step on the moon. On August 1, as part of its ongoing coverage, the *Las Vegas Review-Journal* ran a now-famous wire photo on the front page, showing the lunar module reflected in the helmet visor of moonwalker Edwin "Buzz" Aldrin. What were those editors thinking? The big news for Las Vegas on August 1 was inside, on page four: Elvis Presley had taken his giant leap for Vegas-kind on the stage of the International Hotel, performing in concert for the first time in nine years.

The appalling news judgment seems scarcely believable now. Astronauts—with the possible exception of those floating from the ceiling of the old Vegas World—never made one thin dime for Las Vegas. But an average day on the Strip can still find Elvis impersonators serenading couples in wedding chapels, passing out valuable coupons as sidewalk casino hawkers, or even plunging from airplanes to celebrate major holidays and shopping center openings.

The Elvis Presley story is an American epic and a Greek tragedy rolled into one. Las Vegas is most associated with the third act: Elvis making a triumphant return, only to slip into drug-ravaged self-parody. But the city is a running thread through all three acts of the play. It was Las Vegas where Presley tested the showroom waters during his breakthrough year of 1956, and discovered that he had not yet captured the tastes of the American mainstream—or at least its nightclub culture. It was Las Vegas where he later came to play and make movies, and Las Vegas where he married his child bride.

Elvis and Vegas needed each other. What would Las Vegas be without "Viva" in front of it? And who would Elvis have been without the sequined jumpsuits, that big old Las Vegas Hilton, and the doomed TVs inside the Elvis Suite? What better mecca for fans to make a pilgrimage to and seek an audience with the King?

"They loved what he did; they loved what he stood for," says Sammy Shore, the comedian who opened Presley's shows at the International Hotel. "He was America. He

> " Bright light city gonna set my soul,
> Gonna set my soul on fire.
> Got a whole lotta money that's ready to burn,
> So set those stakes up higher. "

"Viva Las Vegas"

was a Southern boy who became the world's idol."

The triumph of the '70s Jumpsuit Elvis might not have had the same impact if it weren't for the contrast of the Rocker Elvis' less-than-spectacular Las Vegas debut. It was April 23, 1956, four months after Sun Records' regional singing sensation turned 21 and completed his first recordings for RCA Records. One of them, "Heartbreak Hotel," was starting to drive a wedge between the generations, as the Memphis white boy who sounded black burst from the staid *Dorsey Brothers TV Show* into unsuspecting living rooms, jiggling his hips in a primal communication with American teens.

A Vegas booking became the controversial "Colonel" (the title was self-bestowed) Tom Parker's first attempt to break his young discovery out of the Southern honky-tonks and state fairs and land him some national credibility. "The Atomic Powered Singer," as newspaper ads billed him, was booked as an "extra added attraction" to Freddy Martin and his orchestra and comedian Shecky Greene at the New Frontier Hotel, where a 24-foot cutout of Elvis went up in front of the building.

A more mismatched trio may never have shared a stage—Elvis' April 1956 Las Vegas debut was obviously more accidental than orchestrated.

Today it seems like a strange talent combination, and it was. The New Frontier had an aggressive entertainment buyer named Sammy Lewis who "had the foresight of bringing in people that were in the news for something," Shecky Greene recalls. "A lot of other people wouldn't have touched him [Elvis]." But the hotel probably should have waited. Though Elvis was a grassroots sensation in the South, when he stepped out in front of his trio—slap bass, drums, and electric guitar—to strut his stuff before the cocktail crowd, he went down "like a jug of corn liquor at a champagne party," according to *Newsweek*.

Las Vegas was still firmly dominated by the nightclub tradition. Rock 'n' roll was confined to the lounges, where, *Variety* and *Las Vegas Sun* columnist Bill Willard noted, "One can up and go—fast. But in a dining room, the table-sitter must stay, look, and listen the thing out.

"For the teen-agers, the long, tall Memphis lad is a whiz; for the average Vegas spender or show-goer, a bore. His musical sound with a combo of three is uncouth, matching to a great extent the lyrical content of his nonsensical songs," Willard wrote.

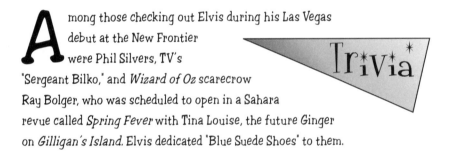

Among those checking out Elvis during his Las Vegas debut at the New Frontier were Phil Silvers, TV's 'Sergeant Bilko,' and *Wizard of Oz* scarecrow Ray Bolger, who was scheduled to open in a Sahara revue called *Spring Fever* with Tina Louise, the future Ginger on *Gilligan's Island*. Elvis dedicated 'Blue Suede Shoes' to them.

Shecky Greene still agrees with Willard's appraisal. "The presentation was terrible," he recalls. "He [Elvis] walked out with three or four guys. It looked like a rehearsal hall. He wasn't ready." Though the comedian took a personal liking to the 21-year-old singer, he could see that "he was scared to death."

Trying to put Presley into context, the New Frontier's press release heralded that he was "unanimously acclaimed by critics as the most important singing find since Johnnie Ray," who was working down the street at the Desert Inn. But, Greene points out, "Johnnie Ray was already a performer; he had worked in joints in New Orleans. Elvis wasn't a performer yet. He really didn't know how to make contact yet with the audience. He didn't say to the audience, 'I'm gonna do this,' or whatever. He just went out there. Boom, boom, boom."

Even though the Colonel had slicked Elvis up with a bow tie and jacket, "he was kind of weird-looking for those people," recalls lounge veteran Freddie Bell. "He had the sideburns and that hair." And he was singing rock 'n' roll, loudly, in Frank's town. "Everything was still too loud for Vegas then," Bell says with a laugh.

True, Bell and his Bellboys had just played on a flatbed truck in front of the Fremont Theater to promote their appearance in *Rock Around the Clock*. But their music still wasn't quite "rock" as Presley came to define it. "We were more R and B," Bell says. "In order to sell our show, we had to do a lot of choreography and dancing besides just doing rock 'n' roll. We had the snappy tuxedos, the showbiz look."

Recordings have surfaced, apparently from closing night, in which Presley tries to "work the room" with some uneasy banter: "We've had a pretty hard time ... uh ... had a pretty good time while we were here," he says at one point. At another, he attempts to josh with bandleader Martin: "Do you know that song, Mr. Martin? 'Get Outta the Stables'? You do? Well, do you know that one about, 'Take Back Your Golden Garter, My Leg Is Turnin' Green'? Did you ever hear that one?"

Trying to salvage the gig, Parker, Sammy Lewis, and Bud Lilly, the New Frontier's publicity director, set up an afternoon matinee for Elvis' teen-age fans to benefit Chuck Hull's Baseball Federation. A dollar donation included soft drinks for everyone. "It's a real bargain-type afternoon," Lilly noted in promoting the April 29 matinee starring the hotel's "nonchalant phenomenon." The event drew about 700 screaming teens, a scene more familiar to Elvis that year.

Presley's two-week stretch in Las Vegas wasn't a total loss. The young rocker apparently enjoyed his break from the road and took a liking to the city. He watched a Western movie and rode the carnival rides at the Western Village, an amusement park that separated the Jetsons-esque New Frontier from the cowboy-themed Last Frontier. He saw a young Jackie Wilson sing "Don't Be Cruel" as part of Billy Ward's Dominoes in the Sahara lounge. And he caught Freddie Bell's show at the Sands, visiting the lounge with a small entourage that included horror hostess Vampira, who was performing in Liberace's show at the Riviera. "They never sat at a table; they always sat at the bar, right in front of me," Bell says.

And Elvis obviously didn't need Vegas during the most important year of his life. He had already signed a deal with Paramount to star in his first movie, *Love Me Tender*. Parker, ever the revisionist, even claimed years later that the hotel wanted to extend the gig but hadn't lived up to an advance deposit the manager demanded after checks for previous acts bounced. At any rate, Hollywood was beckoning Elvis, and the Strip was happy to go back to non-rock nightclub fare. *Las Vegas Sun* columnist Forrest Duke summed up the showroom problem: "With an audience of jaded adults ... he's not quite in his element." Then again, Duke noted with some degree of foresight, "Who needs jaded adults? Elvis Presley?"

Not for 13 more years in Las Vegas, as it would turn out. But Elvis did leave with one valuable parting gift. Bell says the young singer was so impressed by his lounge arrangement of "Hound Dog"—a toned-down version of a tune first recorded by Willie Mae "Big Mama" Thornton—that Bell gave the Colonel a copy of a single that had been a regional hit for him in the East. He hoped that if Elvis recorded it, he might reap some benefit when his own version was released on an album. Alas, few people today have heard Freddie's take on the song.

Even a bow tie and jacket couldn't mute the raw sex appeal of a 21-year-old "Atomic Powered Singer" enough to appease older casino patrons.

"[The Colonel] promised me that if I would give him the song, the next time Elvis went on tour, I would be the opening act for him—which never happened," Bell says.

Elvis did come back to Las Vegas in 1956, but he was in the audience, not in the spotlight. In November, not long after 54 million people saw him on the *Ed Sullivan Show,* he went to see Liberace, who, with his brother George, had come to check Elvis out at the New Frontier. (The pianist watched the show "looking incredulous," according to Willard's *Daily Variety* column.) Elvis lingered after the show to pose for a now-famous photo in which he and the pianist switched jackets and instruments: Elvis at the piano in gold lamé, Liberace strumming a guitar in a striped jacket. "I didn't pose them. They did that all by their little lonesome," photographer Jerry Abbott, of the Las Vegas News Bureau, later recalled.

During the next year, Presley was romantically linked with several Vegas

# The Odd Couple

Both are pop-culture icons, though one is more universal than the other.

One is the young Elvis, with black hair, sideburns, and a killer smile that burned its image into a generation.

The other had black hair, too. It was long and parted in the middle, and framed a killer smile of a different sort. The other is Vampira, the original Hollywood horror hostess. Few people these days have seen the Elvira prototype's TV broadcasts from the '50s; TV was a more fleeting medium back then. Fortunately, Vampira was immortalized in the bad movie classic, *Plan 9 From Outer Space*. She didn't get to speak any of her trademark puns, but at least got to flex cartoonishly long talons from a body that veered into a 4-inch waist.

Only in Vegas could Elvis and Vampira meet, by a quiet hotel swimming pool, "softly giving off a blue light." Maila Nurmi, the lady who played Vampira, recalled the fabled week when Elvis made his infamous debut at the New Frontier while she was working in Liberace's show at the Riviera. In fact, it was opening night.

"Lee took me out with this large group," she recalled. "We were going to see as many of the shows as we could that night before we actually opened at the Riviera."

As Nurmi watched the New Frontier show, "This one kid walked in from the wings carrying his guitar. He sort of stood there by the microphone, and he proceeded to sing with all this eye shadow on. There was much hip-thrusting, you know. He was extremely good and I was stunned. ... The audience was stunned because they didn't know what to make of it. Finally somebody booed. And then everyone started to boo."

Nurmi told Liberace she had a headache and was bowing out. "But actually," she said, "I was looking for Elvis because I'm the great Earth Mother, you know. I had to go help heal this wounded soul." Eventually she found him out by the swimming pool, wearing a canary yellow jacket he hadn't worn onstage. "He came out alone and looked around as if he had an appointment, and looked into the darkness. I said, 'I'm over here.' I said, 'Well, I'm a performer. I just saw your show, and what they did was terrible.'"

And Elvis told her: "You know, every night before I go onstage, I pray. I talk to God. When I'm standing in the wings

Vampira was Liberace's foil in his 1956 show at the Riviera, but she was more captivated by Elvis Presley offstage.

waiting to go out, I talk to God. I pray for a nice show and He always answers me. Tonight He didn't answer me. That's the first time He didn't answer me." Elvis had never played to old people before, he told her. When he saw "all those white heads and all those glasses," he knew he was in trouble.

Nurmi consoled him and predicted that even adults soon would be kissing up to him. They sat and talked about life's rejections. He told her that his high-school class had voted him "Most Likely to Succeed"—as a joke. The two hung out during the rest of the engagement. "We played the bumper cars [in the New Frontier's Western Village]. I'd smash him. 'Here I come, Elvis'—bang!"

But, she says, that's the only bang they shared: "He was too young for me."

entertainers: singer Kitty Dolen, showgirl Marilyn Evans, and Dunes stripper Tempest Storm. "He really liked her," longtime Elvis sidekick Lamar Fike said of the latter, "because she was a very neat lady." When "The Pelvis" cruised up for his Army physical in January 1957, the passenger in his Cadillac was Dotty Harmony, a Sahara Hotel chorus girl who had been invited to spend Christmas at home in Memphis.

## Love and marriage on the Strip

Loyal fans waited patiently for Presley to finish his career-shattering two-year hitch in the Army, after which he reported for duty in a string of cheesy movies. His lukewarm showroom reception in 1956 meant that he could, for a few years anyway, give up on Vegas as a business proposition and use the city the same way as any well-heeled tourist would: whooping it up as a paying customer.

"I remember when he came out of the service, I was sitting in the lounge at the Sahara and I got a tap on the shoulder," Freddie Bell says. "I turned around and it was Elvis. He says, 'You got any good songs for me?'"

Las Vegas excursions always came in the company of bodyguards, cronies, and coattail holders known as "The Memphis Mafia," or more simply as "the guys." Sonny West, a key member of the circle since 1958, remembers Las Vegas as both a weekend break during the filming of movies and an extended detour "on the way home" from Hollywood to Memphis when filming wrapped.

Freddie Bell remembers, "Every weekend he'd come in, he'd have a beauty with him, a gorgeous starlet." The Sahara was home base because it was owned by Milton Prell, the Colonel's friend and Palm Springs neighbor.

Elvis and Nicky Blair take a pensive time-out on the set of *Viva Las Vegas* in 1963.

Priscilla Presley later had nothing good to remember of her 1967 wedding. Orchestrated by Colonel Tom Parker, the affair was held at the Aladdin Hotel, which was owned by his buddy Milton Prell.

"We'd rent a theater and go down at two o'clock in the morning and watch previews of his films," Bell recalls. "He would ask me, 'How do you think I did there?' If I told anybody Elvis asked me what I thought of him, they'd think I was insane."

Since those movies hadn't been released yet, "the security back then wasn't near as critical as it was once he started performing," Sonny West recalls. "We would go to places [such as] shopping centers and a small crowd would gather, but he wasn't in the public eye like he was later."

Presley would often check out Bell's lounge show, but would sneak out when Bell began to imitate him. "He was afraid I was going to introduce him," Bell says. Elvis would, however, "come backstage and do karate exhibitions. He'd always have these two guys that traveled with him. He'd throw these two guys all over the place. I said, 'They gotta be gettin' paid [to take a dive].'"

Given such good times in Sin City, it seems almost divine providence that arguably the best of the '60s Elvis movies was *Viva Las Vegas,* which required two weeks of location work in late July 1963. The film brought Elvis his most dynamic co-star in Ann-Margret, who many believe may have been the one true love of his life.

Regardless of what happened between Elvis and Ann-Margret or any other Hollywood starlet, it was Priscilla Anne Beaulieu, 21, whom Elvis, 32, married on May 1, 1967. Elvis met Priscilla while stationed in Germany; she'd lived at Graceland since 1963 as a young maiden-in-waiting. They flew into town in the wee hours and obtained their marriage license at 3:30 a.m.

The Colonel's old friend Milton Prell hosted the wedding at his new hotel, the Aladdin. The ceremony was performed before a few friends and relatives in Prell's private suite in the three-story Camelot building, before the party opened up to include 100 additional guests for a celebration breakfast. *Las Vegas Sun* reporter Jeff Rice (who later wrote *The Night Stalker*) noted that the menu included "ham, eggs, and Southern-fried chicken, oysters Rockefeller, roast suckling pig, poached and candied salmon, lobster, eggs Minnette, and champagne."

In her biography *Elvis and Me,* Priscilla recalls the ceremony being as hideous as her Cleopatra eye makeup. It was an omen of sour things to come: The marriage would be over by 1972.

Matrimony and the imminent birth of daughter Lisa Marie aside, 1967 was not a good year for Elvis Presley. The Beatles, The Who, and the Rolling Stones had given a new meaning to rock music, and "Clambake" was not part of the definition.

Presley's yearning to restore his credibility as a live performer led to the "Elvis TV Special" (often referred to as "the Singer Special" or "the '68 Comeback Special"), which taped in the summer of 1968 and aired that December. A leather-clad Elvis electrified TV audiences, reminding fans of their rockabilly memories and introducing them to a more accomplished and versatile present.

Lamar Fike, a close confidant in the circle of friends known as "The Memphis Mafia," remembers the first talk of playing Las Vegas this way: "We had just finished 'the Singer Special'—everybody calls it a comeback special, but it really wasn't—and had flown into Vegas for a rest, because we'd worked real hard on that. The Colonel was in the front seat of the limo with his driver, and I was in the back with Elvis. The Colonel turned around with his cigar and said, 'You know, we can take that show you just did and put it in Vegas and make a lot of money.' Elvis looked at me, shrugged his shoulders, and said, 'Sounds like we're playing Vegas.'"

But it would not be that simple. Elvis hadn't performed outside television or film in nine years, and the stakes were high. Billionaire Kirk Kerkorian was building the International Hotel (now the Las Vegas Hilton); its 1,519 rooms made it the biggest

Barbra Streisand made her Las Vegas debut as Liberace's opening act in July 1963, at the same time that Elvis was filming *Viva Las Vegas* in town. Streisand visited Presley at the Hilton in August 1974 to talk with him about acting in her remake of *A Star Is Born.* The Colonel nixed the idea. Stories vary as to the reason, whether it was the usual wrangling over money or whether playing an over-the-hill rocker would hurt Elvis' "image." The part went to Kris Kristofferson.

Trivia

Elvis was still every bit the cool cat when he signed his deal to perform at the International Hotel, but the act that became a long-running hit was no longer at odds with the city's musical tastes.

hotel in the world. A nearly 2,000-seat showroom (with balcony) dwarfed anything else in Vegas. The hotel's short list of big attractions to open the room included Frank Sinatra and Barbra Streisand, as well as Elvis.

Streisand ended up opening the hotel as the result of a decision that today is a matter of dispute. Parker claimed before his death that he deliberately held his client back because the room was an unknown commodity and the sound and lighting kinks hadn't been worked out. "I never like to open a brand-new place," he said. "Let somebody else try out the equipment." But Nick Naff, the International's executive director of advertising and publicity, said the Colonel put the same kind of spin on that tale as he did on most others.

Streisand was hot, Naff says, coming off her famous concert in Central Park and an Academy Award for *Funny Girl*. Elvis, on the other hand, was "really unknown as a stage property in Las Vegas. He had been doing nothing but making these lousy pictures, and he hadn't worked on a stage for years. He was very unsure of himself."

That much, at least, was indisputable. "Elvis was nervous because the last time he was in Vegas, he lost his ass and didn't do a damned thing," Fike says. "It rattled him. He was bothered by it." Despite all that had happened since, Fike—today a Nashville country music agent and publisher—says that for Presley, returning to Vegas was like "getting on your father's horse that had thrown you through a wall when you were a little kid. Even though you're older, you wouldn't be in a hurry to get back on it."

But Elvis and those around him did their homework. On a quest to reinvent himself, Elvis decided to investigate Tom Jones. The Welsh sex machine was packing the

Flamingo, the hotel Kerkorian had acquired at a fire-sale price and used as a training ground for the International's management team. "Joe Esposito [another inner-circle member who became Elvis' crew chief] came to me and said, 'We'd like to go see a couple of performances of Tom Jones,'" Naff recalls. "I knew Elvis was planning what he was going to do." The staff arranged for Elvis to enter the Flamingo showroom after the lights went down and to watch Jones from the back of the room. "And he did watch," Naff attests, "in two performances that I know of, in my presence. What he was trying to do was see what sells."

Despite the stripped-down, back-to-basics feel of "the Singer Special," Elvis decided he would have a lot of company on the Hilton's massive stage. For the first time in his career he would be backed by both rock band and stage orchestra, and by both male and female gospel vocal groups. (The female Sweet Inspirations included Cissy Houston, Whitney's mother.) He even hired Sammy Shore as the opening act after seeing the comedian warm up Tom Jones' casino audience.

Opening night on July 31, 1969, was a private show attended by celebrities, casino high rollers, and the press. The room still had its sound bugs, as Shore realized when he walked onstage after a few songs from the Sweet Inspirations and discovered that his microphone was dead. When he was handed a second one, he says, "I pretended that one was off, too." The gag won the crowd over for his 25-minute set. "It was so easy to bomb in that room," he adds. "I was so happy to get off but thrilled to have done as well as I did."

L ounge entertainment was hot during Elvis' comeback weekend. At Presley's request, the International hosted his old friend Wayne Cochran, as well as the Ike and Tina Turner revue during his engagement. More of his '50s contemporaries—the Everly Brothers and Frankie Avalon—were found at the top of the Landmark across the street. Vic Damone, who was working the Sands during Presley's 1956 debut, was appearing in the lounge at the Frontier. And Shecky Greene, co-billed with Presley in '56, was working the Riviera's lounge.

*Trivia*

As Shore walked off, Presley was standing in the wings waiting to go on. He extended a hand. "His hand was clammy," Shore recalls. "He was as nervous as I was." A drum roll called Elvis onstage. Clad in black with an acoustic guitar slung around his neck, he struck a familiar pose: "Well it's one for the money, two for the show, three to get ready, and go cat go!"

The Elvis that the audience saw that night—and for many nights to come—was not

Elvis meets the press after his opening night at the International on July 31, 1969. It was the only news conference he would ever consent to in Las Vegas.

the hip-swiveling youngster of the '50s, but not entirely a rip-off of a '60s-groovy, pelvis-thrusting Tom Jones either. "Jones was among the horniest men I ever knew," Naff says. "Elvis couldn't project that sex image. But he could say to females, 'Love me; I'm the nicest guy in the world.' That's the very reason they love him today. He played on his own projected qualities—the nice guy, the shy guy."

"It's the first time I've worked in front of people for nine years, and it may be the last. I don't know," Elvis told the preview-night audience. The singer churned and burned his way through a medley of his old rockabilly hits, but closed the 15-song show with a six-minute version of his most recent single, the brass-powered "Suspicious Minds."

Afterward, he appeared at a news conference—the only one he would ever sit through in Las Vegas. He told the reporters, "It was getting harder and harder to perform to a movie camera. The inspiration wasn't there." He seemed relaxed and cracked a few jokes, including the fact that he was "tired of playing a guy singing to the guy he's beating up" in the movies.

The Colonel had at least been right on one count when he told Naff, "You just wait till Elvis gets in. You don't know what's going to happen to your hotel." Legend has it that the very next day, hotel president Alex Shoofey and the Colonel struck a five-year deal, offering Elvis twice-annual engagements at $125,000 per week. (Former publicist Bruce Banke says there was never a signed contract, only a handshake deal.) The annual three-week "Summer Festivals" of performances in August and return engagements during the winter soon became a bonanza that neither side would want to spoil.

# A star is reborn

"It will never be again; I don't care how big the star is," Joe Guercio says of the Elvis years at the Las Vegas Hilton. As the hotel's musical director, Guercio arranged the charts and conducted a 30-piece orchestra for most of Elvis' Las Vegas dates and tours in the '70s. "It was another world. You can't get that going again."

Elvis may have suffered from bad timing in 1956, but he couldn't have picked a better window of opportunity than 1969. Big as it was, the International lacked a theme like most major resorts have today and drew much of its year-round trade from the Convention Center next door. Elvis gave the Hilton not only a theme but, twice a year, a convention as well. Reservations would come from Japan, England, Germany.

"Just like we need a new hotel every so often, we need a new star," noted *Las Vegas Sun* entertainment columnist Joe Delaney. Presley's opening-weekend competition on the Strip included Paul Anka, Ed Ames, Dinah Shore, Jerry Vale, Steve and Eydie, and, yes, even Shecky Greene, all from nightclubs or the staid world of variety television that Elvis once left all shook up.

Yet, at the same time, Vegas tradition helped define a new direction for Presley. When Elvis got out of the Army, Frank Sinatra and the Rat Pack hosted the now-infamous "Welcome Home" special, taped March 26, 1960, at Miami's Fontainebleu Hotel and aired May 8 on ABC. At one point, Sinatra sang "Love Me Tender" in counterpoint to Presley's take on Sinatra's "Witchcraft"—"We're working the same way only in different areas," Sinatra explained to the camera.

By the '70s, the contrast was no longer so awkward, and Sinatra's words were more prophetic than the ad-libbed line suggested at the time. "His [Elvis'] audiences were now ready," said Bill Willard. "The kids had grown up and now had the nostalgia thing going." They still screamed and clawed their way to the stage in hopes of being annointed with a kiss and a scarf while Elvis muddled through "Love Me Tender," but now they could afford hotel rooms, souvenirs, and gambling money.

By aging along with their hero, Elvis maniacs could now see beyond "Hound Dog" and allow their idol to expand his rock, gospel, and soul roots to the pop hits of the day. "B.J. Thomas has a new record out," Presley tells fans in *That's the Way It Is,* the concert film capturing a 1970 summer stint at the International. "And I don't particularly like it," he adds, with a nightclub comic's timing, before singing "I Just Can't Help Believing." Presley may not have learned "Witchcraft" from the Rat Pack, but he had learned how to work a room Vegas-style.

Elvis clowning backstage with longtime musical director Joe Guercio. The pose comes from an old joke in which a zoo ape pulls down his lower eyelid as a means of communicating, "Screw you."

"Sinatra was a show," says Joe Guercio. "Elvis was a happening." He would draw as many as 100,000 fans for each engagement (counting returnees; like rhinestone Deadheads, Elvis fans tried to catch as many shows as possible). At a Friday midnight show in February 1970, upward of 2,000 people were turned away—more than the number seated inside.

And yet, even with dinner entrées of steak, prime rib, or baked lobster tail going for a then-handsome fee of $15, "Elvis' showroom didn't make any money," Naff says. Nor did the singer draw the pinkie-ring high rollers like Sinatra did. "The real value of Elvis to the hotel was that he put the International on the map, period. In the old days, publicity was the thing for Las Vegas, not advertising." The International was inconveniently located a few blocks east of the Strip, "so the showroom meant everything to the casino." All headliners—Elvis included—were put on a grueling schedule of two 90-minute shows per night, so the casino could fill up with two "show breaks" each night. "When you have volume, you're gonna get play. Even the Elvis fans would play the slots," Naff adds.

The Colonel did what he could to make sure each engagement remained an event. Coming in a week or two early as the advance man, Parker would host a huge breakfast in his fourth-floor International suite, summoning every radio station's advertising rep and negotiating each contract for airtime buys. He also put the name "Elvis" on every billboard in town; frustrated political candidates weren't able to buy billboard space for the 1972 election because the Colonel had it all sewn up.

The night before Elvis' first show, the Colonel, in deference to the preceding headliner, would wait until the audience had entered the showroom, then would proceed to plaster every square inch of the hotel with Elvis posters. "By the time people came out [of the showroom], they'd be walking into a different casino than when they came in," Banke says. "He [the Colonel] prided himself on never leaving an empty spot" on the walls.

Parker also had his own racket working at the hotel's souvenir stands. He staffed them with volunteers from a local charity and cut the charity a generous check after every engagement, while still pocketing more cash than he would have if he'd paid the concessionaires. Ever the carnival huckster, Parker included among the souvenirs framed posters. "He called them original Renaldis from Italy," Naff remembers. "Where the other posters might cost ten dollars, these might cost forty or fifty." The kicker? "There was a guy in our carpenter shop named Renaldi who'd be turning these goddamned frames out all during the engagement!"

Las Vegas was even good for Elvis Presley—at first. For two years, he seemed happy to be back in direct contact with his fans, and the Hilton made a solid home base when he wasn't touring large arenas. The 30th-floor Imperial Suite was intended for all headliners, but it eventually became known to both the staff and the public as the "Elvis Suite." Lamar Fike remembers one stay that lasted for seven weeks. "I felt like I lived [there], for chrissakes," he says.

"What did he [Elvis] like about Vegas? The freedom. And the women, in that order," Fike adds. "He could still keep the hours he wanted to. Elvis was a vampire. He had to get back to the room [by sunrise]."

In the days after his engagement ended, but before he left town, Elvis and the guys would check out the next act to come into the Hilton or other acts on the Strip: Glenn Campbell, Redd Foxx, the Checkmates, Don Rickles, Wayne Cochran, and Bobbie Gentry. The latter had a wacky opening act named John Byner—who, it just happened, did a killer Elvis impression (as did Freddie Bell, Brendan Boyer, the Mary Kaye Trio, and any number of lounge acts Elvis just "happened to go see" over the years). "We went to see Byner three or four times in a week. Elvis just loved it," Sonny West recalls.

West remembers one memorable trip to see Bobby Darin, whom Elvis recognized as the "showman" he was aspiring to be. "He's in his tux and everything, looking real sharp," West recalls. "We're clapping and everything. He knows we're out there. So he comes to a part of his show where he was getting ready to do a medley of his old hits. And he says, 'I feel like I've grown past this.'

"All of a sudden, this voice booms out, 'Don't knock what made ya, Bobby!'" Upon hearing the voice of the King, "Bobby crunched his shoulders up and says, 'Man, you know something? He's right!' Boom! 'Splish splash, I was takin' a bath …'"

Over the years, the Vegas routine became more refined. When Elvis would land by private plane at the Howard Hughes Charter Terminal, road manager Joe Esposito would phone ahead to advise Hilton officials of the landing time so hotel limousines could be dispatched to the private airfield. By the time the limos arrived to whisk the entourage to the hotel's north laundry entrance, "there'd be five hundred fans there," Banke recalls with a laugh. "I thought, 'How do they know this?'"

Elvis and the guys sported custom jewelry with the logo "TCB," which even casual fans know means "Takin' Care of Business." But Naff says the logo had a double meaning, and the second one perhaps even came first: "Takin' Care of the Broads." Showroom maître d' Emilio Muscelli and his staff had their marching orders: Line the massive stage with "good-looking, middle-aged, Elvis maniacs, not screaming youngsters," Naff recalls. The same rules didn't always apply in the dressing room beneath the stage.

Getting someone into the dressing room to meet Elvis was "a complicated protocol," Naff says. "I didn't abuse it, [but] one time I had agreed with a newspaper in Honolulu to send the winner of a beauty pageant and her escort on a trip to Las Vegas that included a stay at the hotel and a meeting with Elvis." Both the winner and her escort were, predictably, gorgeous.

"I took them down there the first night," Naff recalls. "There's always four or five guys hanging around, and I say, 'Elvis, I want you to meet [the women]. I'm not going to impose on you, but if you could just spare five minutes, et cetera, et cetera.'" Presley sat and chatted away with the women, and after a while looked up and said, "Hey, Nick, you can go."

"I promised to have them out of there in five minutes, but I didn't see those girls for two more days," Naff says, shaking his head. "They just sucked them up. They disappeared."

The Vegas show grew to a level so parodied that it's hard to see in a serious light today. The first engagement's black karate outfit was replaced by the now universally recognized jumpsuit, adorned with sequins and sometimes topped off by a cape. Bandleader Guercio came up with a theme fit for a king when he and his wife went to see a reissue of *2001: A Space Odyssey.* During the opening sequence set to Strauss' "Also Sprach Zarathustra," Guercio's wife leaned over and said, "Don't you get the feeling Elvis is about to walk out?" From that point on, he never walked out to anything else. (Guercio also continues to receive royalties when comedians or talk shows use his brief "Elvis Theme," a three-note rise and fall written so the band would have something to play while Presley was taking his bows.)

Though Presley was now working with strings and horns, he wouldn't be confined. "Ever let the air out of a balloon?" Guercio asks, his eyes following an imaginary one around the room. Presley would try to stump the band on what song he'd launch into next. Guercio ordered oversized music stands for his players and separated the charts with cardboard tabs labeling each song for quick access. "When [Elvis] got hip to it, he loved it," Guercio says. "It was like a fencing contest. He got off on it. I never did."

Elvis and the boys did love a good prank. Guercio once jokingly complained that the billboards always said "Elvis" and didn't mention the band. Driving toward the hotel one day, he spotted a billboard that read "The Joe Guercio Orchestra," with the word "Elvis" in tiny letters in one corner. Another time, Sammy Shore turned around in the middle of his monologue to see a life-size and lifelike mannequin plummet to a hanging death from the Hilton balcony.

But no one was laughing in January 1971, when opening night was clouded by a Memphis newspaper's revelation that Presley had received death threats. Security was unusually tight and "the whole room was in chaos," Shore said. "I made it funny. I kept saying, 'Remember, I'm just a comic. Don't shoot.'"

Post-Charles Manson hysteria convinced Clark County Sheriff's officials that it was acceptable to issue the guys concealed weapon permits, which may explain how the private elevator to the Elvis Suite wound up with a bullet hole—and how a TV screen or two met their fates.

Two years later, Presley got to be the ultimate badass right onstage, when four men rushed the stage from their ringside seats. By one newspaper account, Elvis sent the first one flying off the stage into the audience: "Presley's precise punch palls pugilistic Peruvian," read one headline. The four men were arrested on drunk charges and later filed suit, claiming they were just trying to shake hands.

"Everyone was riding a crest," Shore says. "No one thought it was ever going to end. I remember feeling like I never wanted this to stop."

# Winding down

The crest ended for Shore before it did for Elvis. In a 1972 misunderstanding, Shore agreed, with the Colonel's consent, to play the Hilton's show lounge for more money. What the Colonel didn't tell him was that it would mean being replaced by fellow comic Jackie Kahane in the showroom. "A few years later when I went to see [the show], I felt really sad," Shore recalls. "[Elvis] just didn't care anymore. It was like showing up and doing a job now. I thought, 'Why are you letting this all slip away?'"

Most people now know why. But at the time, the rumors of drug abuse were written off by both the King (of Denial?) and his fans as the evil rantings of hippies and liberals out to destroy him. A widely circulated tape, apparently recorded on the Hilton soundboard during a performance, has the King confronting the rumors head-on: "I don't pay attention to rumors. I don't pay attention to movie magazines. ... I don't read 'em, because they're all junk. [Audience applause.] Now I-I-I don't mean to put anybody's job down. They got a job to do, they gotta write something, so if they don't know anything, they make it up. [More applause.] In my case they make it up. But I hear rumors flying around. I got sick in the hospital. ... In this day and time, you can't even get sick. You are 'strung out.' Well, by God, I'll tell you something, friend. I have never been strung out on anything in my life, except music.

In the final era of Presley's career, this Nassau arena concert photo (autographed to Joe Guercio) shows the King almost unrecognizably overweight in his trademark white jumpsuit.

"When I got sick here in the hotel ... one night I had a hundred and two [degree] temperature ... from three different sources I heard, I was 'strung out' on heroin. All across this town, 'strung out.' I swear to God. Hotel employees, Jack ... bellboys, freaks who carry your luggage up to the hotel room ... maids. ... All across this town, 'strung out.'

"Now don't you get offended, ladies and gentlemen, because I'm talking to somebody else. If I find, or hear, the individual that has said that about me, I'm gonna break your goddamned neck, you son of a bitch! [Wild applause.] That is dangerous; that is damaging to myself, to my little daughter, to my father, to my doctor. ... I will pull your goddamned tongue out by the *roots!* [More applause.] ... Thank you very much. Now anyway, how many of you people saw the movie *Blue Hawaii?* Probably the most requested song—let me get out of this mood—probably the most requested song in this movie was 'Hawaiian Wedding Song.'"

By now most Elvisphiles agree that Presley did not consider his up-and-down cycles of amphetamine and narcotics to be drug abuse, since his pills were prescribed. (After Presley's death, it was George "Dr. Nick" Nichopolous who was in the hot seat. But Elvis was fond enough of his Las Vegas physician, Dr. Elias Ghanem, to give him a $38,500 Stutz Blackhawk coupe.) At the time, Elvis watchers could see only his change in attitude.

"What audiences see in the flesh is a rather somnolent, lackadaisical superstar attired in bejeweled jumpsuit and who, with almost sleepwalking fervor, makes his rounds kissing little girls and throwing scarves," Bill Willard, who had been so wrong about Elvis in the '50s, wrote in August 1973. "Everyone's been there before, even to the 'new' tunes inserted. They sound old and mid-'50sish." Willard concluded, somewhat ominously, that the Colonel's "windup toy is winding down."

In late August 1974, Presley canceled the Hilton shows, citing pneumonia. It was his first cancellation at the Hilton, and only the fifth in his entire career, he told reporters. The following summer, he canceled most of a Hilton engagement to fly back to Memphis for hospitalization and treatment for fatigue. It was reported as his fifth hospitalization since 1973, only two years earlier.

Health problems and an obvious weight gain were compounded by a discernible lack of enthusiasm. "By nineteen seventy-five, he was bored," says veteran *Sun* columnist Delaney, who wrote his first less-than-glowing column after Presley wisecracked and insulted band members for most of a show before cutting it short. "The attitude was just terrible," Delaney remembers.

If Elvis was bored, so was the general public. By the mid-'70s, wider interest had waned—as it had 10 years earlier. "The last two years he still filled the house, but it was the die-hards at that point," Delaney recalls.

"The ship had already sailed; he couldn't get any bigger than he already was," Shore says. "It's always the journey. When you get there, it's over with. There are no more mountains to climb."

"It got to be kind of pathetic at the end," says Naff, who remembers the King strolling around backstage in a head-to-ankle boxer's robe with the hood pulled tight like a turban. One night, CEO Barron Hilton and other corporate officials decided to give Presley a jeweled belt as a birthday present. (Elvis usually opened at the hotel in January, soon after his birthday on the eighth.) The dressing room had a public living-room area with a well-stocked bar that was separated from the actual private dressing area. "We got into the dressing room right away and sat there, fifteen or twenty minutes," Naff recalls. "It was uncomfortable. Nobody wanted to leave. ... Then he [Elvis] comes out with his robe. It was embarrassing. He could hardly talk. If you think he slurred when he normally talked, you should have heard him that night. That's when we knew: This can't go on."

Explanations vary as to why Elvis felt the pressure to continue. The ones most cited are debts from excessive spending, bad business management by his father Vernon, and the Colonel's gambling habit—the simple explanation for Parker's loyalty to the Hilton. "He would take over a whole roulette table for hours," Delaney recalls.

It was clear that Presley needed a long break from the Vegas and concert tour ordeal. Two shows a night are almost unheard of on the modern-day Strip but were still a norm for the Elvis engagements, even in the later years. Elvis performed at 8 p.m. and midnight. At least once during the early engagements, a third show was added at 3 a.m. to accommodate fans who were being turned away from the showroom—even after the aisles were packed with extra chairs, by some accounts. (Fire inspectors, responsible for enforcing occupancy limits, were notorious for eyesight as poor as that of pro-wrestling referees.)

"The Colonel had him on a brutal schedule," Lamar Fike says. "If somebody did it now, they'd die onstage. … It was the most cruel thing I've ever seen in my life." The town where Elvis came to play ended up working him into a cycle of bad habits. "I think Vegas contributed as much to his demise as anything else," Fike adds. "He literally worked himself to death."

Presley's 1976 winter engagement at the Hilton began on December 2. Just as comedian Kahane was finishing his routine, a voice signaled him through the curtains to stretch the act. In his column about opening night, Joe Delaney reported: "Presley finally came onstage at 10:02 p.m. and sang until 11:47 p.m. … He is still a little heavier than he should be but not as heavy as on his previous visit. The capacity crowd could [not] care less about this."

Freddie Bell, Presley's Las Vegas friend from the '50s, took his mother to one of those final shows but declined Joe Esposito's offer to go backstage. "I couldn't go," Bell says. "To see such a deterioration—and I knew what the problem was, too. I was sick, because here's a kid that was so clean. Never would drink or smoke. I was a

## Elvis Shows in Vegas

New Frontier: April 23-May 6, 1956
The International (renamed the Las Vegas Hilton in 1971):
July 31-August 28, 1969
January 26-February 23 and August 10-September 7, 1970
January 26-February 23 and August 9-September 6, 1971
January 26-February 23 and August 4-September 4, 1972
January 23-February 23 and August 6-September 3, 1973
January 26-February 9 and August 19-September 2, 1974
March 18-April 1, August 18-20, and December 2-15, 1975
December 2-12, 1976

drinker in those days, a wild kid. And he used to tell me I was crazy the way I behaved. He used to tell me to clean up, start working out."

The 11-day, 15-show engagement ended on December 12. It was the last Las Vegas would see of the real Elvis Presley.

# The final curtain

On August 16, 1977, Joe Guercio and his wife were stopping by the Boulevard Mall for some last-minute items before flying to Portland, Maine, to join the band when he heard the news.

Bruce Banke took a call from an Associated Press reporter, who said there were unconfirmed reports that Elvis Presley had died. Banke recalls: "I told him that with certain stars, rumors start all the time. 'If you hear anything else, call me back.' He called back. I could hear the bells in the background," sounding the "urgent" code on the AP's old teletype machines.

Banke barged in on a meeting between Barron Hilton and the hotel's executive staff. "I must have been white," he says. "I hadn't been in the room a minute when the phone rang. It was Colonel Parker calling Barron to confirm it." Banke and his staff "proceeded to answer calls until eleven that night. My entire staff had no voice left. ... As a PR person, that was without a doubt the longest day of my life."

> Elvis was just an illusion. He wasn't real, just something you saw through a piece of glass.
>
> George Sidney, director
> *Viva Las Vegas*

Ghanem told reporters that he "personally gave [Presley] a physical examination for insurance reasons only recently. ... Why, he was in perfect health." Ghanem traveled to Memphis to take stock of the situation, as reports of drug abuse flew.

"He didn't take dope," local performer Sonny King told a crowd of mourners. "His dope was you, the people. You were his narcotic."

"Some people had to die," says Joe Guercio. "Marilyn Monroe had to die. James Dean had to die. I can't see E.P. at sixty years old, just like I can't see Marilyn at eighty. That's the way it is."

The flag in front of the Hilton flew at half-staff on August 16, 1977. And the next day, the *Review-Journal* reported that an inch and a half of rain poured from the sky in a three-hour period that began shortly after midnight, causing the roofs of "countless businesses and homes [to] collapse under the weight of constant rainfall during the night," as a city mourned the fall of its King.

# Tom Jones: The Eternal Sex Machine

People often wonder what Elvis would be like today if he hadn't died in 1977. By now, it's safe to say that the King could only have hoped for a best-case scenario summed up in two words: Tom Jones.

By far the coolest cat to endure as a 30-year headliner on the Strip, Jones has remained a certified sex machine. And he's done this, at least in recent years, while never crossing too far over the line of self-parody. Even if he's no longer packaging the merchandise in spandex-tight pants or karate-kicking "Delilah" with quite as much vigor, how many 60-year-olds can get a crowd on its feet by belting out Lennie Kravitz's "Are You Gonna Go My Way"?

The mutual affair between Tom Jones and Vegas began when he first played the Flamingo on March 21, 1968. It came just after a breathtaking climb in which the young singer, who had fancied himself a Welsh soul brother, was steered into a groovier brand of British pop by his songwriting manager, Gordon Mills.

In 1965, Jones recalls, "We were looking for a rock 'n' roll tune to do, [something] hard-hitting." Jones recorded a demo of Mills' song "It's Not Unusual," which was intended for a female singer. "I said, 'This sounds like a hit song.' [Mills] said, 'Yeah, but not for you.' It was a lot milder when we first did it. It didn't have the brass going. It was softer, like a Brazil '66 [arrangement]."

When Jones insisted,

A 1984 publicity photo of Tom Jones when he was 44—already older than Elvis was when he died—no doubt benefits from retouching, but it still suggests the future that might have been for Presley.

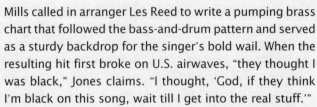

Mills called in arranger Les Reed to write a pumping brass chart that followed the bass-and-drum pattern and served as a sturdy backdrop for the singer's bold wail. When the resulting hit first broke on U.S. airwaves, "they thought I was black," Jones claims. "I thought, 'God, if they think I'm black on this song, wait till I get into the real stuff.'"

But the real stuff would have to wait a little longer. The B-side of "It's Not Unusual" was a Burt Bacharach song called "To Wait for Love." Bacharach liked what he heard and wanted the young singer to do his next movie anthem, "What's New, Pussycat?" He told Jones: "It's a crazy song for a crazy movie. But in order to give it credibility, I need you to sing it." When Jones first heard the song, he says, "I thought [Bacharach] was joking. ... I said, 'I want to go a different way. I want to go into R and B.' He said, 'You've got plenty of time for that.'"

And thus began the wildly schizo career of Tom Jones. "The problem I've always had has been my versatility," he says. "When I hear a song I like, I want to do it. Sometimes it doesn't fit into what people might think I would do."

He first visited Vegas during that breakthrough year of 1965, en route to an *Ed Sullivan Show* taping in Los Angeles. "I came to Vegas to have a look at it and see what it was all about," he said. "I thought, 'Christ, this would be a good place to work.' But it took three years." That's how long it took a New York-based agent to suggest to Jones that he was ready to make the move from the Dick Clark "teen" circuit in the States to the nightclubs.

As luck would have it, the wife of Flamingo General Manager Alex Shoofey saw Jones at New York's Copacabana club and urged her husband to book him, remembers Nick Naff, publicist for the Flamingo and later for the Hilton. "He was virtually unknown" in Vegas and required some "building up" as a headliner, Naff recalls, which explains a hotel press release for the month-long engagement: "Las Vegas has seen them all, from the biggest names on Broadway to the million-dollar film queens. But few have generated the excitement that seems to be surrounding the premier Las Vegas engagement of British song star Tom Jones." Mrs. Shoofey even posed with Jones in a photo, "welcoming" him to the city.

In reality, casino types thought he was "a pop singer, trying to be a nightclub entertainer," Jones recalls. They hedged their bet by teaming him with comedian Kaye Ballard, "America's Favorite Mother-in-Law." But management knew it had made the right call, Naff says, when "the wives of the pit bosses came to stand in the back and watch him. ... In those days, he was young and vigorous and had all the moves. He did things that more or less weren't done before."

Not that the Strip didn't require a little time to adapt. First came the confusion caused by "Tom Jones"—a 50-minute topless cabaret spoof of the Henry Fielding novel and the movie that the singer took his stage name from—playing in the Desert Inn lounge. "The movie was so big that [people] thought I was going to act in a play," he recalls. And Kaye Ballard perhaps wished that it had been a play. "She was very upset because the same audience was coming to see me every night," Jones says. "She was trying to do these [same] jokes, and they're the same people out there." More than half of the audience were repeat customers.

From that first engagement, Jones leveled out his white soul excursions ("I Can't Stop Loving You," Bobby Blue Bland's "Turn On Your Love Light") with such work-the-room variety numbers as "Hello, Young Lovers," "Danny Boy," and "Old Black Magic." No question lingered as to whether the hotel would honor the remaining engagements in its three-year contract.

The next year brought a legendary visit from another Vegas greenhorn: Elvis

The line between mentor and protégé blurred when Elvis came to check out Tom Jones at the Flamingo, while readying his own act for the International. The two became friends even though Presley borrowed some of Jones' athletic stage moves.

Presley. "He wanted to see what I was doing to be successful in Las Vegas," Jones recalls. "He was honest about it when he came backstage after the show. ... He said seeing me gave him more confidence to make a comeback in live shows, which he did," Jones adds. "He said he felt we were similar in our approach. ... Why was I successful in sixty-eight when he wasn't in fifty-six? But times had changed by then."

Presley took the lessons to heart: The brassy arrangements, the karate kicks, and the sex appeal swathed in a veneer of nightclub respectability all became elements of Elvis' Vegas revue.

As for Jones, he cut a *Live in Las Vegas* album at the Flamingo in 1968, capturing a stage show that included "Hey Jude," as well as "Hard to Handle" (years before the Black Crowes remade it). The following February, *This Is Tom Jones* debuted on ABC. "Then it was pandemonium," he says of his stateside popularity.

Jones was promoted to the newer and larger International, then jumped ship to Caesars Palace in April 1971. A non-bylined newspaper report that may or may not have been a hotel press release (it was sometimes hard to tell in those days) claimed that the opening weekend "mobs" were so great that the hotel had to take the "unprecedented step" of opening its reservation windows at 9 a.m.—"an hour considered almost nocturnal in the round-the-clock entertainment capital." Inside the showroom, "women stood in the aisles and danced, some on table tops," while guards tried to keep other ladies off the stage. A "woman from Michigan was stopped at the [dressing room] door when security noticed she had a handcuff clipped to her wrist. She later explained that the open cuff was to entrap Jones."

The *Live at Caesars Palace* album captures the macho madness of the era and features Jones' best album cover of all time: He is posing in a Roman robe and hoisting a goblet, while being tended to by a quartet of toga-clad, grape-feeding babes. The photo fueled Jones' decadent image as a lady's man, but the swingin' singer said his drinking had to be severely curbed while in Vegas.

"The only thing I had to watch was alcohol, because it's so dry here and alcohol dehydrates you anyway," he said. "If you're going to do two shows a night for a month straight in Las Vegas, alcohol's got to go. I tried it the other way, but it didn't work," he added with a laugh. "My cousins would come out from Wales, where I was always known as a beer drinker. And my cousins said, 'If the boys back home could see you ...'"

But Vegas was well worth the sacrifice, sustaining Jones long past his peak years. He became one of the great showroom interpreters, but not of the Cole Porter and Harold Arlen classics already well-covered by the Rat Pack. Instead, a Tom Jones show in the '80s was more a place for his fans to hear—perhaps for

Jones remained the once and future sex machine in 1998, forging on with his sometimes loopy, but always invigorating, brand of blue-eyed soul.

the first time—covers of contemporary hits: Prince's "Purple Rain," Sting's "We'll Be Together," or the Escape Club's "Wild, Wild West" ("There's so many bloody words in it," Jones noted). When INXS caught wind that Jones was covering "Need You Tonight," the group encored a Las Vegas concert with "It's Not Unusual."

It was another cover tune that eventually leaked beyond Jones' insulated following and revived his career. Anne Dudley—producing and performing under the name Art of Noise—caught Jones singing Prince's "Kiss" on a British talk show and invited him to sing on her own offbeat synthetic version. "I don't think I've gone into left field or anything," Jones said after the song became a hit in late 1988. "There's a part of me that is a rock 'n' roll singer." However, he changed a key word: Prince may sing, "Women not girls rule my world," but "women *and* girls" rule the world of Tom Jones. "Why would he want to leave out the girls?" Jones pondered.

For the "Kiss" video, Jones donned a looser-fitting black wardrobe and jettisoned the trademark pants that fit like leotards from the knees up but managed to flair into cuffs somewhere around the ankles. He decided to retain the baggier look for his stage shows. And while he hasn't been opposed to dropping his 1994 dance single, "If I Only Knew," like a 40-megaton bomb on a showroom crowd, he has otherwise retreated from the Top 40 hits to the soul standards that remain his first love. "I've gone back to what I started with," he said. "If there are no uptempo songs out that I think fit the bill, I fall back to soul."

Lately, he's even been finishing the "you and your pussy ... [cat]" lyric that he used to leave hanging when singing "What's New, Pussycat?" And most of the time, he doesn't even bother to savor the panties tossed onstage. But don't take this as newfound Puritanism. "I don't mind people throwin' underwear," he said. "I used to really do the business and all that, [but] it got old because I was getting reviewed on not what songs I was singing but how many pairs of bloody underwear" ended up onstage.

"I want people to take my voice seriously, but in doing so, I still like to have fun with it," he noted of appearances on *The Simpsons* and in the movie *The Jerky Boys.*

Living well in deluxe high-roller suites during his six to eight weeks in Vegas each year, Jones is the rare veteran who doesn't think the town was better when the mob ran it. "It didn't do much for the show to have a lot of hoodlums around here," he says. "It didn't affect me in the showroom. My audience is regular people."

That could be "regular" in the sense of an underwear-throwing fanatic, or a conventioneer who decides to check him out on the spur of the moment. "There's no such thing as a Vegas crowd, because it can change nightly," Jones says. But the singer prefers to see that as a challenge. "It doesn't bother me if the show is filled with convention people, as long as I can get to them," he says. "It doesn't matter to me when it is, but it'll happen somewhere in the show. I will get them."

# THE LAS VEGAS DRIVE-IN

An odd but indisputable truth emerges from the movies set in Las Vegas: The best of them have little or nothing to do with gambling. The city's main claim to fame has been relegated more to forgotten melodramas such as the Ryan O'Neal bomb *Fever Pitch* in 1985. The movies people *really* remember deal more with the decorative edges, the distractions used to bait the trap. It doesn't matter whether it's show business, a showgirl, or perhaps just the trippy architecture of the casino itself.

The poster for the 1969 generation-gap comedy *Where It's At* bills "Brenda Vaccaro as Molly, Don Rickles as Willie, and Caesars Palace as CAESARS PALACE." Talk about product placement. By the time of *Mars Attacks!* in 1996, however, Vegas had evolved beyond the art design dreams of even such a demented genius as director Tim Burton. Why build something so extravagant as a pyramid on a back lot when there's already one sitting in the desert?

"The definition of surrealism in Vegas is very wide. At what point are you into the area of the surreal in this town?" writer-director Andrew Bergman asked in 1992, when his comedy *Honeymoon in Vegas* ushered in the modern era of Vegas depicted more as a twisted theme park than as a seedy place where losers come to live or die at the tables.

Las Vegas is so full of "visual information," as Bergman put it, that even movies like *Con Air*—which has no plot-related reason to be within the city limits—take on a luster they don't deserve. *Honeymoon in Vegas* was "the first [movie] I wrote as the director, thinking as much about where the scene was taking place and what was going on in the background as what [the characters] were actually saying," Bergman added.

*Honeymoon* inadvertently reveals another priceless asset of shot-on-location Vegas movies. Though it was made in the '90s, the closing sequence of Elvis impersonators parachuting into Bally's parking lot will show future generations that there was indeed a parking lot in front of Bally's, not the electric Slinky that now shuffles pedestrians in from the sidewalk. Or perhaps some day it will prove that there once *was* a hotel called Bally's. The same sequence shows the Dunes sign standing proudly across the street—not to mention the Dunes itself—instead of the Bellagio.

In other words, movies preserve the architecture that Vegas doesn't. In *Honeymoon,* Nicolas Cage runs down Fremont Street beneath a wide-open sky. Five summers later in *Con Air,* he's sprinting under a Fremont Street Experience canopy with LED-animated jets soaring above him. For those who can recall these recent changes, older movies such as *Meet Me in Las Vegas* and *Las Vegas Story* might as well have been filmed on Mars. It's a struggle to recognize a reference point—anything familiar—in the background. Even in 1971, when James Bond heads west on Flamingo Road in *Diamonds Are Forever,* the position of the Dunes sign indicates that the camera was on top of the late hotel. But where's Bond headed? There's no Barbary Coast. No Bourbon Street, no Maxim. Not even an MGM Grand (later Bally's). It's just bare desert.

Beyond showing how Las Vegas has exploded, the movies explain what it used to be. The rambling landscaped driveways leading up to the Strip hotels in *Ocean's Eleven* and the luxurious Flamingo swimming pool surrounded by graceful bungalows in *Viva Las Vegas* speak volumes about the non-gambling appeal of the young Vegas. It was indeed a desert oasis, a mirage on a dusty highway where peaceful days by the pool leveled off the high-adrenaline evenings.

The list of movies filmed in Vegas is growing with the city, but most of the attention here will focus on three certified classics—at least in the *Cult Vegas* sense. Though none is considered a great movie by conventional wisdom, their enduring popularity quashes their faults and critics. *Ocean's Eleven, Viva Las Vegas,* and *Diamonds Are Forever* each capture something quintessentially cool about Vegas. The rest of the made-in-Vegas movies just have to fall in line.

# *Ocean's Eleven*

(Warner Brothers, 1960. Produced and directed by Lewis Milestone. Written by Harry Brown and Charles Lederer. Starring Frank Sinatra, Dean Martin, and Sammy Davis Jr.)

*"The eleven of us cats against this one little city."*

If ever a movie's behind-the-scenes story was more interesting than the finished product, it was that of *Ocean's Eleven.* The energy that went into the Rat Pack's fabled evenings at the Sands is noticeably missing in the film, along with any real sense of urgency. It's not a musical but does squeeze in two memorable songs. It's not quite funny enough to be a flat-out comedy and not thrilling enough to be a caper drama. Leisurely directed to the point of disinterest, *Ocean's Eleven* falls somewhere in the maddening middle.

Why, then, is it the ultimate Vegas movie?

The answer comes with words used hesitantly, for they are far too pretentious for the movies discussed here. *Verisimilitude. Milieu.* What the uppity French refer to as "social" or "cultural" setting: a movie's way of reading between the lines. But just call it "cool." *Ocean's Eleven* shows, in wide-screen and living color, what it really was like to roam around Frank Sinatra's Strip in its 1960 heyday. The history was captured accidentally; the movie is too much into its stars to be aware of its historical value, though Warner Brothers publicists did play up the location shooting in the press book by noting that this was the real Vegas and not some soundstage.

But there's another milieu at work here: the Rat Pack vibe, the sheer attitude that unifies the movie. It's the casual swagger, the flick of a cigarette, the snappy patter. It's easier to forgive the shortcomings of *Ocean's Eleven* if you see it for what it is: a conceit. Not a movie that made the boys look good, but a movie they thought would make them look good. The final product screams for the magical sense of anarchy that was played out each night in the showroom. Any armchair scriptwriter could conjure a vastly more even and entertaining film by recasting Danny Ocean and his entire gang, not just Dino's lounge singer character, as Vegas entertainers who become more innocently embroiled in their plan to rob five casinos; think *Some Like It Hot* without the dresses.

But that wouldn't have been cool. At least not as cool as imagining yourselves to be playboys who served together in the 82nd Airborne. The movie was a vanity effort by Sinatra's own Dorchester Productions, so the premise had to tickle Frank's fancy. And what could be better than putting aside the show-biz grind and pretending to be a war hero capable of pulling off a commando raid between martinis? If they want to see the showroom act, let them come to Vegas.

Peter Lawford is usually credited with bringing the basic premise of war buddies conspiring to rob Vegas to Sinatra's attention. The Warner Brothers studio records, available through the University of Southern California film archives, attribute a first draft titled *The Hard Way* to Daniel Fuchs. But no matter who hatched the caper movie, studio records indicate that the casual air of the finished product extended back two years to what young filmmakers now call "development hell."

A late-December 1958 memo from studio executive Walter MacEwen suggested that the project was slow-rolling, in part because director Lewis Milestone, then 62, preferred staying home to showing up at the studio to meet with screenwriter Richard Breen. "Frank seems in fine fettle and very cooperative," MacEwen wrote. "If Milly

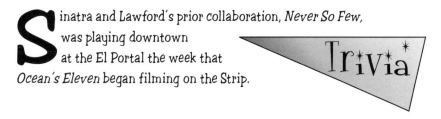

**S**inatra and Lawford's prior collaboration, *Never So Few,* was playing downtown at the El Portal the week that *Ocean's Eleven* began filming on the Strip.

[Milestone] comes in daily as he said he is willing to do, then Breen will show regularly, too, and this whole project will get on a more businesslike footing."

Studio records also show that Milestone and Breen wanted to view three movies in their research. *The Lavender Hill Mob,* a British caper comedy about timid bank clerks molding gold into Eiffel Tower souvenirs, foreshadowed the tone of *Ocean's Eleven* far better than the French Foreign Legion drama, *Legion of the Doomed,* or Stanley Kubrick's early classic, *The Killing*—although the latter was about an elaborate robbery. Breen also needed to visit Vegas "to survey the terrain carefully," with "all necessary arrangements made by Sinatra," as another MacEwen note pointed out in September 1958.

"It seems Breen has never been to Las Vegas, but carefully concealed this fact from Sinatra," MacEwen wrote. It almost goes without saying that Breen's name does not appear in the eventual movie, which instead gives screenplay credit to veteran screenwriters Harry Brown (*Sands of Iwo Jima, D-Day, The Sixth of June*) and Charles Lederer (*Can-Can*), based on a story by George Clayton Johnson (the infamous *Logan's Run*) and Jack Golden Russell.

With so many writers involved, it's no wonder that the movie struggles so mightily to find its tone, and that minor characters and subplots are brought up, then abandoned. It even begins with a bit of narration—"Christmas in Beverly Hills ..."—though the narrator (Richard Boone) is never heard from again. However, great things are promised through the snappy animated titles by Saul Bass—who gave so many '60s films their distinctive opening visuals—and a breezy overture based on the recurring "Eee-O-Eleven" theme by Nelson Riddle. (The animated titles replaced the screenplay's proposal to have toys in a Beverly Hills store window suggest the major characters.)

The first half-hour unfolds slowly. The characters are introduced gradually as they're brought together for some type of scheme, but the gradual clues merely bore modern viewers already familiar with the caper. Spyros Acebos (Akim Tamiroff) is the Beverly Hills mastermind who thinks up great crimes but hires others to pull them off. He's hatched a plot so brilliant that it requires "Mushy" (Joey Bishop) to reunite the members of the 82nd Airborne once commanded by Danny Ocean. The gang is constantly getting Acebos' goat ("Why don't those fellows respect me? ... Why should I be treated like I'm stupid and they're smart?"), which is the lamest humor in the movie.

But the introduction of Sinatra and Lawford is some of the best. Vince Foster (Lawford) is getting a very James Bondian backrub from a babe in an Arizona hotel when Sinatra enters in a fleecy orange pullover. "If you're not careful, buddy boy, she'll rub you out," Ocean notes with a flick of his cigarette as the camera pulls back to reveal a second babe waiting to rub his shoulders. The two men talk business briefly, ignoring their hot masseuses, until Ocean lightly pats one on the rear and says, "All right, girls, time for your nap. Beat it." He pours himself a drink—an array of booze bottles adorns nearly every interior scene—and squirts Foster with a shot of seltzer to get him up and running. It's all shamelessly sexist, even without the cut Lawford line: "If there's one thing I hate, you succulent thing, it's to be cold."

As both the head of Dorchester Productions and a partner in the Sands, Sinatra—seen here on the casino floor—was able to put the two together with the filming of *Ocean's Eleven*.

Mushy goes to the airport to greet lounge singer Sam Harmon (Dean Martin), who, it's explained, is Ocean's closest friend because Ocean saved his life during the war. Meanwhile, Sinatra and Lawford head to a Phoenix burlesque club (a back-lot set at Warners) to round up Vince Massler (showroom comedian Buddy Lester), who is working as the club's emcee. It turns out that the stripper—dancing to the strains of "The Tender Trap"—is Massler's wife, and a bar fight breaks out after a drunk rube comes on to her with the quaint pickup line, "I'd like to wrap you up, take you home, and spread you on my waffle."

Meanwhile, the last two major players make their appearances. (As the title promises, there are indeed 11 conspirators all told, but fortunately the movie didn't flesh out parts for all of them.) Anthony Bergdorf (Richard Conte) is meant to be the dramatic focus, a just-paroled electrical genius who wants to go straight for the benefit of his wife and son, but needs the money because of bad news from his health-care provider: "Doc, give it to me straight. Is it the Big Casino?"

Josh Howard (Sammy Davis Jr.) is found driving a garbage truck and singing the bluesy theme song "Eee-O-Eleven" (the name comes from a crapshooter's good-luck chant). His hopes of playing professional baseball were curtailed by the prospect of minor leagues in the South: "Can you imagine a one-eyed third baseman in Mobile?" Josh is intrigued by the payoff of $1 million each and likes the odds: "The eleven of us cats against this one little city." Though he's a black garbageman, the Josh character's warm, equal, and "colorblind" treatment by the other characters was subtly progressive for the movie's day, and a sharp contrast to all the Jewish and Negro jokes in the Rat Pack's stage act.

Late in this busy agenda comes an attempt to flesh out Ocean's character by introducing Angie Dickinson as his estranged wife Bea. Their marriage "drowned in champagne," she tells him before shooting down his bid for "a little hey-hey." Finally, when Foster goes to hit up his rich mother for more allowance money, viewers meet Caesar Romero as Duke Santos. He's a millionaire, self-made by dubious means, and the latest in the string of mom's many husbands. Foster is embarrassed to always be begging for change, but he acknowledges that "money is a hard habit to break."

**A**ngie Dickinson's part was longer in the script. A cut sequence had Ocean and his wife briefly reuniting in Ocean's suite on New Year's Eve, tussling on the bed. "I just want you to quit this life," she tells him. "I'm not letting you dump the cart on me," he replies. Since their relationship is not resolved anyway—and doesn't really jibe with the film's fraternal tone—the already long movie was probably wise to leave her character in Los Angeles with a suggestion of reconciliation.

*Trivia*

At last the screenplay gets to the pivotal scene in Acebos' basement poolroom. The lesser characters—including future "Mr. Roper," Norman Fell—are presented, along with the scheme to rob Vegas. The male bonding over a pool table, the haze of cigarette smoke, and a chorus of clanking glasses combine for one of macho cinema's defining moments. Though a bit of the script's talkiness was axed, Milestone was slow enough with the scissors to preserve most of the chatty repartee—full of one-liners that were no doubt borrowed from the nightclub act—and certainly more than would have survived a non-Sinatra production. Frank volunteers "to do something for world peace, like buying the Miss Universe pageant." Lawford (then John F. Kennedy's brother-in-law) thinks he'll "buy some votes and go into politics." Dino wants to "repeal the Fourteenth and Twentieth amendments—take the vote away from the women and make slaves out of them."

W hen JFK visited the *Ocean's Eleven* location in January 1960, his campaign was just building momentum. It's less known that his opponent, Richard M. Nixon, tried to steal the thunder from the movie's debut by passing through Nevada on the day before the big premiere.

Trivia

Finally, the business at hand—the caper—is improbably unveiled on a large, two-colored handkerchief that Sinatra produces with the flourish of a stage magician. The hanky map bears the logos of the five targeted casinos: the Sahara, Riviera, Sands, Desert Inn, and Flamingo. "This is our objective," Lawford says with his dramatic British accent. "Our mission: liberate millions of dollars."

The plan: On New Year's Eve, in the one minute and 38 seconds it takes to sing "Auld Lang Syne," the gang will blow the power transformer that feeds the Strip. During the blackout, before emergency power is restored, "inside" men at each casino will rob the cage. Only Dino is skeptical: "I got a suggestion. Forget it," he tells them. "I'm the only guy here who knows Las Vegas. And I'm telling you, the percentage is always with the house." When he can't change their minds, he lightens up: "I'm not gonna let you bums try to pull the job without your best man." They pile hands, baseball team style, on the pool table. All for one and one for all.

Fade in, Las Vegas. A quick shot of downtown, then shots of each hotel, target by target, as the gang members get down to business. They infiltrate each casino, marking the way to the cage with infrared paint. As the gang goes about marking the power switch boxes and casino cages, Milestone's leisurely 127-minute pace (and now, wide-screen TV airings) offers unbelievable tours of the Flamingo, Sands, and Sahara. (The Riviera and Desert Inn are short-shrifted at first; only exteriors are shown.)

Sammy's garbage truck is the traveling command post. At one point, he and Lester trade an extremely inside Vegas joke at the Sands loading dock: "Why so many [garbage] barrels?" Sammy asks. "It's them whole dinners," replies Lester, who is wearing a waiter's uniform. "When it's à la carte, we get sensible garbage." There's more joking when Sinatra, after walking through the Sands like he owned the place—hey, he did own a piece of it—stands bemused at the casino cage while Red Skelton, in a celebrity cameo, is comically denied credit. It's a real "Twilight Zone" moment for those who know that virtually the same incident, with Frank on the receiving end, would cause Sinatra to trash the Sands in 1967 and turn his back on the hotel forever.

Another joke from the script, however, was cut. Sammy and Norman Fell pull up in front of the Desert Inn, where the Louis Prima and Keely Smith show is advertised on the marquee. Fell was to say, "Man, you ought to see the show they got in here. ... It was banned by three different bishops." A studio memo noted that pressure from church groups "has had quite an effect on the Las Vegas casinos in recent months. The

Desert Inn may not appreciate the humor of this dialogue." Sinatra always was a true Las Vegas citizen (considering his movie suggested that the place could be robbed clean), and the line was deleted.

The movie is generous with footage of Martin and the Red Norvo Band performing in the Sahara's Casbar Lounge (of Prima and Rickles fame). Martin is singing the second Jimmy Van Heusen and Sammy Cahn original, "Ain't That a Kick in the Head" (inspired by one of Dino's favorite expressions), to a trio of ladies who are "drooling over him," as the script notes. "You girls look like you've got combat fatigue. You've been on the line a long time," Martin tells them with a dismissive smile. No time for dames today.

Meeting to compare notes at a bowling alley (not a Las Vegas location), the gang determines that all is ready, despite a major complication: A suspicious Santos has turned up in Vegas with Foster's mother.

The clockwork timing of the heist is threatened only by another dame: a drunken Shirley MacLaine, who delays Martin outside the door of the Sahara's power room. "I thought he said it was a lady's drink. I think he meant a lady horse," she hiccups as she staggers into Dino's arms. "I'm so drunk, I don't think I could lie down without holding on." Since MacLaine has swiped the whole Joe E. Lewis drunk bit that would later become his shtick, Martin has to play the suave straight man. But he gets in one quip: "I used to be Ricky Nelson. I'm Perry Como now."

The heist is finally consummated in a briskly paced sequence that goes unmatched by the rest of the film. It's fast because the caper goes "too easy," as Ocean notes, worried that something must have gone wrong. It has. As a goateed "Don Murphy" of KLAS-TV breathlessly reports the heist to viewers, Bergdorf staggers out of the Riviera clutching his chest, then collapses on the sidewalk, dead from a heart attack. Never one to be accused of overacting in this picture, Sinatra can manage only a grimace as Martin leads him away from the gathering crowd.

The millions of dollars go into trash cans, which are collected and hauled out of town by Sammy. He's stopped at the city limits by a roadblock, but is condescendingly told to "get this truck out of here" by a deputy (played by 1920s cowboy star Hoot Gibson). "Yessir, I'll do that," Sammy replies in a Steppin Fetchit voice, and the audience laughs with him as he sings "Eee-O-Eleven" all the way to the landfill in the early morning hours.

The movie slows down once again, with the final act taking longer than necessary to unfold. But one scene does make the audience squirm: Santos puts two and two together, and confronts Ocean and Harmon to demand 50 percent of the loot. They don't know that he's playing both ends from the middle, having already promised the casino owners their money back in exchange for a 30 percent service charge. Duke's meeting with the casino heads is the only place where mob control of Las Vegas can be inferred (as previously noted, Sinatra was a respectful guest): "We all have partners to answer to, right?" one owner asks.

After Duke drops his bomb, Sinatra and Martin nervously invade the service bar, looking for solace and solutions. There's a little more of Sinatra-Dino pally-hood in the shooting script: "Whenever I feel like some exercise, I take a long walk through your head," Martin says. "Careful you don't find yourself in a minefield," Sinatra warns. "I do all the time," replies Martin. "I'm always getting blown up by your crazy ambitions." In the shortened final version, however, the booze inspires a plan.

Cut to the whole Rat Pack riding abreast in Josh's trash truck, all of them except Sammy applying shoe polish to their faces. "I knew this color would come in handy one day," he tells them. When asked, "How do you get this stuff off?" he starts to reply, then freezes—realizing he's the victim of the movie's only "get Sammy" joke.

The gang transfers the money to an incongruous, decidedly non-Vegas back-lot chapel, where they plan to smuggle it out of town in Bergdorf's coffin. Santos, however, has anticipated such action. He's already paid a funeral parlor informant (Hank Henry) to be on the watch for suspicious activity around the body. The discarded paper band from a $10,000 wad of cash, thoughtfully appropriated by Sammy for the widow and son, triggers a call to Santos and sets the stage for a memorable finale.

The gang attends Bergdorf's funeral, all crowded into one church pew, with Santos literally breathing down their necks from the row behind. At one end of the pew, Bishop whispers, "What's that noise?" The question is relayed all the way down the pew to day-player Nicky Blair at the other end. "The deceased is bein' cremated," he announces. One by one, each head turns to the other, until the realization is finally transmitted back up the pew to Bishop. There was no need for Sinatra's wisely excised line: "That tore it; we're broke!"

The attempt to cut a 149-page script—pushing the bloated vanity of one of today's

A photo taken on the funeral parlor set of *Ocean's Eleven* shows the Rat Pack ready to shoot the famous surprise ending. From left: Peter Lawford, Dean Martin, Sammy Davis Jr., Frank Sinatra, and Nicky Blair, who delivered the scene's key line.

inatra's pal Nicky Blair was best known for his Sunset Boulevard restaurant in the '80s. One signed photo from Sinatra that adorned the walls was addressed to his "favorite star" from Blair's favorite "bit player." Blair spent his last years in Las Vegas, trying to repeat his restaurant success. He died of cancer in November 1998.

Trivia

Kevin Costner vehicles—also resulted in a brilliantly improvised closing shot to replace a belabored ending. The crew originally was to "amble gloomily" along the Strip until the camera tilted up to a Piper Cub helicopter scattering Bergdorf's ashes to the winds. The final shot was to show Acebos going postal and racing into the camera as "The End" flashed onscreen. What replaced it was sheer genius.

Sammy walks along the sidewalk in front of the Sands, tie pulled down and dragging on a cig, as his offscreen singing voice intones: "Show me a man without a dream ... and I'll show you a man that's dead. Real dead. My dream has been kicked in the head. Real dead." The others saunter past him, leaving Sammy trailing behind until the Sands marquee gradually comes into the shot. To break the downer tone, the marquee reveals the Rat Pack's names for the *Summit at the Sands* showroom engagement, reminding everyone that it was just a movie after all. The boys lost, but at least the widow got some dough.

His name in lights: The end of *Ocean's Eleven* is the most memorable use of the Sands marquee, but not the only time that a Vegas movie deliberately violated its own laws of reality for a wink at the audience. In the 1956 Martin and Lewis road comedy *Hollywood or Bust,* the duo drive through Las Vegas and spot their real names on the Sands marquee. The reverse was true of the 1964 Billy Wilder comedy *Kiss Me, Stupid:* The Sands marquee was changed to promote the appearance of some "fictional" lounge singer named Dino.

Sheriff's deputies shield the Rat Pack from locals who jammed Fremont Street for the August 3, 1960, premiere of *Ocean's Eleven.*

The legend behind *Ocean's Eleven* thrives on how the Rat Pack managed to wreak havoc all night, then somehow show up for filming the next day. Production records housed at USC solve the mystery but debunk the legend: During the 28 days of Las Vegas location work, the principals were seldom needed more than two or three hours per day. Sinatra's longest day was February 3, during which he was on hand at the Sands from 9:30 a.m. to 6:30 p.m. for filming both indoor and outdoor scenes, including the Skelton sequence. Martin's longest day was January 22, when the "Kick in the Head" scene in the Casbar Lounge was shot from 9:30 a.m. to 3:45 p.m. More typical was the first night of shooting on January 18, which detained Sinatra (for the Bergdorf death scene) from only 6 p.m. to 8 p.m. On January 28, he worked inside and outside the Desert Inn from 5 p.m. to 6:40 p.m. On February 6, he was needed inside the Sands from 5 a.m. to 7:15 a.m. Hell, why go to bed?

Perhaps typically, it was Sammy who bore the brunt of the location work, with all those scenes of driving what the script finally calls "the garbage truck we already know so well." Since he was also the most high-energy performer of the bunch, it's not surprising that columnist Ralph Pearl reported on February 2 that Davis "passed out colder than a refrigerated mackerel early Sunday morning from too much bubbly water, lack of sleep, and a hard day and night behind the movie cameras and Copa Room footlights." (On January 30, Davis had filmed the dump scenes from 10 a.m. to 5:30 p.m.)

Most of the first and last thirds of the movie—including scenes involving Santos' and Ocean's hotel suites, the cashiers cages, and the funeral home—were filmed later on the Warners lot in Burbank, once the showroom run ended and the boys were safely out of Vegas.

The movie debuted at the Fremont Theatre on August 3, 1960. Hundreds of locals were given party hats and noisemakers as they jammed Fremont Street for a gander at the stars. The cast and visiting celebs were royally paraded in by sheriff's deputies for a midnight screening, which followed a cocktail party and Rat Pack dinner show at the Sands. Hank Henry introduced the stars to the rabble from a small stage in front of the theater. As the lights dimmed, Sammy shouted, "Let's have the Martin and Lewis picture!"

Local reporters were fired up by the event but lukewarm about the movie, though some of them rightly predicted that it would go on to become one of the year's top grossers. Coming when it did, *Ocean's Eleven* couldn't miss at the box office and joined *Psycho* as one of the big money-makers in the year of the surprise ending. Continued interest in the movie's mystique led to Steven Soderbergh's all-star remake in 2001. Mostly, people still agree: Too long, too flat. But, man, was it cool! Even if it was the wrong way to go about making a movie, the film captured the right time.

# *Viva Las Vegas*

(Metro-Goldwyn-Mayer, 1964. Produced by Jack Cummings and George Sidney. Directed by George Sidney. Written by Sally Benson. Starring Elvis Presley, Ann-Margret, Cesare Danova, and William Demarest.)

*"The lady loves me, but she doesn't know it yet."*

How's this for a first date? You drop by the dance class at the college gym and engage in a little choreographed rock 'n' roll foreplay with the drop-dead gorgeous redhead of your desire. Just to get the juices pumping, you understand. Then it's off with the redhead for some skeet-shooting at the local gun club. After that, a balancing act on motor scooters in the Convention Center parking lot. Then it's time to play dress-up for a mock shootout in a Western-themed village. Finally, the two of you jump in a helicopter for a ride over Hoover Dam (She: "Hey, this is fun!" He: "It's the only way to travel.") and a touchdown on Lake Mead for a little water-skiing.

Offscreen, Elvis Presley never had to work this hard to impress a babe. But Ann-Margret was no ordinary leading lady. She'd already been dubbed "The Female Elvis" when they were teamed for *Viva Las Vegas,* and it's their electric chemistry that makes the movie one of the best and most popular of Elvis' 31 features.

The movie seems to revel in its own silliness. Tapping director George Sidney's background in MGM musicals (*Show Boat, Kiss Me Kate*) and squeezing through the closing door of an era when people could still break into song onscreen, *Viva Las Vegas* maintains a dopey innocent charm. But at the same time, it throws you a naughty wink as it ogles in close on Ann-Margret and gets hot and sweaty with the duo's steamy

The guys chat during a break on the *Viva Las Vegas* set at the Flamingo. From left: Nicky Blair, Elvis Presley, Cesare Danova, and director George Sidney.

gyrations. The songs yo-yo from sweet traditional melodies like "Santa Lucia" to bongos, finger-snapping, and growling surf guitars that undulate in beatnik grooviness.

*Viva Las Vegas* arrived on movie screens in the spring of 1964, after the British invasion but before the Beatles completed their takeover of teen-age minds. Watching the film today, you can almost hear the snappy tunes and stilted dialogue crackle over a tinny drive-in speaker, while the wide-screen "Metrocolor" unfolds beneath a small-town sky—a last little breath of wholesome American pop before the evil charms of Mick, Jimi, and Woodstock seized the nation's children.

A wide-screen copy of the movie unveils the charms of Las Vegas in the early '60s, a "bright-light city" to be sure, but one with a laid-back resort atmosphere and surrounded by natural attractions. "What people don't understand is you don't even have to go near the Strip for a month," director Sidney said of the first Las Vegas movie to show the city's off-Strip excursions. "People think you're just living under the bright lights of the Strip, which you're not. There's a whole other world."

Sidney agreed to make the movie right after helming Ann-Margret's star-making performance in *Bye Bye Birdie*. "MGM had a picture they wanted to do with Elvis about being an oil driller in the desert, somewhere in Europe," Sidney recalled. "They called me and said, 'We need a picture because he's not doing that well with his pictures.'" [*Girls! Girls! Girls!* and *Kid Galahad* had each grossed less than half of *Blue Hawaii* at the box office in 1962.]

"I said, 'Well, you've got the wrong character. Make him a driver.' So I sat down with the writer [Sally Benson] and we wrote a whole different script in ten days." It was Sidney who promoted Las Vegas as the new setting: "Where's the most exciting place in the world? Out in the desert with the sand? Who in the hell needs that?" And with Ann-Margret on board as co-star, he knew he needed a suitably dynamic background. "My God, you put those two together, at least they've got something to bounce off."

The director was "very familiar with Vegas," having visited since 1937 and being tight with Sinatra and the Rat Pack. He directed Sinatra in *Pal Joey* and shot the climax of *Pepe* in Las Vegas at the same time that *Ocean's Eleven* was filming in 1960. (Caesar Romero and the Rat Pack made cameo appearances in the star-studded misfire built around Mexican comedian Cantinflas.) "I said, 'I can make you deals [to shoot] up there.' It worked out fine.

"So we wrote the script. It's not exactly the work of Shakespeare; no one ever accused us of that," Sidney added. "But the point was, it's what I call a 'coat rack'—something you just hang it on. This number, that number, this kind of entertainment … That's what the script served for. You put the whole thing together and you get a good dinner."

Sidney said he "ad-libbed" the now famous title. The continuing popularity of both the phrase and the song turned in by the team of Doc Pomus and Mort Shuman (who also penned the Elvis hits "Little Sister" and "Suspicion") is "amazing," the director acknowledged. "MGM could sue everybody. … Everywhere you go [in Las Vegas], they used the name. They could have made millions with just the title."

The song is first heard over the opening credits. The script's idea was to show Elvis towing his motorless race car to town, with cowboys riding up and inexplicably firing guns toward a helicopter-mounted camera. But that whole business was cut. Instead, the now immortal percussion and twangy guitar sync right into aerial views of the city lights, as an airborne camera first lingers over Fremont Street's hotel signs, then moves down the Strip to the Thunderbird, the Stardust, and finally the Flamingo, where it settles for the opening scene.

It's there that the movie provides its one and only glimpse of a casino; remember, Elvis flicks were targeted to teens and families. But it doesn't quite show Elvis a-sinnin'—the scene cuts just as he has settled at a crap table and raised the dice above it.

The "coat rack" of a plot establishes Elvis as race-car driver Lucky Jackson, who lives up to his name when he wins enough money at the crap table to pay his entry fee into the Las Vegas Grand Prix. He phones his earnest sidekick, Shorty, in Los Angeles

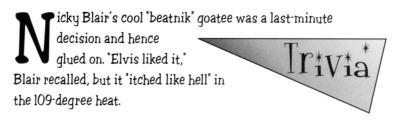

**N**icky Blair's cool "beatnik" goatee was a last-minute decision and hence glued on. "Elvis liked it," Blair recalled, but it "itched like hell" in the 109-degree heat.

Ann-Margret and Nicky Blair mug on the garage set of *Viva Las Vegas*, which was located on the Convention Center parking lot.

with the thumb's up to buy a new engine. The role of Shorty was perhaps the most recognizable part ever played by the late Nicky Blair, who also had the small but crucial cameo in *Ocean's Eleven*. Blair's buddy, Sammy Davis Jr., was up for the part, but the producers eventually decided that three powerhouses would be slicing the musical pie one too many ways. "I freely admit [Sammy] would have done a much better job than me," Blair said years later. From then on, Davis would rib him: "Nicky beat me out of the best part I ever would have had."

At a speedway garage, improbably located on the Convention Center parking lot, Elvis meets Count Elmo Mancini (Cesare Danova), who quickly becomes his friendly rival. Side by side, the two crawl under a race car to set up the memorable arrival of "m-m-m-marvelous" Ann-Margret, as the coming-attractions trailer billed "that ball of fire from *Bye Bye Birdie*." From the undercarriage point of view, the two men see a pair of striking legs in white shorts. Then Sidney switches to a "backdoor" view, before finally showing the b-b-b-beautiful face of "Rusty Martin" looking down on the boys.

"I'd like you to check my motor. It whistles," she says, innocently.

"I don't blame it," Elvis replies.

The screenplay notes that Rusty "swings along in front of them, her wonderful legs stepping proudly, her little behind moving very rhythmically." Sidney drives this home with a tight caboose shot and more bongos. But the redhead is no bimbo. Realizing that she's stepped into the wolves' den, she will tell neither of them where they can find her again.

But both drivers are smitten. They run into each other again at the Sands' Copa Room, where each has independently guessed that Rusty is a showgirl. Unrewarded, together they make their way to every feather show on the Strip—the Thunderbird, Stardust, Flamingo, Tropicana, and Sahara—to no avail. (Exterior signs of each hotel are shown, but only the Tropicana's *Folies Bergere* is featured in a production number, which wasn't called for in the original script.)

The next day, Lucky visits the Count's poolside suite at the Flamingo. Peering out the window, he accidentally discovers that Rusty is no hussy of a showgirl. Instead, she's a wholesome swimming teacher, giving children lessons in the hotel pool. Elvis rushes to serenade her, and at the end of the cute "The Lady Loves Me," she pushes him off the diving board into the pool. Lucky's name betrays him; his casino winnings are sucked into the pool filter. That sets up the major plot complication—if you could call it that—of how he will get the money to buy his engine in time for the race. Short-term, he and Shorty become waiters at the hotel where they were guests minutes before.

Sidney understood the saint-and-sinner dichotomy that was the key to Ann-Margret's sexiness, and he knew how to keep the two sides in balance. He toned down the preachiness of a scripted speech to Lucky about non-Elvisian work ethics: "Do you know how hard it is to *earn* money? Not win it, but make it?" Rusty asks him in the surviving speech. The script goes on to say, "There are thousands of people in this rich country that have never had five-hundred dollars in their hands at one time in their lives. ... They raise families and try to get enough together to buy a little house." Tempering the high-and-mighty lecture, Sidney cuts right to Lucky asking for a date. She tells him to show up at the University of Nevada, Las Vegas gym. ("What're they teaching you?" Elvis wonders. "How to stack cards? Dealing from the bottom of the deck?")

Cut to the gym and Rusty's "hot" side, as she boogies down to the wailing bongo and sax jam "C'mon Everybody"—choreographed by David Winters of *West Side Story* renown—wearing black stockings, high heels, and a red turtleneck. The sweet side comes back into play after their big date, when she introduces Elvis to her dear old dad (William "Uncle Charlie" Demerest of *My Three Sons* fame).

F uture showroom star Glen Campbell was among the studio musicians recording the *Viva Las Vegas* musical tracks at Radio Recorders studios in Los Angeles. "All eyes were on Elvis until Ann-Margret walked in," he recalls.

The rest of the featherweight plot serves mainly to connect musical pieces, both location croonings and the elaborate studio production numbers that Sidney and MGM did best. "Scripts are not to be read; they're just roadmaps. They're not literary work," Sidney noted years later. "It's like cooking a meal. You lay out the food; everything is there. If you're the chef, you just put everything together. And if you're lucky, you don't give everybody indigestion."

The two kids obviously dig each other. But she's worried about him dying in a fiery crash. And then there's that pesky old count, who keeps trying to charm her away. Eventually the two young lovers face off in a Flamingo employee talent show, where Elvis sings the title track again with the help of showgirls. It's a showstopper, but fails to unite the young lovers or solve the financial fix. She wins a pool table; he wins a honeymoon vacation. It looks like Lucky is out of the big race, until help arrives from a mysterious benefactor.

Comedian Jack Carter, who plays himself as the Flamingo talent contest emcee, was headlining the Flamingo showroom (with Leslie Uggams) when the *Viva Las Vegas* film crew was in town.

**Trivia**

For the climactic race, the trailer promised "the most exciting road race ever filmed." Hardly, but it does capture a lot of Southern Nevada scenery from its helicopter points of view. Sidney cut Rusty's scripted line about another driver's wife—"I don't want the look that's on that woman's face"—to keep the tone light and supportive. Current-day Las Vegans tend to watch in amazement as the Grand Prix cars take off at a Henderson drag strip, then show up on Fremont Street to make a left in front of the Golden Nugget downtown, rip from Hoover Dam to Mount Charleston, and end up on Fremont Street again. It almost goes without saying that Elvis is the winner, after most of the competing drivers spin out in fiery crashes.

Once it's revealed that Rusty's dear old dad was the mysterious benefactor, the movie wraps up hastily with a brief wedding scene in front of the Little Church of the West chapel. Though Sidney economically cut an ending that had Lucky and Rusty abandoning a chauffeured limo for the comforts of his own car, it's still assumed that Lucky's race victory has settled all the plot misgivings Rusty once shared about being a driver's wife.

But no matter. The real fun of *Viva Las Vegas* is the location scenery and the hot duets, such as a dynamic remake of Ray Charles' "What'd I Say," with both stars dressed in yellow on the Culver City soundstage. Some of the songs (the title tune and Ann-Margret's rendition of "My Rival") are photographed in a single unflinching shot to add

Some songs recorded for *Viva Las Vegas* didn't make the final cut. Elvis originally was supposed to sing "Do the Vega" at the talent show instead of "Viva Las Vegas." The garden scene, in which Rusty shares her fears of a racing injury, was to include a duet called "I'd Only Love You More." "You're the Boss," a duet with Ann-Margret written by Leiber and Stoller, surfaced later in RCA compilations and was remade in 1998 by Brian Setzer, with Gwen Stefani of No Doubt.

Trivia

to the stagy theatricality of the movie. Most of Elvis' previous leading ladies were "weak," director Sidney noted. But with Elvis and Ann-Margret, "you put a combination together, it's like lighting a firecracker. You light up the sky."

Sidney's doting camera work leaves no guesswork about his infatuation with Ann-Margret, whom he went on to direct a third time in *The Swinger*. "Colonel" Tom Parker, however, was less than pleased. "It's completely true," the director recalled, that Elvis' manager so strongly objected to Ann-Margret being an equal presence that he tried to get her solo numbers cut out of the picture, and later took to comparing her number of close-ups to those of Elvis. "I told him, 'I'm directing the picture,'" Sidney recalled. The director also remembers Parker saying, "We'll get even with you" by not putting out a soundtrack album—as if that would hurt a film director more than a recording artist. But when the movie became a $5 million hit, "everything was forgiven," Sidney said.

It wasn't unusual for an Elvis movie shoot to generate rumors of a romance with his leading lady. Years after his death, Ann-Margret remained politely diplomatic about her relationship with Elvis. "He was just a great man and had such a great sense of humor. God bless his soul," she told veteran journalist Bill Willard in an interview for the UNLV pop-music archives. "I had never seen him before I worked with him. And it was really something, because we found that we sort of worked very much the same. We felt the music the same. It was very interesting."

Most biographers—including some of Elvis' "Memphis mafia" buddies—believe their romance was genuine. "That chemistry happened there, and that chemistry happened after the movie, too," says Sonny West. "If Elvis had not given his word to Priscilla's father and mother that he would marry her when she was old enough, that might have been an interesting outcome there." Alas, Priscilla was already living at Graceland and was not particularly well-protected from media reports of the on-set romance. "They kind of knew it wouldn't have lasted very long because of that situation," West says.

Though most of the crew stayed at the Flamingo, Elvis and his entourage took over the top floor of the Sahara, where he usually stayed in Vegas. The sweet Swedish bombshell quickly became "a favorite of all of us guys and enjoyed being around us,"

Elvis met his hunka-hunka burnin' love equal when he was paired with Ann-Margret in *Viva Las Vegas,* and the electricity crackled from head to toe.

West says. "See, when Elvis wanted his privacy, there was no problem. 'Hey, guys, I'll see ya'll later.' That's it; we're outta there. ... Whenever they wanted to be alone just to talk privately, we were gone. She loved that. The other times when the scene was crazy, and we all had guests there and were cutting up, she loved that, too."

One strange courtship rite was reported by columnist Ralph Pearl. Elvis was spotted at a store called Sherry's, buying chocolate-covered ants, grasshoppers, and caterpillars for his co-star. (Also buying the novelties were Patti Page and Cassius Clay; the latter planned to send them to a sportswriter he didn't like.)

Blair remembered that Elvis and Ann-Margret tried to be "cool" in public about their involvement. But MGM milked the not-so-well-kept secret for publicity. Even before the production left town, it was rumored that the title might be changed to *The Lady Loves Me.* And when the movie was ready for theaters, the trailer teased, "From the hottest spot on Earth comes the hottest love news of the year. ... Elvis meets his love-match!"

Location work on the movie began in Las Vegas in mid-July 1963. The skeet-shooting scene was shot at the Thunderbird Hotel Gun Club on July 21, according to a hotel press release that claimed Ann-Margret had been practicing with a shotgun and had, in fact, "become a real marksman." Also, the Thunderbird's 42-foot yacht was used in the Lake Mead scenes. The mock gunfight in Western garb was filmed in the Old Vegas amusement park, formerly located on Interstate 95 on the way to Lake Mead.

Today, the movie is the best-selling Elvis title on video. It was used as the key to a video promotion tied to the 20th anniversary of his death. The title song barely cracked the Top 30 when released on an EP prior to the movie, but has since been remade by ZZ Top, Bruce Springsteen (for *Honeymoon in Vegas*), and Shawn Colvin (for a Doc Pomus tribute album). One can never predict something like that, Sidney says today. "You hope, but you never know. I mean, Paramount didn't know 'White Christmas' was the song. They had 'The Day After Tomorrow' as the lead song in the picture. ... Anybody tells you they do know—bullshit!"

# *Diamonds Are Forever*
(United Artists, 1971. Produced by Harry Saltzman and Albert R. Broccoli. Directed by Guy Hamilton. Written by Richard Maibaum and Tom Mankiewicz. Starring Sean Connery, Jill St. John, Charles Gray, and Jimmy Dean.)

*"An inelegant trap, obvious and vulgar."*

James Bond. Las Vegas. At first, the two seem to go together like vodka and vermouth. After all, the first James Bond novel was *Casino Royale,* which established a hard-drinking, chain-smoking spy with a zest for high-stakes gambling. And so it was only natural that the hero and the city would cross paths. Alas, Vegas wasn't the French resort setting of *Casino Royale,* no matter how much Steve Wynn later tried to turn the town into a faux Mediterranean. *Diamonds Are Forever,* the novel and film, reflected the true Vegas of their respective days, each of them a place where a British secret agent just might feel a little out of place after all.

The paperback James Bond visited Las Vegas in 1956. It would take another 15 years for the movie spy to follow suit. By then, seven films into the James Bond series, it was getting harder for either Sean Connery or the filmmakers to take poor 007 seriously. *Diamonds,* released for Christmas 1971, nudged the series down the path of slapstick and overt comedy it would travel the rest of the wacky '70s with Roger Moore as Bond.

The first Bond movie filmed extensively in the United States is hard-pressed to make Las Vegas live up to the exotic earlier locations of the series. Take, for example, the obligatory scene where Bond sports a white tux to make a big strike in the Riviera casino and meets the obligatory chippie (Lana Wood, Natalie's sister) spilling out of her evening dress. "I'm Plenty," she says. "But of course you are," he replies with trademark Connery droll as he peers up from the crap table to meet her prominent attributes face-on.

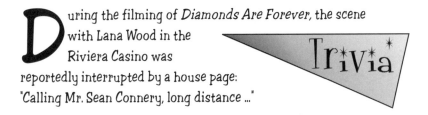

During the filming of *Diamonds Are Forever,* the scene with Lana Wood in the Riviera Casino was reportedly interrupted by a house page: "Calling Mr. Sean Connery, long distance ..."

Connery's white dinner jacket stands out in marked contrast to the polyester jackets and wide ties of the extras in the casino background. If director Guy Hamilton intended it as a visual joke—an overdressed Bond strolling among the rubes—it works even better now. The fact that Vegas was leaving the Rat Pack era behind and sliding into its '70s cheese state was more difficult to conceal than Connery's advancing waistline.

But in that sense, *Diamonds* is more true to Ian Fleming's vision of Bond in Vegas than the superficial plot similarities would suggest. The harder-edged Bond of the books feels as out of place in '50s-era Vegas as an overdressed Connery looks in the Circus Circus arcade.

*Diamonds* was the fourth James Bond novel, and its episodic, travelogue tone doesn't offer the taut suspense of the better Bond yarns. But its leisurely, observational style does make for a detailed and palpable impression of Vegas as seen through the eyes of a worldly, if slightly snooty, British author. Bond's creator visited Las Vegas to research the book for a single night in 1954, and both his snobberies and fascinations— such as an oxygen-dispensing machine at the airport—end up in the novel.

Bond finds Vegas "an inelegant trap, obvious and vulgar," adding that "the noise of

Despite the flaws of *Diamonds,* Bond's adventures in Las Vegas are more exciting than Fleming's 1960 return to the desert mecca in the non-fiction travelogue *Thrilling Cities.* The man who created the high-stakes-gambling Bond spends most of the Vegas chapter detailing a less-than-thrilling bout with a slot machine.

**Trivia**

the [slot] machines had a horrible mechanical ugliness which beat at the brain." He determines that only about one percent of those at the hotel pool "should be allowed to wear bathing suits," and tours a casino that seems more like Arizona Charlie's than the swingin' Sands where Fleming stayed: "Elderly women [sat] at the banks of machines like hens in an egg battery."

In the book, Bond poses as a diamond smuggler to infiltrate a pipeline that stretches from South Africa to the United States. When a racehorse fix at Saratoga, New York, goes awry and fails to generate his payoff, the gangsters he is working for arrange for him to place five winning blackjack bets at the "family" casino in Las Vegas.

A cabdriver ally gives Bond a tour of the Strip, enabling him to ogle a Glass Pool Inn swimmer, and warns, "Nobody wears [jackets] here except to house the artillery." Later, Bond and the driver try unsuccessfully to evade gangsters by hiding out at a drive-in movie along Boulder Highway (unnamed, but presumably the Sky Way, which opened in June 1954).

The book's main action has Bond squaring off against gangsters, including a mob boss who dresses like a cowboy and hides out in a mock Western town. Bond escapes from the gangster's restored Pullman locomotive by fleeing in a hand car, then manages to gun him down somewhere near the ghost town of Rhyolite after the locomotive gives chase. The plot rightly reflects Fleming's—and the world's—preoccupation with Las Vegas' "investors" of that era.

By the swinging '70s, however, gangsters in cowboy suits and antique locomotives

> We're both traveling bad roads, and all bad roads lead to bad towns.
>
> Felix Leiter to James Bond
> in *Diamonds Are Forever*
> (the novel), 1956

didn't cut it. Vegas was going corporate, and the filmmakers found a more topical plot inspiration: the invisible and enigmatic Howard Hughes, who had spent four years methodically buying up huge chunks of the city while holed up on the top floor of the Desert Inn. By the time Hughes suddenly left town without warning on Thanksgiving Eve 1970, no one beyond his closest circle of aides had ever seen him publicly.

*Las Vegas Sun* publisher Hank Greenspun was convinced that Hughes had been kidnapped and ran a banner headline proclaiming, "Howard Hughes

Jill St. John takes a break, while Sean Connery dons his jacket for a scene in *Diamonds Are Forever*. The International (now the Las Vegas Hilton) doubled as the film's "Whyte House."

Vanishes! Mystery Baffles Close Associates." Some conspiracy buffs to this day theorize that Hughes never left Las Vegas alive. Screenwriters Richard Maibaum and Tom Mankiewicz thus tapped into a scenario far more topical than cowboy gangsters: What if Hughes had been kidnapped by Bond's arch nemesis, Ernst Stavro Blofeld?

The first half of *Diamonds* vaguely follows Fleming's smuggling plot. Bond tracks the pipeline by posing as a criminal named Peter Franks. When the real Franks shows up in Amsterdam, Bond kills him in a tense elevator fight, then helps his lovely co-smuggler Tiffany Case (Jill St. John) pose as a bereaved widow to smuggle the diamonds into America inside the coffin carrying Franks' body. Three cartoon gangsters meet Bond at the airport and give him a hearse ride to a remote desert mortuary—the Palm Mortuary on Boulder Highway in Henderson, which is still as it was in the movie, though no longer as remote.

The bad guys shove Bond into a coffin and fire up the crematorium. The super-spy seems genuinely distressed as the smoke begins to rise around him, until the gangsters kill the fire in the nick of time. The diamonds, they've learned, are phony. "You get me the real money, and I'll get you the real diamonds," Bond tells them.

One departure from most Vegas movies may require a second viewing to notice: *Diamonds* skips the obligatory aerial establishing shot of the Strip. The gangsters never mention that Vegas is their destination, though they drive by a state highway sign that reads, "Welcome to Nevada—'Recreation Unlimited.'" The funeral home sequence cuts straight to Bond relaxing in a bath at the Tropicana (without an establishing shot of the hotel), then the city is slowly revealed as he trails the smugglers across town. (Eight hotels are thanked in the end credits, though only the International and Circus Circus are identifiable in the movie.)

One of the mortuary crooks turns out to be a lounge comic named Shady Tree, who is snuffed in his dressing room by an ambiguously gay duo of hired killers, Wint and Kidd, before Bond can confront him. The chief suspect is the mysterious Willard Whyte (country-music sausage-huckster Jimmy Dean, who, *Review-Journal* columnist Forrest Duke claimed, was cast after the producers saw his show at the Landmark Hotel). But it's revealed that Blofeld (Charles Gray) has kidnapped the Hughesian millionaire and assumed his identity while stealing enough diamonds to create a deadly outer-space laser. "The ideal kidnap victim," Bond observes. "No one's seen the man for five years, so who's going to miss someone that's already missing?"

(Was it a complete coincidence that three weeks after *Diamonds* was released, Hughes spoke to reporters by telephone to refute an "as told to" memoir by Clifford Irving, which was eventually exposed as a hoax? Or that *Diamonds* was still packing houses in late shows at the Fremont Theater when Governor Mike O'Callaghan proclaimed in a *Sun* headline, "It's time to meet Hughes"?)

The action leaves Vegas after a chase scene on Fremont Street that seemed fresh in its day but comes off as hackneyed after the car crash epidemic of the '70s, epitomized by *Smokey and the Bandit*. Bond's 1971 Mustang sets police tires a-squealin' as he leads a parade of squad cars on a merry chase around the downtown casinos, finally escaping in the corker stunt of flipping the muscle car on its passenger-side wheels to clear a narrow alley. The actual stunt was filmed on a back lot, but the footage is integrated convincingly enough for those who never actually tried to find such a narrow alley downtown.

The movie's finale leaves Vegas and moves to Blofeld's satellite control base, which is located on an offshore drilling rig. An early script draft, however, called for the climactic sequence to be a chase involving hotel-owned yachts on Lake Mead, culminating in a fight at Hoover Dam. Knowing in retrospect that it was Connery's last "official" turn as Bond (he returned in 1983 to make *Never Say Never Again* outside the official series), it's frustrating that *Diamonds* didn't take itself just a little more seriously. The villains lack the sense of real danger they had in earlier films, and Jill St. John seems to lose I.Q. points as the movie progresses, which throws a bucket of cold water on her swimsuit modeling.

Connery had already quit the series once and was lured back with what was said to be the biggest check ever paid to an actor up to that point: $1.25 million (which he donated to the Scottish International Educational Trust), plus a percentage of the profits and studio financing of two non-Bond films of Connery's choosing. All the more shameful that he seems a bit overweight and detached, though some of the material makes it hard to blame him for not wanting to be more involved. The most embarrassing scene in all of Connery's Bond films has to be the one in which, wearing a terrible pink tie (that's even tied too short), he gets his butt kicked by Bambi and Thumper, two kung fu-fighting female villains.

But Connery still knew how to turn on the charm at the right moments. And in the better parts of *Diamonds*—such as a scene where Bond follows Case as she passes off diamonds amid the distractions of Circus Circus—director Guy Hamilton manages to foreshadow the glitzy amusement park that Las Vegas was starting to become. (Unlike the novel's 007, Connery shows no particular surprise at his surroundings. This, after all, is a man who demolished a fake volcano two pictures earlier.) The extensive location work makes the Strip seem an almost likely place for a secret agent to ride atop an outdoor elevator in a dinner jacket (Connery's sniff of his carnation as he ascends is a perfect nonchalant touch), or to escape from the bad guys by appropriating a moon buggy for a wild ride through the desert.

With the help of John Barry's majestic score, Hamilton does give Vegas a sense of glittery whimsy as he shows the world the relatively new trapeze acts at Circus Circus, or maniacally smashes police cars in front of the neon backdrop of Fremont Street. *Diamonds* also captures the epic scale that Vegas was just starting to embrace by setting the main action at the sprawling International Hotel (now the Las Vegas Hilton), which was then the world's largest hotel and matted to look even larger. While production designer Ken Adam insisted on creating Bond's wildly fanciful "Whyte House" hotel suite on a sound stage, reality has since caught up. All the top Vegas hotels now have mind-boggling high-roller suites for their biggest players that are easily as

**T**he passengers in the outdoor elevator Connery rode to the top of the fictitious "Whyte House" in *Diamonds Are Forever* included journalists visiting the set, hoping to interview him. They never did, even though they spent the better part of two hours inside the elevator only inches below his feet as Bond took his outdoor ride.

*Trivia*

The moon buggy chase offers a bit of ludicrous comic relief in *Diamonds Are Forever.* The scene was filmed at the Johns Manville quarry outside of town.

outlandish as the one where Tiffany rolls around in bubble-bath foam on top of a giant aquarium.

*Diamonds* invaded Las Vegas for nine weeks of shooting on Easter weekend 1971. The Circus Circus location work began on Easter Sunday, followed by the car chase on Fremont Street. The scene where gangsters toss Plenty out the window began in a Tropicana suite, but she lands in the pool at the International. The Johns Manville Gypsum Plant stood in for the moon buggy space-laser factory, while a pipe-laying machine in the desert near Hoover Dam gave Bond a close call with a robotic welding machine.

When not working, Connery golfed at the soon-to-go-private Las Vegas Country Club, and he once was spotted by columnist Duke "sharing a chateaubriand with Producer Cubby Broccoli and Prince Mike Romanoff" at the Riviera's Delmonico gourmet room. Merv Griffin and Riviera headliner Mitzi Gaynor held down an adjacent table, with Vic Damone across the room on that swingin' evening.

As odd as parts of *Diamonds* are, an even odder scene didn't make the final cut: a celebrity cameo from Sammy Davis Jr., who reportedly had hosted Connery on one of his TV specials. In the casino floor scene with Lana Wood, Davis was supposed to have had an argument with the casino manager, said Nicky Blair, whose role as the hotel doorman also was cut. (A still from the scene was displayed in Blair's Las Vegas restaurant.) *Diamonds Are Forever* was the third of the three great Vegas films Davis was to have had a part in, and the second he was aced out of.

# Decade by decade

All movies mirror their times. But those set in Las Vegas seem to do it to distraction, thanks to the ever-changing state of a city that really started to explode only in the second half of the 20th century. When it comes time to measure (or mock) social change, it also helps that Vegas is a resort center constantly reinventing itself, able to plunge headlong into the pop-culture trends that older, more staid cities would have to display discretely amid their skyscrapers and suburbs. Here, then, are some by-the-decade highlights of Vegas on film.

## The '50s: Bombs away

It's a surreal image, that famous photo of the mushroom cloud that seems to explode right over the neon signs of Fremont Street. The bizarre juxtaposition, captured by an enterprising Las Vegas News Bureau photographer, symbolizes a strange chapter of '50s Nevada history: above-ground nuclear testing at the Nevada Test Site, just an hour's drive from Glitter Gulch.

It now seems odd that no serious Hollywood drama tackled the issue. But considering how Las Vegas has fared in the movies, it's perhaps only fitting that two goofy B-movies (only one was a deliberate comedy) inadvertently captured the confused and naive attitudes of the atomic era. The 1954 Mickey Rooney comedy *The Atomic Kid* and Bert I. Gordon's *The Amazing Colossal Man* three years later both take off from the same premise: What would happen if someone were actually exposed to blast radiation but survived?

Just as Stanley Kubrick found dark laughter in nuclear brinksmanship for *Dr. Strangelove (Or How I Learned to Stop Worrying and Love the Bomb),* only a comic genius like Mickey Rooney could see the humor in above-ground testing. Rooney produced, as well as starred in, *The Atomic Kid,* a low-budget Republic feature inspired by the controversial tests that still make headlines today. (The National Cancer Institute reported in August 1997 that fallout from the 100 above-ground tests reached all 48 contiguous states and exposed millions of children to radioactive iodine.)

For a certain aging child star, however, the scenario concocted by writer Blake Edwards (who would go on to direct hits such as *The Pink Panther)* treats radioactivity as a fun thing that makes you glow in the dark and gives you instant power over women and slot machines. Most of the unintentional goose pimples come near the beginning. Rooney, as the dimwitted hero Barnaby "Blix" Waterbury, and his slightly

**T**he Atomic Liquor Store still stands proudly—with an appropriately awesome neon sign—on a rough stretch of Fremont Street populated by hookers and transients. Atomic "wasn't a dirty word like it is today," said Joe Sobchik in reference to the name of the store he converted from a café in 1954, the year *The Atomic Kid* was made. Nevada Test Site employees were "very proud of their work at the time."

Trivia

more cunning pal Stan (Robert Strauss) stumble across the desert in search of uranium and "a peanut butter and pickle sandwich," only to find a lonely suburban tract house instead.

"Maybe this is one of those families that moved all the way out here to get away from the atom bomb," Blix surmises. Instead, the two have wandered into "Atomic City" at the Nevada Test Site. The tract house was inspired by the real-life "Doom Towns" the government actually constructed near ground zero and furnished with food, cars, and refrigerators to see how they would hold up after the blast (your tax dollars at work).

In a creepy moment, Rooney knocks the head off one of the members of the resident mannequin family. Then the two sages decide that Stan should head to town and put down a deposit on the model home. He's intercepted by the military, but only after the lunchmeat-obsessed Blix is toasted in the big ka-boom, depicted by not-so-artfully-blended stock footage.

Miraculously, the only thing that's toast is Blix's sandwich after he digs his way out of the rubble, charred and smoking like the Warner Brothers coyote after a close encounter with the Roadrunner. In fact, Blix is A-OK the Army determines, after hustling him off for observation and the attentions of a nurse (Elaine Davis, one of many Mrs. Rooneys), who manages to get the boy's geiger counter running in a way that no fallout could. "I always pictured my dream man as tall, dark, and handsome," she says. "Now I've got short, red-headed, and radioactive."

The movie was too low-budget for any location work, so a studio casino was used for the scene in which Blix's radioactive touch makes slot machines belch coins in downtown Vegas. Stock footage of the Golden Nugget, Las Vegas Club, and Eldorado casino signs sets the scene. Blix endures a few more half-baked adventures, such as using his new-found fame to endorse "the peanut butter with the built-in atomic protection." But by then, the 86-minute epic has long since lost the interest of modern viewers fascinated more by its utterly cavalier treatment of nuclear radiation.

Rooney must have been fortunate that "B" studio Republic couldn't afford to film at the test site. In 1999 he was still alive and kicking, appearing as the title character in a national tour of *The Wizard of Oz*—unlike John Wayne and the cast of *The Conqueror.*

Researchers claim that those actors were terminally poisoned during location filming in the Utah desert while working on the Howard Hughes-backed 1956 epic.

Low-budget wunderkind Bert I. Gordon returned to the premise for *The Amazing Colossal Man,* which reached Las Vegas theaters in October 1957. Though most film buffs are quick to assume that Gordon was "inspired" by the success of *The Incredible Shrinking Man* that same year, the producer denies it today. "People think along the same lines," he says. *Shrinking Man* author Richard Matheson "read the newspapers, too. I read the newspapers and remember thinking, 'That thing [the test site] is crazy to begin with. Somebody's going to get hurt,'" he recalls of headlines that included accounts of giant mutated rats.

While Gordon's movie is ultimately good for more laughs than *The Atomic Kid,* the first half-hour is surprisingly eerie. The long, grim shadows in the early hospital scenes are either a nod to film noir or symptoms of a low budget, which is soon exposed by the dubious special effects.

Colonel Glenn Manning (Glenn Langan) supervises soldiers at Desert Rock, Nevada, where a plutonium bomb is being triggered at the "Nevada Testing Grounds." For some reason, the bomb doesn't go off after the countdown. In the meantime, a light civilian plane decides to land at the blast site. Ignoring orders, Manning attempts a rescue, only to have the bomb cook him in his tracks. His hair disappears in a flash, and his shirt gets the Doc Savage look. His fiancée—"We were to be married tonight in Las Vegas!"—rushes to be with him in the hospital, but she is denied access as Manning is quarantined, left alone to die.

What a surprise, then, when the next morning Manning looks like he merely stayed out in the sun too long. "He's developed new skin," the doctors explain, pondering radiation's "regenerative or healing power."

The movie gets progressively sillier as Glenn begins to grow 8 feet to 10 feet per day. The Army erects a giant mess tent for Manning to hang

Nuclear testing was a source of pride to most Las Vegans in the '50s, but the *Amazing Colossal Man* brought home a cautionary tale.

out in, but can manage to give the bald colonel only "an expandable sarong" for a uniform. Glenn gets philosophically morose (a direct lift from the better-written *Shrinking Man*), but it's hard to take the existential laments of a bald man too seriously when he's wearing what looks like a diaper.

The doctors race the clock to find a cure. Because Manning's heart isn't growing as fast as the rest of him, they warn that "his mind will go first, then his heart will literally explode." While they track a cure related to his bone marrow and pituitary gland—shrinking elephants as the initial experiment—Manning decides he's had enough and goes AWOL. Curiously, it takes two helicopters and all manner of ground patrol to spot him, and then only after he shows up on the Strip. This forces a local TV reporter named H. Wells (no G?) to retract his mocking dismissals of motorists who claimed to have seen "a giant" in the desert.

First, the overgrown Manning stands eye to eye with the sultan on top of the Dunes sign. As columnist Forrest Duke noted, "The Dunes got off easy—he just gave his fellow giant a puzzled look and strolled toward Downtown."

An incredible tour of the 1957 Strip begins, although the low budget prevented any real location filming and is limited to rough matte shots. Still, the movie offers a look at the original Riviera—then the tallest building in town—when the giant peers into a window of the nine-story tower to terrorize a woman in a bathtub.

He moves on to the Royal Nevada (one of several failed casinos built in the boom year of 1955, eventually annexed by its next-door neighbor, the Stardust), where he lifts the crown from the top of the sign, fortunately choosing not to wear it as a diaper accessory. Then it's on to the Last Frontier Village and adjacent Silver Slipper, where Manning rips said slipper from its pedestal. He gets to the Sands, where the Danny Thomas show is advertised on the marquee. Something about that Sands sign doesn't look the way it should, though. ... Ah, it's only a model for the movie giant to tear apart. Downtown mascot Vegas Vic fares even worse: The waving cowboy sign is reduced from grand neon to cheap cardboard that gets ripped to pieces in Manning's growing rage.

The cowboy's treatment foreshadows Manning's imminent demise. When the crazed colonel moves on to Hoover Dam (still called Boulder Dam back then), his Army colleagues persuade him to quit hoisting around his fiancée like Fay Wray, then reward him with a hail of gunfire. The Amazing Colossal Man tumbles to the bottom of the dam. But we don't see his dead body, because he's due to return—two years later and even uglier—in *War of the Colossal Beast*.

## The '60s: Biker trash and hippie chicks

Vegas, we are nowadays led to believe, became Squaresville incarnate in the late '60s. A photograph taken somewhere in that era, showing Frank and Dino holding up signs that read, "We Want Free Broads," reinforces the image of hipsters fallen just an arm's length out of touch. Despite the grooviest efforts of Sammy Davis Jr., the Strip basically functioned within its own obliviously boozy biosphere and became a symbol

Stand-up comedian Corbett Monica dazzles Jacqueline Bisset with his "pixie" quality in *The Grasshopper.*

of the establishment to the turned-on, tuned-in Woodstock generation. Right?

Well, not if you judge by Hollywood, which seemed to associate the Strip's loose-flowing cash and topless entertainment more with the youth movement during the pivotal year of 1969. The poster blurb for *Where It's At,* released that May, offers this catch line, blazed between a bikini-clad torso and a crap table: "Where it's at for you, Dad [David Janssen, as the owner of Caesars Palace] ... ain't necessarily where it's at for me."

That same year, *The Grasshopper,* a melodrama co-written by Garry Marshall, depicts Vegas as the only place where a free spirit (Jacqueline Bisset) can indulge her restless soul. That Vegas can be so appealing to her while coming off as its stereotypically garish and greedy self to the audience is the movie's magnificent contradiction. Its mixed signals puzzle a modern viewer, though it's clear that the movie was riding a new wave of permissiveness and going for shock value in its scenes of casual nudity, pot smoking, and interracial sex. As Austin Powers would say, "Shag-a-delic, baby!"

As Christine, Bisset embarks from a small Canadian border town with plans to meet her boyfriend in Los Angeles. But she ends up hitchhiking to Vegas with nightclub comic Danny, played by nightclub comic Corbett Monica. "You've got to see Vegas once in our lifetime," he tells her, before proclaiming a few moments later, "There it is, honey. Vegas." Something must have happened to the expected montage of glittering casino lights; instead, there's a single shot of the northern edge of the Strip, dominated by the Tod Motor Motel, a Denny's, and a Gulf station.

Christine is dazzled when the comedian takes her to a penthouse party for a showroom comic, but she temporarily rejects Monica's come-ons: "Yeah, I know. I'm fun, I'm cute, I have a pixie quality. When's the last time you saw a pixie get laid?" he asks her. But soon the straight life with the boyfriend in L.A. bores her, and Christine rushes back to make the comedian one happy pixie. Before long, though, she realizes that two restless free spirits make a bad match. The comedian suggests she stay in Vegas—"It's beautiful here, lotta classy people"—and she takes his advice by begging for a showgirl job from a sleazy producer (Ed Flanders). "I did *Little Women* in school," she tells him.

"Nude?" he quips, explaining, "Showgirls gotta have gigantic tickets."

"Are you trying to tell me my breasts aren't big enough?"

"Hey, they're fine with me. I'm an aesthetic guy. But these morons from out of town, they wanna see freaks."

Christine settles the issue by showing him (but not the audience) her "tickets." She gets a gig wearing a blue wig in the hotel's revue, dancing to the wah-wah vocals of "Jolie Paree" by the Jackie Ward Singers. (The show is the *Casino de Paris* at the Dunes, where much of the film was made. But the hotel may not have been happy with the final product. Though show producer Frederic Apcar's name appears in some shots, the Dunes isn't acknowledged, and its name and marquee are blocked out of most scenes.)

Christine makes friends with a gay guy in the show, gets high with a way-out band called the Ice Pack, and eventually marries a retired football player turned casino greeter (Jim Brown). But their happiness—epitomized by a carousel ride in front of Circus Circus—is short-lived. The movie starts its violent downward spiral when Christine is beaten and raped. Her husband pounds the sleazeball perpetrator, only to get gunned down by his vengeful assistant. Christine becomes a "hustler"—defined as a girl who "makes more money standing around a crap table than lying on her back"— which leads to being "kept" by a rich older man (Joseph Cotton).

Eventually she returns to one of the rock musicians (Christopher Stone), who shows his love by pimping her out for $50 tricks. The movie ends with the supposedly uplifting, very '60s sequence of Christine and a pot-smoking biplane pilot skywriting "Fuck It" in the air for all the fogies stuck on the ground to see. Yeah, baby! But the final scene freeze-frames on a down note: the jaded look on Christine's face as she awaits booking in the jailhouse for the prank.

The ending sums up the movie's schizophrenia. Co-writer Garry Marshall went on to become known for comedies and no doubt provided the humor that sees *The Grasshopper* through the rough spots. At one point, a sleazy producer barks orders to a worker atop a marquee: "Hey, I want bigger letters on 'Nude.' Nude's gotta be the biggest word. The rest you can write up there with a pencil!" But in the long run, *The Grasshopper* can't seem to decide if it's on the side of restless youth, or if it's a pulp morality play warning youngsters away from the corrupting, empty pleasures of Sin City.

In *Hell's Angels '69,* Vegas is seen as a seriously more uptight place. When robbers posing as bikers crash Caesars Palace, a desk clerk tells them, "Caesars Palace is used to informal dress, but this is really off-limits."

The '60s began with one "Let's rob Vegas movie" in *Ocean's Eleven,* so it's only right that the decade ended with one (two, if you count *They Came to Rob Las Vegas,* an Italian production that hit local theaters in February 1969). *Hell's Angels '69,* a lurid and oddly watchable melodrama, has uncanny parallels to an actual June 1969 episode. Real-life bikers had a run-in with the local law between the time of the location filming at Caesars Palace and the movie's theatrical arrival in late September of its title year.

That June, "60 grime-coated outlaw motorcyclists and their mamas"—as the *Las Vegas Sun* so objectively described them—were surrounded and arrested at a rural campsite by about 30 sheriff's deputies. Longtime Clark County Sheriff Ralph Lamb gave the bikers a reception that people would talk about for years. As the *Sun* reported, "The usually dirt-caked outlaws ... were hardly recognizable by either sight or smell after county authorities washed them down, trimmed their scraggly beards, and cut their matted hair."

Once the bikers made bail, Lamb and his boys gave them a police escort out of town. "It might not have been too legal, but the people asked me to do a job and didn't tell me how to get it done," Lamb told *Review-Journal* columnist John L. Smith years later.

The police escort out of town is also a key segment in the movie, even though the Caesars scenes were filmed sometime between late February and early April—judging by a shot that includes the marquee showing Celeste Holm starring in *Mame.* The screenplay turned out to be amazingly prescient, which may or may not help explain why it maintains a curiously neutral respect for both the Angels and the law.

Two rich half-brothers (Tom Stern, also the movie's producer, and Jeremy Slate) infiltrate the Angels to make the bikers unwitting participants in their "just-for-kicks" plan to rob Caesars Palace. "Bright lights, lotsa action, plenty to drink, Tramp. That's my type

The biker melodrama *Hell's Angels '69* has curious parallels to a real-life summer-of-'69 confrontation between bikers and Clark County sheriff's officials.

of town," one of the bikers tells his leader, real-life Angel Terry the Tramp.

The two brothers check into Caesars Palace and deliberately turn heads in the casino with their outlaw duds. After phoning the Angels for help while pretending to be hassled by "the man," the brothers change into business suits and impersonate "citizens" to rob the casino cage, then slip back into biker wear as the Angels arrive at the Palace gates—a distraction that the smooth criminals accurately predicted would tie up the local constabulary.

"We've had a riot and a six hundred thousand dollar robbery. All I need now is an Indian uprising," says the belabored cowboy sheriff (G.D. Spradlin). Portrayed as no redneck or halfwit, the sheriff chills things with the Angels, offering them an escort to the county line, before proceeding to solve the crime. "An escort—that's pretty neat," says Sonny Barger, the Angels' president, eloquently playing himself. Since the movie was no doubt made to cash in on the post-*Easy Rider* chopper mania at the drive-ins, the haircuts endured by the real-life bikers weren't even a consideration.

The biggest laugh today comes from the willing participation of Caesars Palace. Contrast early-day management's idea of free publicity to the corporate powers of the late '80s: They almost nixed the Oscar-winning *Rain Man* because it featured scenes of an intimidating security staff and a prostitute on Cleopatra's Barge.

## The '70s: Trust no one

"This nut thinks he's a vampire! He's killed four, maybe five women. ... That is *news,* Vincenzo, and we are a *news*paper."

Those words, emphatically spoken by a slightly over-the-hill gumshoe journalist named Carl Kolchak, echoed through millions of living rooms on the night of Tuesday, January 11, 1972. What might have been a typical "ABC Movie of the Week" struck such a deep collective chord that it became the highest-rated made-for-TV feature ever. *The Night Stalker* was a thriller that changed the way the American public perceived both its movie vampires and, it would soon turn out, its own government.

Forget *The X-Files.* Or, like creator Chris Carter, at least acknowledge that it was *The Night Stalker* that first knew the truth was out there. The tale of a vampire stalking Las Vegas and the righteous reporter who tracks him down works on two levels. Consciously, it's an almost plausible yarn about a most unusual manhunt. After all, if there really were vampires, wouldn't they eventually end up in an all-night city with an attractive female work force?

"A vampire could work in a Las Vegas casino on the night shift and never be seen in the daytime, and nobody would think it was odd. A pasty-faced guy in a mohair suit could wander around at four a.m., and nobody would think anything about it," said Jeff Rice, the former *Las Vegas Sun* reporter whose unpublished novel was adapted for the screen.

But *The Night Stalker* resounds on a deeper level. Not only did Rice write a Las Vegas novel that was almost heretically unconcerned with gambling, but his near-paranoid loathing of the city's law-enforcement community—and its cover-up attempts—foreshadowed the Watergate scandal that was to begin later that summer. Trust no one, indeed. Oddly enough, newspaper reporters were the heroes in both sagas.

Rice was 27 when the movie aired and was already acclaimed as an "Outstanding Young Journalist" for his work at the *Sun* from 1966 to 1968. (One of his assignments was Elvis Presley's wedding.) But he obviously spent much of his time frustrated by local officials, judging by the hostility of his novel.

> **"** Women in bikinis and thongs doing their weekly marketing just before sunrise are common sights in Las Vegas. **"**
>
> Jeff Rice
> *The Night Stalker*

Originally titled *The Kolchak Papers* and published only as a paperback tie-in after the movie's success, the novel names real places and addresses almost to distraction. Tracking down a copy at a used bookstore might be fun for longtime locals who could guess the thinly disguised character names. *Sun* publisher Hank Greenspun becomes the *Daily News'* Jake Herman—"Part crusader. Part charlatan. ... Before Howard Hughes came to our fair city, he was one of the state's biggest wheeler-dealers." Henri St. Clair is obviously Frederick Apcar, producer of the *Casino de Paris* at the Dunes, where Rice's father worked.

The book also is peppered with names of places gone by, giving a real feel of what it was like to hang out in a much smaller Las Vegas. Kolchak drinks at the Plush Horse lounge on Sahara (now PT's Pub), within crawling distance of his apartment on Karen Court. He patronizes the ultra-swank Dome of the Sea restaurant at the Dunes, frequents the Tower of Pizza on the Strip (ground later occupied by the Country Star restaurant), and takes beer home from the Mayfair Market, right across the Strip from Foxy's Firehouse Casino (now Holy Cow).

The geographic details and narrative digressions are understandable for a reporter turned novelist. They add a veneer of authenticity to the saga of a manhunt for a supernatural serial killer. But they also slow down the real plot: Kolchak first theorizing that whoever is draining the blood of young women is a psycho who thinks he's a vampire, then gradually realizing that he's up against the real deal. The show producer finally recognizes the killer as Janos Skorzeny, a 70-year-old Romanian he remembered meeting in Europe before World War II and one who "hardly seemed a day older than he'd been in 1939!" Kolchak and the sheriff trace the vampire to his lair—an address given in the book as 3779 Spencer.

There, Kolchak firsts splatters the vampire with holy water that makes his skin "foam and bubble." Then, while the creature is gagging up "bile-colored liquid flecked with black and red," a sheriff's deputy coaxes the reporter into driving the fatal stake. Instead of becoming famous, however, Kolchak is threatened with murder charges by

# Vampires in Vegas

Any self-respecting vampire buff already knows that Las Vegas became part of horror history with *The Night Stalker*. Far less known, however, is that two significant figures in monster moviedom—Bela Lugosi and TV hostess Vampira—had their names up in lights on the Las Vegas Strip a good 15 years before Janos Skorzeny claimed it as a happy hunting ground.

Lugosi's turn came as the star of a burlesque comedy at the Silver Slipper Saloon in February 1954. Vampira's brief showroom fame was a bit more typical of what is thought of as a "Vegas" revue: She was Liberace's showroom guest star at the Riviera two years later, in April 1956.

Lugosi's trip to Vegas was one event in the sad parade of misfortunes marking the final two years of his life. "A bad Hollywood marriage left him broke and mentally disturbed," said Eddie Fox, the promoter who brought Lugosi to town. "His movie career was over, and he was so grateful to work here." Interviewed in 1976, Fox was a bit dismissive (or perhaps completely unaware) of Lugosi's subsequent Ed Wood movies, but the actor did take the Vegas job a few months after Lillian Lugosi won a divorce and custody of their son Bela Jr.

Bela Lugosi was fading fast when he agreed to perform in a saloon-hall burlesque show at the Silver Slipper in 1954.

The Silver Slipper Saloon was part of the Last Frontier, which in 1941 was the second resort to venture away from downtown and settle on the dusty Los Angeles Highway. The opportunity to enjoy the "Early West in Modern Splendor" was a precursor not only to today's themed hotels, but also to Disneyland. In 1947 the resort added the Last Frontier Village, which included bumper cars, a mining train, a jail, and artifacts imported from frontier towns.

The heart of the village was the Silver Slipper, which preserved the burlesque tradition in a frontier saloon-hall atmosphere. In 1950, Eddie Fox coaxed longtime burlesque star Hank Henry to Las Vegas to star in melodramas such as *Revenge of the Klondikes*, with Henry vamping in drag as Little Nell. A half-dozen actors worked above a five-piece band on a stage that was "pretty much on top of the bar," remembered the late Bill Willard, an actor and writer for the group.

After four years, Fox started to book name acts to give the productions fresh doses of momentum and publicity. Willard said that he wasn't sure how Lugosi ended up in the show, but speculated that Fox contacted the horror star through a friend at the William Morris Agency. By the time Lugosi was hired, Willard and Henry were used to banging out quick scripts that recycled old burlesque routines and writing novelty tunes by sitting down at the piano with bandleader George Redman and saying, "This is how it goes."

Advertisements billed the show as "*The Bela Lugosi Revue,* starring Dracula himself." But they were something of a misnomer. "There were hints of the Dracula thing throughout, but he didn't want to do the character," Willard recalled. Instead, Lugosi and Henry combined parodies of drawing-room mysteries with the popular *Dragnet* TV show. The 71-year-old Lugosi played the butler, "which he enjoyed," said Willard. "He thought it was a lot of fun."

Lugosi's character was named Boris Kozloff, parodying the name of Frontier owner Jake Kozloff, as well as that of a certain horror star. Willard said the cast knew that Lugosi had fallen on hard times, and that four shows a night—from 9 p.m. to 2:30 a.m.—were tough on him. But Willard remembered no drug use and said that Lugosi performed his part well: "When you get old actors together, they become part of the whole game. In some of his early years, Lugosi probably had indulged in a little comedy. ... He'd had a long career, so it probably brought back memories, doing a little bit of this burlesque stuff."

The silliness of the script excerpts, one of which follows, is a reminder that Vegas was still only coming into its prime as a hipster mecca. The Sands had just opened a year earlier. (No, Sinatra was not in town while Lugosi was at the Slipper, so there's no easy explanation for why the Chairman later sent money to Lugosi after he institutionalized himself for drug addiction in 1955.) However, the burlesque show did have one equally odd competitor: Ronald Reagan, performing at the adjacent Last Frontier. Alas, there are no documentations of any meetings.

In Willard's script, Lugosi as the butler first frightens Sparky Kaye, dressed as a maid.

**Lugosi**: There's something wrong in this household. And it feels like murder. I'm an expert at murder, you know.

**Sparky**: Yes, there is something wrong in this house. Ever since you've been here. Say—haven't I seen you somewhere before?

**Lugosi** (bloodcurdling laugh): Boo! (The maid runs away.)

Virginia Dew, playing the lady of the house, enters and greets Lugosi as Boris.

**Lugosi**: Madame—do not call me Boris. Call me Kozloff.

Willard, playing Lord Ashley, enters wearing a khaki safari uniform that's torn and covered in blood.

**Lugosi**: Why, Master—have you been shaving yourself again?

Willard explains that he's been poisoned by the African tribe of Mau Mau, then collapses on the bed.

**Lugosi**: And now he's dead (weird laugh)—because of Mau Mau and the Asp. (He calls the police: Henry and co-star Jimmy Cavanaugh, parodying Jack Webb and Harry Morgan as Friday and Smith.)

**Hank**: Where's the corpse? Where's the corpse?

**Lugosi**: You're looking at him.

**Hank**: Hello, corpse.

**Lugosi**: No, not me. Him, over there.

**Hank**: All right, corpse. What did you do with the body? Speak up. Where'd you hide it?

**Joan White** (playing a reporter, puts her arms around Lugosi's neck): I think you're cuter than Jimmy Stewart. Boris, you just kill me.

**Lugosi**: I'd like to.

**Hank** (searching for clues, taking his first real look at Lugosi): Haven't I seen you someplace before? I know—on an old television picture.

**Lugosi**: Don't you remember Dracula?

**Hank**: Dracula? Oh, sure. I remember Dracula. Best stripper the Embassy ever had.

Willard's surviving script is missing a solo routine that Lugosi did center-stage, since it was added later and inserted into the original script. Only the last part of the routine remains:

> You must be flipping your ever-lovin' wig.
> I'm the real gone ghoul the cats all dig.
> The chicks dig me most like Errol Flynn,
> So don't beat your chops, man—just give me some skin!

Puns and cornball jokes were no less a part of Vampira's TV hostess act. The same year that Lugosi played Vegas, Maila Nurmi was catching the attention of Southern California TV audiences as the original wise-cracking horror hostess. She also caught the attention of Liberace, who had grabbed the television masses with his piano theatrics.

By the time Liberace was chosen to open the Riviera in 1955, TV had made him a hot enough attraction that the Riv paid him a then record $50,000 per week to be the first showroom act. When he returned in April 1956, the flamboyant pianist spent $35,000 trying to top his first appearance—in a speculative move to land the revue on network television to make back his costs. (Apparently, it never happened; no tape of the broadcast remains.) The 75-minute revue included seven complete production numbers, all tied together by Vampira under the theme "Come As You Were."

Liberace opened the show, then moved to a small set to the side of the main stage for his banter with Vampira. The crypt sideset was adorned with a placard reading "Tomb Sweet Tomb."

The idea was that she hypnotized the pianist to take him into the past—King George's Court, the Imperial Palace of Vienna, and so forth. Eventually Lee awoke from his trance for a finale that included "Beer Barrel Polka" and Les Baxter's reigning national hit, "The Poor People of Paris."

Supposedly a native of Tombstone, Arizona, the Vampira character never wrote letters because they always ended up in the dead-letter office. When she got married, her towels were monogrammed "His" and "Hearse." She liked for her friends to have colds so she could hear them coffin. And she had lots of friends: the morgue the merrier. Vampira wasn't afraid of aging because, she said, "When I grow too old to scream, I'll have you to dismember."

Horror hostess Vampira helped Liberace with his punsmanship in his elaborate 1956 revue, *Come As You Were,* at the Riviera.

the Las Vegas power structure and run out of town.

Rice's agent wisely believed the novel to be more salable as a screen property, and producer Dan Curtis saw its potential. He knew a thing or two about the commercial prospect of vampires, having struck pop-culture gold by introducing the suave bloodsucker Barnabas Collins into his struggling ABC soap, *Dark Shadows,* a few years earlier.

Veteran fantasy screenwriter Richard Matheson cut the deadwood and molded the story into a taut, fast-paced thriller that managed to balance the humor with the thrills, the jaded reporter with the conspiring politicos, all within a tight 72 minutes. The movie remains a detective story with voice-over narration. The vampire—played with silent menace by Barry Atwater, who resembles Jack Palance with a Moe haircut— possessed a hissing animal brutality that had antecedents in horror films (Christopher Lee's *Dracula*) but had never been seen on network televison. And Matheson wisely decided to eliminate one tell-tale characteristic the vampire had in the novel: disgusting bad breath that gags everyone who crosses his path, at one point forcing him into a gift shop in search of breath spray.

The movie begins with the ambush of the first victim in a Fremont Street location shot. Darren McGavin, heading a "dream team" of craggy veteran character actors, is introduced as Kolchak in the first of many scenes in which he cruises the Strip in his convertible. (The scenes, which show the Dunes and El Morocco at different points, were obviously filmed in one session.) Although Kolchak is "a big-time reporter condemned to the sticks with journalistic rubes," as he's condescendingly told over a poolside beer at the Sahara, McGavin invests the reporter with a dignity the wardrobe department didn't share. He's particularly effective in the few scenes establishing his May-December romance with young casino worker Carol Linley.

Kolchak gradually links the ensuing murders—including that of a showgirl who is "125 luscious pounds, less the weight of 12 pints of blood"—with some mysterious blood-bank robberies. The concept of a "vampire killer in Las Vegas" grows more plausible by the day. But it's "bad for the police, it's bad for the people, and it's bad for business," declares a pious district attorney (Kent Smith), in one of the few lines lifted almost straight from the book. With logic that predated *Jaws* by three years, the powers that be decide to suppress the gory details: "The people in Las Vegas would come unglued if they knew."

The suspenseful climax much improves on the novel. Kolchak alone discovers the home of Skorzeny, and the vampire catches him red-handed as he attempts to free one of the missing but still-alive female victims. The suspense as he explores the *Psycho*-like house almost forgives the use of a Gothic, two-story, back-lot estate instead of the more plausible one-bedroom cinderblock house described in the novel.

But Kolchak is no better rewarded in the movie than in the book. His story is killed, and his girlfriend is gone. "We just asked the young lady if she'd be good enough to leave town," the authorities explain, proceeding to convince Kolchak that it would

Darren McGavin as intrepid gumshoe reporter Carl Kolchak and Barry Atwater as a hissing vampire made memorable foes in *The Night Stalker*. The story was conceived by Jeff Rice, a former *Las Vegas Sun* reporter.

be smart for him to do likewise. The vampire news is squelched; the cover-up begins. And unlike in Watergate, the reporter is the victim instead of the hero.

But the story continued, in life as on television. Kolchak returned to battle *The Night Strangler* in Seattle before landing his own television series for a season. Dan Curtis moved on to the most famous vampire of all, producing a respectable remake of *Dracula* with Jack Palance (sans the Moe haircut). But the TV movie was bumped, oddly enough, by live coverage of the resignation of Spiro Agnew. As Kolchak says, "Try to tell yourself, it couldn't happen here."

## The '80s: Stallone snoozers

The '80s were largely downtime for Vegas, and not coincidentally the city's most ignored years in Hollywood. Not until the Oscar-winning *Rain Man* in 1988 would the Strip be seen in a high-profile movie, which happened to coincide with the opening of the Mirage and the beginning of the mega-resort era. However, the Strip was not ignored by one of the biggest stars of the '80s: Sylvester Stallone.

Vegas plays a background role in two movies that gave people good reason to quit thinking of Stallone as a dramatic actor and to start seeing him as a cartoon character starring in glorified drive-in trash. Stallone directed *Rocky IV* (1985), one of the last movies in which Hollywood could portray the Soviet Union as a hissable villain. The movie extended the popularity of Stallone's *Rambo* films in the Reagan era, a time that invented "action heroes" who could sidestep complicated world politics by blowing away bad guys as a one-man army.

*Rocky IV* sends Stallone on a mission to kick a little Commie ass after a steroid-fueled monster (Dolph Lundgren) kills his buddy Apollo Creed (Carl Weathers) in the ring. What starts as a "friendly exhibition bout" takes place at the old MGM Grand Hotel (now Bally's) and is billed below Wayne Newton on the hotel marquee. James Brown's memorable "Living in America" number uses ramps, props, and showgirls from the *Jubilee!* revue. The astonished Commie is temporarily bewildered by the sight of Apollo Creed rising to the stage atop the pagan head from the "Samson and Delilah" number.

Stallone returned to Las Vegas for *Over the Top* (1987), a sentimental reworking of *The Champ* that casts him as a trucker trying to bond with his estranged son. The relationship part of the movie is immediately torpedoed by the fact that dad's an arm wrestler, which means that various ugly guys with names like Blaster and Smasher turn up to challenge him. The road leads father and son to the Las Vegas Hilton, which hosts the "International Arm Wrestling Championships" to the strains of cheesy '80s rock tunes, such as Sammy Hagar's "Winner Takes It All."

## The '90s: Elvis and envy

Hollywood calls it "independent creation" when two fictional properties come up with the same plot. Moviegoers called it just plain weird in 1992 and '93, when *Honeymoon in Vegas* and *Indecent Proposal* turned out to have the same plot: A virtuous woman has to shack up with a smarmy, but charming, rich guy to pay off the gambling debts of the poor schmuck who brought her to Vegas. Both movies turned out to be comedies. Only one was meant to be.

As the deliberate comedy, *Honeymoon in Vegas* was no home run, but it did deliver fairly consistent chuckles. *Indecent Proposal* was the campy melodrama, but Redford's comeback role as a handsome rake charmed female viewers and helped the film's perpetrators laugh all the way to the bank. The movie grossed more than $100 million.

*Honeymoon* writer-director Andrew Bergman says the idea of a guy losing his fiancée in a poker game was easily combined with the desire to set a movie in Vegas, which figured into his screenplay for 1984's *Oh, God! You Devil*. The movie's very title is meant to inspire chuckles, reflecting many people's view of Vegas as the antichrist of love and romance, despite the fact that wedding chapels are a cottage industry.

Into the Fire, the skydiving club used in *Honeymoon in Vegas*, was so infatuated with the paratrooping Elvis concept that club members got some jumpsuits and wigs, and started hiring themselves out as "The Flying Elvi." One of the members was seriously injured in early 1993, when he slammed into a parked car at a jump celebrating the grand opening of a blood bank.

Trivia

*Honeymoon in Vegas* inspired one troupe of Las Vegas entrepreneurs to brand themselves "The Flying Elvi" to meet the anticipated need for parachuting Elvises.

"If Vegas is a twenty-four-hour circus and it's so bizarre ... why do people get married here?" star Nicolas Cage pondered out loud during *Honeymoon's* promotional junket. "I don't know the answer to that. I think it might be because it's fast, and you do not have much time to think about it."

Cage's character hopes so. Jack Singer is a New York private detective with a commitment problem, thanks to seedy divorce investigations and the dying wish of his mother (Anne Bancroft) that he never get married. But Jack realizes that he'll lose his girlfriend Betsy (Sarah Jessica Parker) if he doesn't. "Let's just get on a plane, go to Vegas, and do it!" he proclaims.

"If I'd just said 'City Hall,' the story would end here," he appends in voice-over. Before they can even check into Bally's, a ball-busting (literally) high roller named Tommy Korman (James Caan) spots Betsy as a dead ringer for his late wife and conspires to possess her by fixing a poker game and luring Jack into it. The game evolves into a tense scene, despite the presence of an Elvis—the hotel is crawling with them during an impersonators convention—and the hound-dog face of former UNLV basketball coach Jerry Tarkanian. "The description in the script was a guy who looks very much like Jerry Tarkanian," Bergman explained later. "We looked at pictures of guys and realized very early on the only person who looks like Jerry Tarkanian is Jerry Tarkanian."

Jack winds up owing $65,000 to Korman, who will erase the debt if Betsy will spend the weekend with him in Hawaii. If not, he'll erase Jack. Removing Betsy to the tropical charm of Kauai, Korman charms her with lies, while keeping an ever-befuddled Jack at arm's length. When Korman escorts her back to Vegas after convincing her to tie the knot, Jack resorts to desperate measures to intercept them: hitching a ride with the "Flying Elvises" parachute team and skydiving into the Bally's parking lot to rescue his lady love. (The first draft called for Jack to catch a ride with Siegfried and Roy, and their white tigers. The idea "was funny," Bergman says, "but he wasn't doing anything heroic to get the girl back.")

The continual background presence of Elvis impersonators often steals laughter from the main plot. The impersonators were well aware that Cage had played *Wild at Heart* as a twisted Elvis movie, and between *Honeymoon* takes, Cage recalled, "They kept saying, 'Hey, man, let's get a beer and talk about E.'" Though Cage took the part to get away from psycho roles and play something "a little more sunny," Jack becomes increasingly bug-eyed and manic, the perfect embodiment of anyone driven to the edge by the sound of slot machines.

"I like to gamble, but I don't like gambling with a deck of cards. I like to gamble with work a little bit," Cage said. And his subsequent career gamble in Vegas, the Oscar-winning *Leaving Las Vegas,* paid off better than his roulette system during the *Honeymoon* shoot: "I had this system, which I will not be doing again." He bet on red at the roulette table and doubled his bet if he lost. "There was one streak when I lost thirteen times consecutively. Finally, I got it [the money] back, but I was sweating."

*Indecent Proposal* takes the same three basic characters and plays the situation for melodrama. Bad-movie buffs know from the opening line that the laughs will be unintended: "Losing Diana was like losing a part of me," pines Woody Harrelson in a voice-over that flashes back to the turmoil.

Architect David and his wife Diana (Demi Moore, never looking better) find their storybook marriage going awry when a recession crimps their plan to build his "dream house" on a piece of Santa Monica beachfront property that somehow managed to remain previously undiscovered over the years. Boo hoo, you cry. But it gets better.

David borrows $5,000 from his poor old beer-bellied father, who wears a white T-shirt and suspenders, and appears to live a long way from Santa Monica. "It wasn't enough. We needed fifty thousand," David narrates as the violins tug at the heartstrings. Writhing in his sleep, he suddenly wakes up with a fevered inspiration: "Get up. Get dressed. I've got an idea."

Cut to the requisite helicopter shot of the Strip, albeit this time without the strains of "Viva Las Vegas" heard in *Honeymoon*. With a methodic ease that serious players are still rewinding their VCRs to figure out, David hits the crap table to parlay his $5,000 into $25,000. "We're halfway there. ... I figure about two hours tomorrow and we'll be home free," he declares, and it's only 16 minutes into the movie.

Unfortunately, the movie is 119 minutes long. And it never gets better than the signature scene of the two showering their hotel bed with cash and making soft-focus whoopee while rolling around in the loot. It's a scene that sums up the usually unspoken sexual charge that comes with filthy lucre quickly gained, and so, in its own overheated way, is the only true moment in the movie. (One of *Proposal's* other rare virtues is that it depicted—presciently, as it turned out—Vegas and casino gambling as glamorous to

# Vegas Movies and Me

When *Fear and Loathing in Las Vegas* hit town for a fast and furious three-week movie shoot in August 1997—25 years after the counter-culture classic was published—the set was closed to the press. This was one of the movie's many commercial missteps, though perhaps a minor one compared to opening in wide release during Memorial Day weekend of 1998—the same time as *Godzilla*. The hands-off attitude of director Terry Gilliam and Universal Studios no doubt spared millions of readers bad "gonzo" location reports by journalists unable to resist a chance to mimic Thompson's electric prose. But it also cost the movie reams of free press from print cheerleaders who cherish a book that served as a career rosetta stone, one that painted the idea that it's somehow possible to live as an arrested adolescent and still contribute occasional insights to society.

The book nails the coffin lid on the '60s, as Thompson regales readers with Vegas drug antics in his "savage journey to the heart of the American dream." Thompson combined two separate trips to Vegas with Lord knows how much fiction to create his lurid saga.

Numbering among the legion inspired by the book, I felt somehow compelled to take two days off from my job so I could make $45 per day baking in the 110-degree heat of the dry lake bed near Jean, Nevada, as a *Fear and Loathing* extra. Also, it was the only way to crack the set.

The author (right) and *Review-Journal* staff artist David Stroud spent two days in the desert as *Fear and Loathing* extras. They were barely glimpsed in the final cut of the movie, but at least were rewarded with a close-up view of the infamous "Red Shark" convertible.

My intent was not to write one of those pseudo-Thompson pieces, though it would indeed be interesting to see how the real Thompson would have recounted the sight of Gilliam running around in a white Bedouin robe and turban, or of a pissy self-inflated assistant director screaming, "I'm getting very angry!" at the collected extras inside the "press-tent" location while the crew mocked him behind his back.

Instead, the desire was to witness firsthand what I hoped would be the magic combination of a gifted director and a classic book. Besides, movies have become such a forceful part of the American economy, if not the American dream, that I personally believe everyone should get to be in at least one.

And there was another reason, too. I'd caught the bug during my first brush with a blink-and-you'll-miss-me cameo in a film by a great director. Trying out for a speaking role in *Casino* led to an honest-to-God audition with Robert De Niro and Martin Scorsese. Rumors of their perfectionism proved true: The duo spent countless hours auditioning amateurs for bit parts, such as the business journalist who briefly interviews De Niro. The part rightly went to longtime Las Vegas news anchor Gwen Castaldi, who probably didn't squirm all the way out of a leather sofa and crawl up to the ceiling while talking to the two greats, unlike a certain print journalist who'd been in only one high-school play.

"How are you?" casting director Ellen Lewis asked as I waited outside the audition room on the verge of hyperventilation.

"I should've started with something smaller, like *Ernest Goes to Camp,*" I told her.

She found the line amusing enough to share with Scorsese and De Niro, who were laughing about it when I entered the room. "Isn't there a seal movie? You could have been in that," Scorsese told me (talking about *Andre*), before relaying an urban legend relating to seals and nature documentaries that, alas, is potentially libelous to a certain corporate conglomerate with a benign family image. He and De Niro chuckled mightily, then immediately snapped out of it, as if to say, "Now try to settle down and do this, chump!"

Throwing lines with Bobby, as I now call my close personal friend, did not win me the coveted part. But it did lead to a consolation cameo—perhaps related to the duo's savvy way of throwing bones to people who could potentially help them down the road—as another reporter in a different scene. This lesser role placed me amid a stereotypical pack of media wolves, the kind you'd more likely find at the White House or the O.J. trial than at an old airport in Las Vegas. In a scene shot in one morning at the Hughes Charter Terminal, the jackals ambush Kevin Pollack and surround him with microphones as he steps off a plane, just after Joe Pesci shoots a woman (veteran showgirl den mother Fluff Le Coque) squarely in the head: "Mr. Green! Mr. Green! Have you ever heard of the 22-Caliber Killer?"

Anyway, my VIP treatment on *Casino*—a trailer with my brown polyester suit all laid out and a series of residual checks for a half-day of work—suckered me into two hot and dusty 12-hour days in the extras' tent on *Fear and Loathing*. And my experience, coincidentally, is emblematic of the quality of both movies. The immaculate level of detail in *Casino* creates a sure sense of reality as the film recounts the tale of casino operator Frank Rosenthal and the wane of mob power in the '70s. And it's the absence of that reality that undermines *Fear and Loathing*.

It must be noted that Scorsese (who, oddly, tried to make *Fear and Loathing* at one point in the '70s) had a huge budget for *Casino*, while Gilliam, as quoted in the *Fear* pressbook, "began this movie trying to be as cheap as possible." Both movies cover roughly the same era of post-Rat Pack Vegas, and both were faced with the fact that much of '70s Vegas was gone, a victim of implosion fever on the Strip. *Casino* had more money—and a couple of years' head start—to re-create the early '70s with amazing detail and all on Nevada locations. *Fear and Loathing*, however, had to cut corners and do the best job it could: A credible shot of a pre-canopied Fremont Street was pulled off via a composite of live action and a computer-generated matte.

Nevertheless, both movies share a more ironic feature: They are most memorable in their first halves, before running out of steam. Scorsese devotees may argue with most reviewers—and apparently the ticket-buying public—who found *Casino* overlong, repellently violent, and too reminiscent of the superior *Goodfellas*. However, critics agreed that the movie's most mesmerizing hour is the first one, which hypnotically details the inner workings of a casino like no other movie has ever done. It's a dizzying piece of filmmaking, in which the truth revealed in the face of every extra validates all the hours spent auditioning real casino dealers and doormen.

This acute sense of detail is what's missing from *Fear and Loathing*. Yes, it boasts an uncanny performance from Johnny Depp. But it was otherwise tied down by a budget that required too much wallowing in hotel suites and not enough time on the town. Too much gonzo, not enough journalism. Too much fear and loathing, not enough insight.

The sad part is, the detail seemed to be there on the set despite the budget. The Mint 400 sequence I took part in was well-considered, down to the shotgun shells in the sand at the Mint Gun Club and the Jim Beam memorial Mint 400 decanter on the bar in the press tent. The race sequence was a logical chance for the movie to slow down and illustrate Thompson's idea that "Vegas is so full of natural freaks—people who are genuinely twisted—that drugs aren't really a problem." Instead, the race was glossed over, unfolding at the same feverish pace as the drug scenes.

Circus Circus (perhaps understandably) declined to participate in the filming of *Fear and Loathing in Las Vegas,* so the Stardust stood in as an unbilled location. A sinister clown's face was added as a prop entrance to the renamed "Bazooka Circus" casino.

Admittedly, this opinion might be tainted by the sour grapes of someone who spent two days in a lime-green polyester jacket—sprayed down in a cloud of Fuller's Earth—just to appear for a fraction of a second onscreen. More of the race sequence is included with a batch of deleted scenes on the DVD edition of the movie. The trimmed material doesn't increase my camera time, but one of the scenes—a long bar sequence in which Depp and Benicio Del Toro bullshit a law enforcement agent—hints at the extra depth the movie could have had if Gilliam had taken the time to savor his subjects the way that, say, Robert Altman did in *Nashville.*

Judging by its indifferent public and critical reception, I still liked *Fear and Loathing* better than most people did. Even though the second half of the movie is full of missed opportunities, the first half crackles with the book's energy, and the "Bazooka Circus" sequence alone confirms the director's vision.

The first night of shooting involved Depp and Del Toro's ether-snorting entrance to the Stardust Hotel, redecorated with a menacing clown facade (Circus Circus wanted no part of the movie). Tourists—not too different from the suckers mocked in *Fear and Loathing*—were scoffing at Depp: "He doesn't look drunk." "Boring," they declared before heading back to the nickel slots. In the finished product, however, the scene is appropriately twisted as it plays beneath Depp's narration.

As for *Casino,* I have to share the opinion of the movie's supporting player,

Don Rickles, who believed his effort will endure beyond its short box-office life. "It's the kind of movie that will always come back. People will remember it before they remember *Leaving Las Vegas*," he noted in 1996. "It's such a cult thing and so descriptive of what went on in those years that people will turn back to it."

I'm willing to venture that the same will be true of *Fear and Loathing* as well. Both movies will become significant pieces of Cult Vegas—despite having me in them.

## How much of *Fear* was true?

How wild a ride did Hunter Thompson really take in Las Vegas? Some secrets may forever remain between him and certain rental car companies. Thompson has freely admitted that his biggest conceit was to combine two separate trips to Las Vegas into one: a trip to attend the Mint 400 Del Webb Desert Rally, March 21-23, 1971, and another for the National District Attorneys Association convention at the Dunes, April 25-29. But newspapers of the day do at least jibe with much of the sordid account.

**Thompson**: "We drove over to the Desert Inn to catch the Debbie Reynolds/ Harry James show," only to be tossed out for laughing at Debbie as she "yukked across the stage in a silver Afro wig ... to the tune of 'Sergeant Pepper' from the golden trumpet of Harry James."

**Reality**: Debbie did indeed do the Desert Inn on the Mint 400 weekend, and as she told *Sun* columnist Joe Delaney, "We're doing three big production numbers: a rock medley, an *Unsinkable Molly Brown* segment, and the finale from *Applause*." The possible stretch: Harry James was in the DI lounge, not billed as part of Debbie's show.

**Thompson**: In Chapter 9 of *Fear and Loathing*, a perusal of the *Las Vegas Sun* newspaper prompts Thompson to reel off the atrocities of the unholy year 1971—a 19-year-old "beauty" stuffed in a refrigerator after a heroin overdose, a photo of cops fighting with antiwar protestors, and the "torture tales" of Vietnamese prisoners.

**Reality**: Wrong paper, but the front-page quotes did, with a bit of compression, come from page one of the April 28 *Review-Journal*.

**Thompson**: Edward R. Bloomquist, the keynote speaker for the National District Attorneys Association convention at the Dunes, dispenses such "Reefer Madness" wisdom as, "The reefer butt is called a 'roach' because it resembles a cockroach."

**Reality**: Bloomquist's speech, as reported in the *Review-Journal*, didn't sound so Stone Age. When pot smokers can prove the drug is harmless, Bloomquist will "eat humble pie gladly," the paper reported. He did, however, note that marijuana was linked to "perpetuated immaturity" and a tendency toward suicide.

The lounge singer in the introductory Vegas montage of *Indecent Proposal* is Kristine Weitz, a statuesque, former college athlete who became a longtime Hilton fixture with the act Kristine and The Sting. Three years after the movie, she became a gay icon—tarted up like a drag queen, who just happened to be a real woman—singing dance hits such as "Feel What You Want" in chic New York and European nightclubs.

young adults, at a time when the Excalibur was generating press about the city as a family destination.)

But the next day dawns, as it always does in bad melodramas. Because of their inability to recognize a hot streak and quit while they're ahead, no one is really surprised or sorry for the couple when they switch their game to roulette and start to lose their stash. Retreating to assess their losses, David and Diana become the rare L.A. tourists to discover the delightful charms of Huntridge Liquor & Cocktails and its adjacent drugstore, a living anachronism at Charleston Boulevard and Maryland Parkway (in the movie, of course, meant to epitomize down and out). There they agree to return to the Hilton for one more attempt, and even the Huntridge waitress shakes her head, along with the viewer, knowing what's bound to happen next.

Fortunately, one witness to their fatal last turn at the wheel is suave millionaire John Gage (Robert Redford), who had earlier ogled Diana in a hotel dress shop. "That sonofabitch must get more pussy than you can shake a stick at," observes future *Sling Blade* Oscar-winner Billy Bob Thornton, as he and Woody stand with the gawkers to watch Gage's baccarat game in the high-roller pit. When Diana kisses the rich showoff's dice to help him win a cool million in one throw at the crap table, Gage invites the couple up to his suite for a philosophical debate over a game of pool.

"You can't buy people," Diana tells him.

"Let's test that cliché," he replys, offering her a quick million to spend the night with him.

It's here that the movie basically paints itself into a corner. Ticket-buyers were lured to the theater on the central premise: Would you or wouldn't you? But c'mon, a million dollars? To sleep with Robert Redford, looking more suave than he has in years? The central question is settled in minutes.

The couple makes the decision together: She will do it, then never speak of it again. But the moment he drops off his wife at Gage's suite, David has second thoughts. He gets a little delirious, as the casino that once reveled in a luster not seen since *Diamonds Are Forever* is suddenly full of ... Shriners! In fezzes!

When the animatronic tiki gods in the Hilton's Benihana restaurant start to sing

"Help Me Make It Through the Night," David snaps (and who could blame him). He goes tearing back to the suite in a frenzy that is amazingly similar to Cage's *Honeymoon* hysteria. Too late. Gage is already whisking Diana away via a helicopter on the roof (a downtown roof, to the amusement of locals, who spot Main Street Station and the Lady Luck Hotel as the chopper supposedly lifts off from the Hilton).

By no mere coincidence, the movie isn't as luridly riveting once the action leaves Vegas. David gets jealous, that pesky Gage won't leave them alone, and the architect nearly loses his lady love before realizing—gasp!—that money can't buy happiness. At least not the happiness of teaching architecture at the community college where David ends up. He doesn't get to jump out of an airplane to rescue his wife, or even enlist the aid of Siegfried and Roy's white tigers. But animals do figure in, when David wins back his gal by popping the whole million down on a hippopotamus at a zoo foundation fundraiser.

I n a departure from most Vegas movies, flamboyant funnyman Rip Taylor—a Vegas fixture since the early '60s and the original "prop" comic—does not play himself or even appear in the Las Vegas sequences of *Indecent Proposal.* Instead, he turns up minus his outlandish toupees as Demi Moore's abusive boss in L.A.

Trivia

The two "proposal" movies were interesting parallels for Cage and Harrelson. Cage was trying to play more of a leading man and action hero—"I understand my work in the past wouldn't really suggest me being an everyday guy," he noted—but Harrelson's bug-eyed performance showed him the path from the naive country boy he played on *Cheers* to even seedier and nuttier roles in *Natural Born Killers* and *The People vs. Larry Flynt.*

Harrelson had the last laugh three years later in the juvenile but hilarious *Kingpin,* where comedian Chris Elliot parodies the Redford character. Elliot offers a million dollars to Harrelson and road buddy Randy Quaid—bowlers who are down and out in Reno—to have sex. With each other.

# Fear the worst: The three stooges

Cult movies need no one to make excuses for them. By their very definition, movies that mainstream critics and audiences dismiss as pure garbage are usually the ones that find an immortal afterlife. Bad-movie freaks are drawn to unintentional humor, laughable special effects (almost a virtue in today's world of amazing effects unburdened by story), or guilty pleasures like gratuitous sex or nudity. The "worse" a movie supposedly is, the more likely it is to endure beyond one that's merely boring or forgettable.

The first part of this chapter did as much to expose the warts of the three Las Vegas classics as it did to celebrate their charms. If they are the best that Las Vegas movies have to offer, then you might wonder, what could be the worst?

Heh, heh, heh.

In 1995, Las Vegas gave birth to *Showgirls,* a stinker par excellence. It provoked an almost venomous wave of hatred, but should justifiably take its place as a camp classic once given the wisdom and perspective of time. But it would be anticlimactic not to start with two earlier films—the comparably benign *Las Vegas Hillbillys* and the more easily forgettable *Lookin' to Get Out*—and work up (or down) to the big kahuna.

If there is such a thing as a bad movie not living up to the full debacle of its promise, *Las Vegas Hillbillys* is it. The mere title is enough to titillate the bad-movie connoisseur, but the real come-on in 1966 was the epic meeting of its co-billed blonde bombshells, Jayne Mansfield and Mamie Van Doren. Alas, the two are never quite seen in the same shot, and the title is a tease. God knows where the movie was filmed, but except for one memorable shot, it weren't in no Vegas. It's all done on sparsely furnished sets or hilly outdoor locations, probably in the South.

A bare-bones plot provides the vehicle for a parade of pre-Nashville Network Grand Ole Opry stars to plant their feet and sing; there probably weren't a lot of color TVs around rural drive-in country even as late as 1966. Ferlin Husky and Don Bowman play two Tennessee moonshiners who think they've hit the big time when they inherit what turns out to be a dilapidated Vegas casino: "Beats the devil out o' choppin' wood," says Husky.

En route, they stop near Hoover Dam to help out nightclub singer Mansfield—"the biggest star you'll ever meet in Vegas"—when they find her stranded next to her convertible. That sets up a music rivalry with Van Doren as Boots Malone, the "Fresh Out of Lovin'" bargirl they inherit with the casino. Striking an alliance, Husky tells Mamie, "I'll do the country songs and you do the fast—whatcha call 'em?—go-go things." Billie Bird, the movie's version of *The Beverly Hillbillies'* Granny, eventually unites all forces and turns the casino into a country music showcase.

The movie lives up to its Vegas promise in only one golden sequence: The boys' jalopy—a stripped-down truck with a picnic-table parasol sprouting from the top and Roman candle-like explosions coming from the back of it—cruises the Strip around the Dunes, Stardust, Thunderbird (where Van Doren performed in real life), and Silver Slipper. One can only imagine what Sinatra would have said if he'd looked out his window one day to see the umbrella-capped creation on the Strip.

The accompanying song has yet to supplant "Viva Las

> " No fancy long-legged Las Vegas showgirl could ever turn me away from you. "
>
> Jeepers (Don Bowman) to his hometown sweetie in *Las Vegas Hillbillys*

Mamie Van Doren got to play the down-to-earth gal for a change as singing bargirl Boots Malone in the backwoods cheapie *Las Vegas Hillbillys.* Ferlin Husky (left) and Don Bowman also starred in the movie.

Vegas" as the city's anthem: "Yippy-ay-yo, Las Vegas. We made it, yessirree. In a beat-up car we traveled, from the hills of Tennessee. ... Yippy-ay-yo, Las Vegas. We'll stay till we get rich. Smokin' big cigars, drivin' real fine cars on the Las Vegas Strip!"

Siegfried and Roy (before they were headliners) perform to cheesy disco over the opening credits of *Lookin' to Get Out,* and the 1981 movie goes downhill from there. Pinpointing why it's damned near unwatchable is difficult, as it threatens to turn into a good movie at several points and was directed by the usually talented Hal Ashby (*Bound for Glory, Coming Home*).

Jon Voight, the movie's co-writer, who starred with Dustin Hoffman in the film *Midnight Cowboy,* apparently must have been scratching a long-simmering itch to play a Ratso Rizzo-type character by creating his own like-minded sleazeball. Voight's sidekick is Burt Young, reprising his popular Paulie shtick from the *Rocky* movies. They're *Lookin' to Get Out* of New York to escape from mobsters trying to collect $10,000 in gambling debts.

"We're goin' to Vegas," Voight tells Young.

"Las Vegas?"

"I don't know any other Vegas."

There's historical value, at least, in a sight-seeing tour of the *Hallelujah Hollywood* revue and other highlights of the original MGM Grand Hotel (now Bally's) before its big 1981 fire. The two men lie their way into the "Doctor Zhivago Suite" to bask in luxury in a scene that would be echoed in the superior *Rain Man*. Ann-Margret proves you can't go home again—or at least back to Vegas—playing Voight's ex with a wooden lifelessness that is perhaps the movie's greatest sin. The slapstick (but not bloodless) violence and endless shouting in the climactic casino scenes are spellbindingly awful, proving that no Vegas movie worth its salt should revolve around gambling.

Ah, but it pales in comparison to *Showgirls*. If *Lookin' to Get Out* merely seems anemic, clumsy, and miscalculated, *Showgirls* dive-bombs with reckless, carefree abandon, plunging into its sleaze and bad taste with all the zeal of a John Waters movie.

The jury's still out on whether *Showgirls* will be remembered only as another example of Hollywood ego, waste, and indulgence, or whether bad-movie buffs will peel away the layers of this smelly onion to savor its joys in repeated viewings. When it was released, the sense of betrayal and fraud was too overwhelming for most audiences to laugh, although there was a desperate attempt to re-release it in West Hollywood as a midnight movie (advertised as *Ho-girls*) and recoup some of the $39 million squandered on this megabomb.

If *Showgirls* had been some little direct-to-video exploitation movie, it would have raised nary an eyebrow. It attracted attention—and eventual vitriol—because it was a major studio effort from the *Basic Instinct* team: writer Joe Eszterhas (who received $3 million for *Basic Instinct*) and director Paul Verhoeven, who had delivered steamy and stylish sex in the earlier hit and still slipped by with an R rating. This time, the duo conned United Artists into playing up the sleaze element—"So erotic, so controversial, that we can't show you a thing except the title," went one teaser campaign—and sticking with the movie's NC-17 rating as a matter of anti-censorship pride. Imagine the studio's embarrassment when these A-list filmmakers delivered the kind of soft-core nudie melodrama that plays on pay cable in the pre-dawn hours.

Instead of *Instinct's* steamy eroticism, audiences were bombarded with school-yard vulgarities ("Life sucks? Shit happens? Where do you get this stuff? Off of T-shirts?" one of the more intelligent characters finally asks) and crude violence. But viewers who live in Vegas were especially amazed, particularly those with any ties to the city's production shows. It's not as though you go through *Showgirls* and nitpick various little inaccuracies, such as the Stardust's "entertainment director"—a middle management gig at most casinos—having a lavish mansion and backyard pool worthy of the CEO.

Nope, this one is big-picture wrong—or at least grossly stereotyped—in virtually every idea and plot turn, starting with the title subject. Showgirls do remain in Vegas, but almost as an afterthought. Author Larry McMurtry had no trouble seeing them as one of his favorite themes—the dying breed—in *The Desert Rose*, a novel that came a full 12 years earlier (1983). Interestingly enough, both stories were set at the Stardust. (Duped into believing that *Showgirls* would be a hit and generate positive publicity, the Stardust tried to follow the movie's lead by hiring a "Showgirl of the 21st Century" named Aki for its *Enter the Night* production. No one seemed to much care.)

Granted, the "showkids" who remain on the Strip still operate to some degree in their own late-night world, well-insulated from the residential Las Vegas that's increasingly independent of the Strip. A movie about their lives might still be fascinating. But not a single character in *Showgirls* rings true. It's weird, even a little surreal, to watch a movie filmed extensively in the actual, modern-day Las Vegas inhabited entirely by these play-acting stereotypes, all of them laughably predictable, with one exception: the heroine.

One of the more brilliant touches—deliberate or not—is the predatory, feral nature of Nomi (Elizabeth Berkley), who spends much of the movie topless. In the opening scene she hitchhikes, then pulls a switchblade on the guy with Elvis hair who gives her a lift. Later, this Typhoid Mary smiles with satisfaction after kicking a future friend in the nuts and starting a brawl in a disco (the defunct Shark Club). At least she can hold her own when she has to take a job at a topless club while waiting for her big dancing break on the Strip.

The real-life topless joint Cheetah's got free advertising when it was used for exteriors (a set was used for inside). It's oddly referred to as "The Cheetah" in the movie, where Nomi gives the Stardust's entertainment director (Kyle McLachlan) a totally nude, full-contact, lap dance the real club is not licensed to offer.

The producers paid a *Las Vegas Sun* reporter a handsome fee to research the inner workings of topless clubs, then ignored her findings to embrace obvious or outdated clichés: the scumbag manager ("This is a class joint"), or the Totie Fields-like comedienne, a job position most clubs no longer bother with. Again, a serious movie might have explored some new ground—the idea that nude and topless clubs in Las Vegas have become a big industry that's all but killed the feathers-and-sequins revues on the Strip. If Nomi had danced in a showroom revue, then stopped by the strip joints to earn extra cash on her way home, that would have been more novel and realistic. Instead, Eszterhas sticks with the clichéd, '60s notion that the showroom job is coveted enough to lead to *All About Eve* backstage melodrama.

*Showgirls* doesn't reach its full hilarity until the arrival of Gina Gershon as the icy, bisexual star of *Goddess*. Gershon's deliciously over-the-top performance suggests that she's the only cast member who smelled a future *Valley of the Dolls* in the fermentation process. She sets Nomi up for a fall by arranging an audition with the show's producer (Alan Rachins of *L.A. Law*), who gets all the best lines: "I am a prick. I don't care whether you live or die. I wanna see you dance and I wanna see you smile," he tells the hopefuls. "Come back when you fuck some of this baby fat off," he says to one. "I'm erect. Why aren't you erect?" he asks Nomi, then offers her ice cubes to make her nipples stand up. The show itself (staged inside the Horizon in Lake Tahoe) is way nuder and—at the time the movie came out—more erotic and interesting than any of the real production shows on the Strip.

The plot goes the way of *The Terminator* meets *All About Eve* as Nomi wreaks destruction for all who cross her path, be it Gershon's ice queen or the Michael Bolton-esque rock star who gets a *Faster Pussycat*-style, jack-booted ass-whippin' after he rapes Nomi's best friend. The ending, again, is open to debate on whether it was intentional. Nomi, the machine of destruction, hitches a ride to … yes, the highway sign confirms … the only city worthy of her wrath: Los Angeles.

The only thing more ludicrous than the movie itself is its press kit, which answers the vital question: What the hell could have taken over the rational minds of Verhoeven and Eszterhas while they were making this piece of shit?

Two words: lap dancing.

"The concept of a naked woman dancing privately for one man alone in a room captured the filmmakers' imaginations," a press release declares. "Eszterhas was the first to try lap dancing—but only if he were allowed to bring the female researcher along with him." Eszterhas insisted Verhoeven try it as well: "And, in the end, he couldn't resist because it's as far as you can push that envelope. Vegas takes the whole phenomenon of lap dancing and nude dancing to its absolute zenith," the proud screenwriter proclaimed.

# Cult value: The best of the rest

As Vegas grew into a broad-based destination resort, more and more movies paid attention. There isn't room enough in this book for all of them, but this overview tries to single out the best, worst, and memorably weirdest. The definition of "cult" is liberal here. It allows some movies to slide in for sheer archeological interest—the excuse being, perhaps, that "Old Vegas" is developing a cult of its own.

Others make it by nature of a star, a director, or curiosity value that ties them into an existing underground following. The rules are admittedly arbitrary: If it's got Wayne Newton, it's in. However, the definition is enforced enough to exclude *Rain Man* and *Leaving Las Vegas,* by the logic that their Oscar-winning status makes them too widespread in their appeal, or at least too well-remembered, to have the kind of fanatical loyalists or rabid pockets of interest that qualify for cultdom.

### Austin Powers: International Man of Mystery (1997)

"Vegas, baby, Vegas!" declares Michael Meyers' most quotable creation since *Wayne's World.* Powers is a combination of several '60s fascinations—secret agent, fashion photographer, and pop star—who wakes up after 30 years in a cryogenic freezer to battle his old adversary, Dr. Evil (also Meyers). The James Bond spoof ends up in Las Vegas for no real reason, except that it makes sense in a *Diamonds Are Forever* kind of way.

Several scenes were filmed in and around the Riviera and Stardust. The most memorable is Powers romancing co-star Elizabeth Hurley on top of a double-decker bus that's cruising the north Strip, serenaded by Burt Bacharach singing "What the World Needs Now Is Love."

"That was great fun," Bacharach recalled in 1998. "Getting onto that bus, just being pulled down the Strip at one o'clock in the morning, playing the piano up there while they're dancing and eating dinner, and watching these people out on the Strip looking in amazement at this old English bus being pulled down the Strip like an apparition."

Almost as much fun is the parody of the archetypal Bond casino showdown, as Powers confronts white-tuxedoed villain Robert Wagner at a Stardust low-roller table and proves himself something less than a blackjack player. Locals will also laugh at an impossible juxtaposition showing Meyers and Hurley in a landscaped area near the front of Circus Circus, staking out a severe-looking office building labeled "Virtucon" (the legitimate business facade to Dr. Evil's empire). The Algiers motel, one of the last original buildings on the Strip, makes its way into the inevitable montage of casino signs—which is at least done as a send-up. "Viva Las Vegas, baby. Yeah!"

## Best of the Best II (1992)

The sincerity of this action melodrama kind of pulls you in, even if you start watching just to heckle its ridiculous premise: When city building inspectors were looking the other way (OK—maybe that's not so ridiculous), a Fremont Street nightclub managed to build an underground arena where martial-arts gladiators fight to the death. Wayne Newton, hot on a streak of sleazeball roles (*Licence to Kill, The Adventures of Ford Fairlane*), shines in another one as the ringmaster.

## Con Air (1997)

The Sands makes its final film appearance in this *Die Hard*-meets-*Airport* potboiler, which is so willfully stupid that it periodically winks at audiences to make sure they're in on the joke. The Sands "implosion" isn't used in the movie, which was filmed there after the hotel closed but before its demolition in November 1996. Instead, a mock aircraft fuselage was carefully rammed through a casino entrance after the prison transport plane of the title crash-lands on the Strip, taking out a scale model of the Hard Rock Hotel's giant guitar sign in the process. The nostalgic can take solace in the fact that the Rat Pack never walked in the plane-violated area, a '90s addition built gracelessly out to the sidewalk. But it's still a little sad to see the '60s-era circular lighting clusters over the valet portico and know that neither they nor the '68 circular hotel tower are around anymore.

*Con Air* also boasts the wackiest disregard for actual Vegas geography since the *Vegas* TV show. People who live in Chicago, New York, or other movie-location meccas probably have the same complaints when, for example, a car turns from one street into a different part of town. Yet Vegas is so widely visited, you'd think people would

The Sands Hotel, awaiting demolition in 1996, gets one last moment of dubious glory as the crash point for "Con Air." A mock fuselage was placed in front of the hotel for the crash scenes.

be distracted by the lack of continuity in the climactic chase scene.

As Nicolas Cage pursues the bad guys, scenes near the Sands are indiscriminately spliced with footage of downtown's Fremont Street Experience (the first time it was used in a movie), the Debbie Reynolds Hotel (another defunct property near the Las Vegas Convention Center), and a long tunnel that doesn't exist anywhere in town. Viewers can get whiplash: Now they're downtown! Now they're on the Strip! No comment about the drill press that appears out of nowhere just in time to crush a bad guy's head.

## Cool World (1992)

It was hiding in plain sight and s-o-o-o obvious: The key to a parallel dimension is found on the electric sign on top of the Union Plaza (since renamed Jackie Gaughan's Plaza), a grand addition to downtown in 1972 that now slowly molds over as a graveyard for oldsters and low rollers. The other world is *Fritz the Cat* animator Ralph Bakshi's version of Disney's Toontown, where humans co-mingle with sexy cartoon characters.

Bakshi's origins in underground comics and midnight movie favorites such as *Heavy Traffic* ensure him a continued cult following, yet *Cool World* helps explain why mainstream success eludes him. Despite the great promise of Kim Basinger as an animated Jessica Rabbit, this tale of a Las Vegas comic book artist (Gabriel Byrne) and his fantasy-girl-come-to-life falls in the uneven "interesting failure" category of most Bakshi efforts. The stylish animation is deflated by a cold, off-putting approach to storytelling.

## Corvette Summer (1978)

No wonder Vegas got a bad rap in the '70s. This coming-of-age comedy starring Mark Hamill (who must have shot it before *Star Wars* went through the roof, judging by a marquee for *Lido '77*) is no Chamber of Commerce endorsement. As Kenny, the car-obsessed high-school graduate trying to track down a stolen Stingray that had been refurbished by his auto mechanics class, Hamill endures perhaps the sleaziest Vegas ever put on film.

First, he gets his pocket picked on the Circus Circus midway by a guy who uses a bimbo to distract him. After he gets caught taking shelter in a U-Haul on a gas station parking lot, the station owner feels sorry for him and gives him a job. But soon the owner demands that Kenny start ripping off customers, telling him to put Alka Seltzer in the battery of a station wagon driven by a woman with her children. When Hamill goes soft, explaining, "She lost all her money playing blackjack," the woman rips off cans of motor oil and drives away without paying for gas.

All the women in the casino scenes dress like hookers—lots of hot pants, halters, and '70s eye shadow—and Kenny's love interest (Annie Potts) aspires to be one. When he's looking for her at one point, he ducks into an establishment right on Fremont Street bearing the sign "Good Company Escort Service." Most of the movie is set in Vegas, but some of the nondescript locations appear to have been filmed in the San Fernando Valley, where the opening is set. The locations blend well enough to fool the modern viewer. A chase sequence in which Hamill tries to follow the Corvette with a bicycle shows that the Strip's density still hadn't filled in between resort hotels, and there's a startling amount of undeveloped land. As Hamill's character says, "I will find that Corvette sooner or later. I'm not worried ... because Las Vegas isn't all that big!"

## The Electric Horseman (1979)

Apologies for stretching the "cult movie" definition here. This romantic pairing of Robert Redford and Jane Fonda at the height of their appeal was a mainstream hit in its day, but the movie has been largely forgotten since then. Still, it's worth a look to see not only how the Strip has changed, but also how the movie seemed to realize that the '70s were almost over. Vegas is equated with polyester and disco, neither of which are viewed favorably here. The city's affinity for trade shows even makes it sort of an extended metaphor for corporate evil. Redford's a fallen rodeo champ who saves a racehorse from a tyrannical conglomerate (don't ask). He steals the horse from the showroom stage as showgirls cavort to "Disco Magic," then rides it through Caesars Palace, up the Strip, and away to saintly Utah.

Willie Nelson, the Strip's most laid-back regular, steals the movie with one memorable line spoken poolside at Caesars: "I don't know what you're gonna do, but I'm gonna get me a bottle of tequila [and] one of those little keno girls that can suck the chrome off a trailer hitch, and kinda kick back."

## Elvis and Me (1988)

This is Cilla's side of the story, in a made-for-TV movie adapted from Priscilla Presley's tell-all (or at least tell-some) memoir. It was filmed at the Las Vegas Hilton just before Christmas 1987. Various areas of the Hilton doubled for the Sahara—Presley Party Headquarters in the early '60s—as well as for the Aladdin's wedding suite. Dale Midkiff (*Pet Sematary*) and Susan Walters star in an ordinary TV bio that showcased the Hilton showroom and backstage area, as well as the "Elvis Suite," before the hotel mutilated them beyond recognition. Despite former Elvis crony Jerry Schilling as technical adviser, details were compromised for budget or drama. (For instance, Elvis never had to go through the kitchen to get onstage. Headliners have an elevator right outside the dressing room.) Explaining that the movie would pull no punches in showing the King's decline, director Larry Peerce announced: "We hope it's going to make a strong anti-drug statement. Priscilla feels very strongly that it should, and so do I."

## The Gauntlet (1977)

This freewheeling Clint Eastwood blow-'em-up is remembered mainly for two delirious sequences in which a house and a bus are each shot to pieces. Corrupt cops in Phoenix send dimwitted officer Clint to Las Vegas to bring back a hooker (Sondra Locke) for grand jury testimony, figuring that they can off them both somewhere along the way. The odds on whether the two will make it are even posted at race books under the code names of horses. Clint caused a big stir among City Hall and Clark County Courthouse employees by first scouting locations, then filming downtown in early 1977.

## Harley Davidson and the Marlboro Man (1991)

An entertainingly bad macho shoot-'em-up brings Don Johnson and Mickey Rourke—as scruffy rodeo cowboy and biker, respectively—to Vegas for one sequence. Trying to elude machine gun-toting baddies, Johnson and Rourke are tracked to the roof of the Dunes. Mimicking the cliff jump from *Butch Cassidy and the Sundance Kid,* the boys psyche each other into jumping into a swimming pool below. Exactly which pool is uncertain, but it wasn't the Dunes'. However, footage of the casino, a hotel room, and the roof at least afford some final views of the doomed hotel.

## Honey, I Blew Up the Kid (1992)

Disney's comic sequel to *Honey, I Shrunk the Kids* revisits the climax to *The Amazing Colossal Man,* setting a giant baby loose on Fremont Street—one of the last times it was filmed uncovered, before the canopy went up. When this movie was being shot, local extras ran in terror from a giant baby shoe dangling from a crane (the rest was matted in). By day, the shoe was parked on a side street to no great curiosity from downtown gamblers. Early scenes also make *Kid* the first Vegas movie to recognize that locals live in Southern California-style subdivisions. White stucco houses with red tile roofs—the ordinary, homogenized reality of daily life for most residents—somehow don't make it onscreen as often as the Strip.

## *Kill Me Again* (1988)

This low-budget, film-noir thriller is an overlooked sleeper worth seeking out, particularly for fans of thrillers in the hard-boiled vein of Quentin Tarantino or crime writer Jim Thompson. A private eye (an early role for Val Kilmer) follows a femme fatale (Joanna Whaley) from Reno to Las Vegas, where the Las Vegas Hilton, Lake Mead, and Valley of Fire are shown to good effect amid violent plot twists in a mean-spirited, savvy melodrama.

## *Las Vegas Story* (1952)

Las Vegas was just starting to hit its stride when Howard Hughes—weirdly foreshadowing his interest in the city—produced this melodrama for leading lady Jane Russell. It's like a Vegas version of *Casablanca,* only without the charismatic leads, World War II backdrop, and unforgettable dialogue. In fact, only two elements raise it above pure tedium: Vincent Price, and location shots that provide a real sense of a downtown accessed by railroad and the budding Strip surrounded by desert.

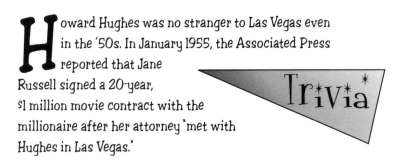

Howard Hughes was no stranger to Las Vegas even in the '50s. In January 1955, the Associated Press reported that Jane Russell signed a 20-year, $1 million movie contract with the millionaire after her attorney "met with Hughes in Las Vegas."

Price plays Russell's new husband, a suave cad who brings his bride on a Vegas honeymoon to escape a suspicious past. Price's gentlemanly performance keeps viewers guessing whether or not he's the bad guy. "What a beautiful picture: moonlight, sagebrush, my wife with a stranger," he purrs after catching her with leading man Victor Mature, who plays the Bogart from her past.

Hoagy Carmichael takes on the Dooley Wilson role, singing two songs (one of them the classic "I Get Along Without You Very Well") and dropping bizarre bits of non-wisdom, such as the opening narration: "Clark County, Nevada. Folks who live here

This is a windy town. People blow in, people blow out.

Victor Mature
*Las Vegas Story*

think it's bigger than the state of Texas. But it ain't." The Flamingo is the primary location, but for some reason it's referred to only as "the Fabulous."

## Las Vegas Weekend (1985)

This is one of those I-can't-believe-I'm-staying-up-to-watch-it cheapies. Most location filming took place at the California Hotel, an undistinguished downtown hotel-casino that extorted producer-writer-director Dale Trevillion into playing an ad jingle during a casino scene that's full of lingering close-ups of the hotel logo. When a naive computer genius/nerd (Barry Hickey) loses his research funding, his girlfriend decides that it might de-geek him a bit if he tests his winning blackjack strategy in Las Vegas.

He cruises Fremont Street, where pedestrians take an unusual interest in him—like no one's ever seen a nerd on Fremont Street. He checks into the California ("That's where I live—I'll stay there"), wins 20 blackjack hands in a row, and falls in with the usual gamut of lowlifes and topless chippies that nerds tend to meet in movies airing on cable in the middle of the night.

## Lost in America (1985)

Albert Brooks has a cult following for his distinct and personal comic vision, and this movie is his best to date. A yuppie couple (Brooks, Julie Hagerty) decide to drop out of the corporate rat race and see America in an RV. Their Vegas stop offers an insightful, informed look at the city in relatively little screen time.

The Desert Inn becomes an unfortunate second-honeymoon stop when Hagerty blows the couple's nest egg in the casino. Drawing on his background as a slick ad man, Brooks tries to convince a casino executive (*The Grasshopper* co-writer Garry Marshall) to give them back the money as a public-relations gesture. He even comes up with an impromptu ad jingle: "The Desert Inn has heart!" Brooks digs himself in deeper and deeper, explaining that he's not just some schmuck "who's here to see Wayne Newton."

"I like Wayne Newton," Marshall replies, deadpan.

The movie also provides a hilarious argument over the fallen nest egg, which is staged on top of Hoover Dam.

The Desert Inn held on to its '70s hipness all the way to 1997, when it fell victim to the plague of Italianate/Mediterranean makeovers spawned by construction of the Bellagio. Then, in the summer of 2000, Bellagio perpetrator Steve Wynn sold his Mirage Resorts properties and bought the Desert Inn, almost immediately announcing plans to tear down the hotel that had been remodeled to copy his previous properties. Albert Brooks, are you paying attention?

The unique architecture of the doomed Landmark Hotel so captivated *Mars Attacks!* director Tim Burton that he filmed the hotel's November 1995 implosion even before principal photography began for the rest of the movie.

## *Mars Attacks!* (1996)

This is a mad movie making full use of a mad town. Any film in which a character asks Tom Jones, "Tom, are you sure you can fly this [plane]?" should have been an instant classic. Instead, Tim Burton's demented sci-fi homage was trounced at the box office by *Independence Day* in the summer of 1996, though it's so much brighter that it almost plays like a parody of the competition. As in the bigger movie, invaders from space threaten a cross-section of America, from the president himself (Jack Nicholson) to an old lady listening to Slim Whitman records in a rural Kansas rest home.

If the Landmark Hotel had to go down in a pile of dust, at least its "implosion" was fittingly preserved by one of the few directors who could appreciate its inspired Jetsonsstyle architecture. Better yet, Burton throws in a subtle nod to the dear-departed Vegas World hotel-casino by renaming the Landmark the "Galaxy Hotel," the dreamchild of a white-trash developer—who is also played by Nicholson. In "the event of some intergalactic emergency, the people still want to roll them bones," he tells his investors, just before the building is zapped. The only bummer is that the real implosion looks like another special effect after being so heavily matted with processed opticals.

Burton honed right in on the city's most surreal pop-art architecture. As the hero, Jim Brown—playing a washed-up boxer turned casino greeter à la Joe Louis—poses with tourists (nuns, namely) at the Luxor. That's where he hooks up with showroom star Jones (a living piece of pop art) for a daring standoff against the Martians in the Young Electric Sign Company's now defunct "neon graveyard." And it's probably no accident that scenes of the Martians wreaking mayhem on the Strip are staged in front of the La Concha motel, a 1962 piece of expressionism that still thumbs its nose at "progress" along the Strip.

## Meet Me in Las Vegas (1956)

This fanciful MGM musical served as the city's best cinematic commercial until *Ocean's Eleven* four years later. While both movies offer generous CinemaScope tours of the Sands, their separate agendas put different spins on Vegas. *Ocean's* showed Sinatra's town as a swanky, exclusive place. *Meet Me* uses the MGM tradition to portray the city not unlike today's imaging campaigns: safe, happy, and colorful, albeit a little more folksy and country-leaning than people would pretend today. "Yippie yi, yippie yay. Everyone's headin' to Nevada today," the Four Aces sing over the opening credits.

The Sands' full cooperation was ensured by a May 1955 story outline for what was then titled *Weekend at Las Vegas*: "He loves the place. He always has fun. When you gamble, you have to expect to lose—and anyway, this time he's going to win!" it says of the luckless hero.

The Sands is depicted as a resort glamorous enough to host a visiting ballet dancer named Maria Corvier (Cyd Charisse), yet homey enough for her to meet a rancher (Dan Dailey), whose notoriously bad luck at the tables turns around as long as he holds the ballerina's hand while betting. "Normally they'd never even meet," notes the story treatment. "But things don't work normally in Las Vegas—that's what's so great about the place."

"While I'm dancing, people will be drinking?" the ballerina asks the Sands manager, played by Jim Backus.

"You say 'art' to them, they say, 'Art who?'" he replies.

When Lady Luck brings the odd couple together, even a sophisticated ballerina is willing to keep winning money, as long as the cowboy quits "calling me 'Baby,' or 'Honey,' or 'Bunny.'" The two predictably fall for each other in a leisurely musical-revue plot that gives Vegas buffs time to check out the Sands. You see the casino with the mural over its long bar, the doorway to the Copa Room, and the Sunrise Terrace coffee shop.

The world premiere of MGM's fanciful *Meet Me in Las Vegas* was staged February 21, 1956, at the El Portal theater on Fremont Street.

The performance allegedly happening inside the Copa Room cuts to ridiculously large soundstages back at MGM studios, where Hermes Pan choreographs an elaborate ballet. Slightly more plausible are vocal numbers from showroom regulars Frankie Laine and Lena Horne, and—best of all—a dance production of "Frankie and Johnny" to the recorded vocals of Sammy Davis Jr.: "Frankie and Johnny were lovers. Man, how those two cats could love. ..."

The obligatory montage of hotel marquees includes the Joe E. Lewis and Lili St. Cyr double-bill at the El Rancho, and Louis Prima and Keely Smith billed almost equally to Sahara headliner Donald O'Connor. *Meet Me* also features a silent "double-take" cameo from Frank Sinatra as a slot player and a one-line cameo from Peter Lorre at a blackjack table. Lyricist Sammy Cahn would do better in *Ocean's Eleven* than he did with the title song here: "By car or plane, by bus or train, meet me in Las Vegas. It's in Nevada. Nevada, USA."

## One From the Heart (1982)

This is a movie that inspires love or hate reactions, repeated viewings for some and complete indifference for others. Bad publicity surrounding director Francis Ford Coppola's waste and rampant ego—"Why shoot on Fremont Street? We can build our own!"—helped torpedo a movie that was uneven, but certainly not terrible. Technically, *One From the Heart* doesn't belong on a "filmed-in-Vegas" list, since Coppola squandered millions to re-create Fremont Street and everything else in the movie—even McCarran airport—on the soundstages of Hollywood's Lion's Gate Studios, which he renamed

Zoetrope in an effort to rekindle the studio system. Unfortunately, the film was ahead of its time when it came to spending its money on visuals, not on the script. While that doesn't seem to bother audiences of the MTV generation, hardly anyone back then saw the movie, and Coppola lost his studio.

The stylized formula might even have made *One From the Heart* a hit today: pretty pictures, empty emotions. At least in this movie the look seems to serve a purpose. Coppola blurs the line between fantasy and reality by confronting cinema's underlying dream state. As he would do years later in *Bram Stoker's Dracula,* Coppola celebrates society's long fascination with movie magic by using low-tech special effects (scrim dissolves, painted skies) and by deliberately creating that state of non-reality a modern viewer gets from watching old movies filmed on a back lot.

It's all to enliven the simple story of a bickering, unappealing couple (Teri Garr and a miscast Frederic Forrest), who break up to spend a magical night in the arms of fantasy lovers: the late Raul Julia as a charming waiter for her, Nastassia Kinski as a circus girl for him. The bad dialogue and cinematic shorthand that slight the relationship don't seem so bad in today's sub-literate movie climate. Garr is charming, and Forrest wins viewers over after he's loved and lost at the end. But the real strengths are Tom Waits' boozy, beguiling Greek-chorus soundtrack and the hyper-stylized vision of Vegas—all pastel skylines, hot neon, and twinkling lightbulbs. Perhaps someday Las Vegas will have a real building that lives up to Dean Tavoularis' sets.

Forrest's character works at a junkyard called Reality Wrecking (get it?), a surrealistic take on the Young Electric Sign Company's graveyard for fallen casino signs. (The real neon graveyard is seen in *Mars Attacks!).* That, and the detailed miniatures of grand old casino signs built for the opening credits—including signs for the Sands, Dunes, and Thunderbird—almost make up for a dancing-in-the-streets sequence that looks like it came from *Roller Boogie* or that other early '80s musical flop, *Xanadu.*

## The Stand (1994)

One of Stephen King's best-loved books was adapted into a well-meaning but ultimately disappointing TV movie, its epic scope compromised by some cheap special effects and a campy villain (the miscast Jamey Sheridan). When a lab accident unleashes a deadly flu that decimates most of the world's population, the remaining good guys head to heavenly Boulder, Colorado, while the bad guys meet up in ... Terre Haute, Indiana? Sorry, just kidding. (King used to live in Boulder and was said to have a place in Vegas; he was sometimes spotted at movie theaters and at other off-Strip haunts.)

Fremont Street hosts the climactic showdown between good and evil. The MGM Grand had the honors in the book, but the denser Fremont Street was a more controllable location for a TV production. Glitter Gulch read just as well as the Strip on film, despite the cheap fountain prop in front of the Union Plaza, which hosted the near crucifixion of two good guys. (In the book, the two heroes were handcuffed and almost pulled into pieces by two flatbed trucks.)

The movie's budget, which seemed to diminish progressively from its impressive beginning, got a little free help from Mother Nature when troublesome, but suitably eerie, high winds blew through the Fremont Street set in June 1993. The Woolworth's on Fremont Street, which closed in mid-1997, doubled for Anytown, America, during the flu/apocalypse scenes. King and director Mick Garris took a break or two in the convenient Fremont Street topless club, Girls of Glitter Gulch. King later made rural Nevada the setting of his 1997 novel *Desperation.*

## *Swingers* (1996)

The retro swing movement broke wide open in the wake of this movie, which unfolds during the days of nouveau swing as a semi-underground scene in Los Angeles. Jon Favreau stars in his own screenplay as a transplanted wanna-be comedian sinking into a swamp of depression after the breakup of a relationship. His buddies' attempts to drag him out make up the minimal plot in the dialogue-intensive comedy. The male-bonding rituals ring as true as the jaundiced eye on L.A. and its singles life. So does a Las Vegas sequence that's very telling (though perhaps unintentionally) of the way Angelinos see their desert playground.

When hipster Trent (Vince Vaughn) decides that a road trip would cheer up the depressed Mike (Favreau), the race is on with Austin Powers for the best use of the line "Vegas, baby, Vegas!"

The Vegas trip comes early in the movie, contrasting the guys' Rat Pack self-image to their full-of-shit, in-their-20s reality. Wearing their best retro suits, they valet park at the Stardust and step into a hotel that inexplicably (except for shared ownership) becomes the interior of the Fremont Hotel downtown.

"I thought Caesars was the dope spot," Mike notes, wondering why his buddy would take him to the geriatric sleepiness of downtown instead of to the Strip (not a lot of product placement for the host property here).

"You don't want all that pirates-of-the-Caribbean horseshit," Trent says dismissively of the modern Vegas. "Guys like you and me gotta kick it here—old school."

A hilarious sequence develops as the duo's plan to be comped like high rollers ("They'll fall all over themselves for a couple of high-class guys like us") disintegrates at a $100 blackjack table. More clichéd is the duo's picking up a cocktail waitress and her friend, and being invited back to—of all things—an Airstream trailer. C'mon. Gorgeous cocktail waitresses can at least afford white stucco apartments—and probably shoot down 20 or more underfinanced L.A. dudes every night.

## *Things Are Tough All Over* (1982)

Only the arguable cult status of (and the author's admitted soft spot for) Cheech and Chong merits mention of this very minor comedy with a very minor stop in Las Vegas. Running from themselves (playing double roles as Arabs), the boys hitch a ride in a convertible driven by Rip Taylor, who keeps Tommy Chong in stitches with such gassers as, "I tried smokin' hash but I couldn't light the corned beef." After all hell breaks loose at a fancy restaurant supposedly inside the Dunes (it probably wasn't), the boys run outside and miraculously emerge on Fremont Street. They duck for cover inside the Flick, a real porn theater of the era. How convenient! It's "Ladies Free," and they happen to be in drag (don't ask).

## Vegas (1978)

Vegas on TV is a subject worthy of its own chapter. But the 90-minute pilot for the *Vegas* (or *VEGA$,* if you prefer) TV show, which ran on ABC from 1978 through 1981 and still turns up on cable, can sneak in as a "movie" here because it was released on video. As written by Michael Mann, who would later revisit the city for the *Crime Story* series, the pilot establishes the formula for the light-hearted private-eye vehicle from producer Aaron Spelling, master of trash TV.

Dan Tanna (Robert Urich) is a studly detective who lives in a costume warehouse owned by his employers at the nearby Maxim Hotel. That the real Maxim had only the tiniest of showrooms—for years playing host to *Playboy's Girls of Rock & Roll*—may explain why the warehouse was as big as, well, a Hollywood soundstage and able to house Tanna's convertible, along with his hep bachelor-pad furnishings. It may also explain why the setting later moved to the slightly more plausible and just refurbished Desert Inn.

Tanna spends a lot of time zipping around town in his convertible, giving the viewer plenty of chances to check out the Barbary Coast while it was still being built and to see who was playing on the Strip (Newhart at the Riviera, Shecky with Florence Henderson at the MGM, Tom Jones at Caesars). Tanna knows everyone in town. He's able to track down a young hooker on behalf of her worried parents by simply dropping off a pizza for a source.

The girl's not happy when Tanna interrupts her wholesome cheerleader number: "I'm a star, baby. The johns love it!" But no sooner does he squire her back to his place (his intentions are noble) than he gets bonked on the head and the girl turns up dead in the desert next to the charred remains of his car. "I didn't like the color anyway," he quips.

Greg Morris, who played a tolerant police lieutenant prone to slipping Tanna confidential information, continued to live in Las Vegas after the show's cancellation until his death in 1997. Also a co-star of the *Mission: Impossible* TV series, Morris lived long enough to walk out of the *M: I* movie in disgust, but he never had to face a big-screen *Vegas* remake.

Trivia

Tanna's now personal mission to find the killer establishes most of the quirks that would become staples of the show. There's the search for a competent secretary, instead of those moonlighting showgirls. There are eccentric sidekicks, such as Harlon Twoleaf (Will Sampson), owner of a "riding ranch"—as in horses—for tourists. And don't forget the *Love Boat*-style celebrity guest bits: Red Buttons as a slot cheat or Scatman Crothers as the "loan officer" Tanna taps to buy a '57 T-Bird. ("Man, you're breakin' my roll!" the Scatman cries when Tanna interrupts his dice game at Caesars.) Best of all, Tanna goes about his work to the gr-ooo-vi-est soundtrack of '70s wacka-wacka cop funk since, well, *Starsky & Hutch.*

## *Vegas Vacation* (1996)

Just how much Vegas has become a warped alternative to Disneyland is shown, for better or worse, in a lowbrow farce that (tellingly) no longer carries the National Lampoon imprint. The Clark Griswald clan that once invaded Wallyworld runs through all the now standard highlights of a middle-class tourist visit. There's mayhem at Hoover Dam, a trip to see Siegfried and Roy, and—in the biggest stretch—Wayne Newton wooing the still sexy Beverly D'Angelo away from hapless husband Chevy Chase. Future generations may find the location footage as amazing as that of, say, *Meet Me in Las Vegas,* but that means only that no one has to watch it again for 20 years.

# As Seen on TV

At first, television and Vegas were good for each other. Why did it go so terribly wrong?

In the early '50s, nightclub performers found a new medium for exposure in TV variety shows. In return, the young medium helped promote the growing Vegas mystique. Even Sinatra gave the boob tube two stabs at an ongoing variety series, in 1950 and 1957.

In time, however, the tube took its toll on supper clubs all over the country. "Television put them out of business," says Buddy Hackett, who recalls a club in Brooklyn having to change its dark night from Monday to Tuesday because of Milton Berle's TV show.

Fear not. The showrooms had their revenge.

To this day, it's hard to say what possesses sit-com stars and game-show hosts to risk making fools of themselves in Vegas. Not everyone, of course. Certainly not the talk-show hosts who occasionally tape on the Strip, or the long lineage of comedians—from Carson to Seinfeld—who had a solid stand-up act regardless of what they did on TV. It's far more fun to remember those stars who were bound to pursue the nightclub variety formula.

Even here, it's easy to give amnesty to those whose careers on the live stage ran parallel to their TV fame. Yes, there *was* a Jim Nabors—who played the Sahara with Kay Starr in '61—before there was a Gomer Pyle, even if nobody cared until he started the whole "Shazam" bit two years later. And Don Adams was an insult comic before *Get Smart,* but conceded the obvious and promoted his 1968 and 1969 shows at the Sands with publicity photos that showed him juggling sticks of dynamite and various weapons.

But of more lurid fascination are those who clearly saw a nightclub act as an easy way to cash in on their TV fame. Barbara Eden already had the most famous belly button on television when the *I Dream of Jeannie* star became George Burns' opening act at the Frontier in August 1969. But satisfyingly enough, the public didn't buy it. No matter how many Bob Mackie gowns she wore, Eden was no Juliet Prowse. Following is a "dirty dozen" of other TV-land faces gone Vegas, with the emphasis on those who tried to spin a showroom act from their TV fame.

**1. Irene "Granny" Ryan**—Earthy comedian Irene Ryan had appeared in Vegas as far back as 1951, sharing the Thunderbird stage with Tennessee Ernie Ford. But by 1965, "Hillbilly" fever had swept the nation, and the 90-pound comedian went unrecognized without her granny costume from *The Beverly Hillbillies.* TV seasons were longer back then, so Ryan had to commute when she played the

Sahara in April 1965.

"Since my hillbilly wardrobe and granny make-up are part of my [show] opening, I wear them on the plane trip to Las Vegas," she stated in a hotel publicity release. "My second show closes about two a.m.," she added. "I catch a morning plane for Los Angeles and sleep all the way back." Co-billed with Andy Russell, Ryan was able to shed the granny garb long enough to clown to "Along Came Joe" and pay tribute to entertainers such as Fanny Brice, Eddie Cantor, and Al Jolson.

Lorne Greene, star of the TV series *Bonanza,* displayed an unusual means of thanking conductor Joe Guercio for his part in a 1971 Vegas gig.

**2. Lorne Greene**— Who else to play the Hotel Bonanza (which once occupied the homestead of Bally's)? Though the six-foot-three Ponderosa boss did have an actual No. 1 hit—"Ringo" in 1964—it wasn't enough to secure a return engagement after his less-than-trailblazing debut in July 1971.

**3. Monty Hall**—The "Let's Make a Deal" man combined a nightclub act with his hosting chores at the Sahara in May 1971. After proving he was up to the high-kicking in a *Mame* production number, Hall devoted the last portion of his act to re-creating the game show and giving away what columnist Forrest Duke heralded as "expensive loot" onstage.

**4. Pat "Mr. Haney" Buttram**—Publicity releases did not mention *Green Acres* when the hyena-voiced Buttram played the Fremont in April 1971. Instead, they likened him to "the late Will Rogers." Sample joke: "They say there's only one man in a million who understands the international situation, and you know, I keep running into him every day." No matter how much people enjoyed Buttram's homespun social commentary, he still obliged crowds by occasionally donning the Mr. Haney costume.

Known as a tippler, Buttram was once carried out of the annual "Night of Stars" bash for charity while complaining, "I've been overserved." Perhaps for that reason, the Fremont upped the wholesome ante with an "Up With People"-styled opening act called "The Establishment." The 10-member troupe, billed as "clean-cut young men and women," tried to live up to their name with a "presentation as all-American as apple pie," according to their publicist.

**5. George "Goober" Lindsey**—Proving the steady appetite for cornpone on the Strip, Lindsey began peddling his homespun *Hee Haw* and *Andy Griffith Show* humor in the late '70s, and opened for "M-M-Mel Tillis" (as he was actually billed on the marquee) at the Riviera in April 1981. Like Buttram before him, Lindsey admitted a fondness for whiskey in his charmingly titled autobiography, *Goober in a Nutshell*. British audiences, he noted, failed to respond properly to hayseed humor. But Vegas crowds were never impaired in their ability to enjoy Lindsey's cultural references to grits or turnip greens.

**6. Suzanne "Chrissy" Somers**—Caesars Palace invested a lot of paychecks, patience, and publicity in a gambit to fashion a new Ann-Margret out of the former *Three's Company* lust object—who was the mother of a grown son by the time she introduced him from the Circus Maximus stage in the summer of 1988. Somers was so sweet and sincere that audiences were actually on her side as she struggled through eight costume changes, covered Buster Poindexter's "Hot, Hot, Hot" in a Carmen Miranda get-up, and saluted pubescent fantasies with a "football" number set in a high-school locker room.

Despite it all, audiences of the late '80s were restless for more than another USO show/"Boogie Woogie Bugle Boy" routine, especially from a performer who was obviously trying too hard. The applause was like that given up by proud parents at a high-school talent show—except that Mom was onstage and the kids were in the audience.

**7. Mary Hart**—The strains of Rod Stewart's "Hot Legs" alternated with the *Entertainment Tonight* theme to welcome the curvaceous co-host to the Golden Nugget in April 1988. But Hart made jaws drop for another reason when she proceeded to cover Boston's "Smokin'" in a manner befitting an "SCTV" parody. Heavy press attention—disproportionate for the usually overlooked job of opening the David Brenner show—resulted in widespread snickering and put an abrupt end to Hart's Las Vegas career.

The ordeal gave her a new appreciation of the entertainers she covered on *E.T.* As she told the Associated Press: "There's a lot of rejection and hard knocks. I'm far more appreciative for having experienced it firsthand." But who could have guessed that her *E.T.* co-host John Tesh would become the more successful live attraction.

**8. Sherman Hemsley**—Who knew that a song-and-dance man lurked behind the feisty facade of George Jefferson? Not many people, judging from the ho-hum reception for Sherman Hemsley at the Sahara in June 1989. Hemsley—who also slummed in a 1986 dinner theater production of *Norman, Is That You?* at the Hacienda—kept his variety leanings in the closet, he explained, because it was better "to do one thing and get that right and get established, and then say, 'Now that you know me ... I'll come up with what I really want to present.'"

That something turned out to be an awkward mix of high-brow aspirations and low-brow shtick. Audiences were rightfully confused by a 16-piece band playing originals that incorporated French-Caribbean influences, followed by a rap spoof in which Hemsley gyrated in a sweatsuit and sported giant gold chains and an oversized boombox.

**9. Jerry "Luther" Van Dyke**—Despite his popularity as Luther Van Dam on *Coach,* Jerry Van Dyke played to near-empty showrooms at the Desert Inn in June 1990. This was even more surprising because Van Dyke had played Las Vegas lounges and showrooms since the early '60s. "It's hard to be a headliner without the [TV] exposure," he explained. But Luther's profile didn't help. Van Dyke's "mule-

From Mayberry to Sin City: Andy Griffith, Don Knotts, and Jerry Van Dyke brought folksy charm to Caesars Palace in the summer of 1968, following the eighth and final season of *The Andy Griffith Show.*

train" routine drew less applause than "Moore's Mess o' Mutts," his co-starring dog act.

**10. Florence "Mrs. Brady" Henderson**—Had *The Brady Bunch* not come calling, Florence Henderson might have become a Las Vegas regular. "I think my first [Las Vegas] date was at the Sands with Alan King," she reminisced during a week as George Burns' opening act in August 1993. "I think it was approximately nineteen sixty-eight, right before *The Brady Bunch.* When I think of playing Vegas, I think of doing two shows a night for a month."

Henderson is as self-deprecating as any sit-com star can get, but occasionally she has to assume a motherly Brady tone to remind everyone that she didn't do only Mrs. Brady. "What people have to remember is you are an actress and you do many other things," she said, including singing Michael Jackson songs ("The Way You Make Me Feel") onstage at Caesars.

**11. Phylicia "Claire Huxtable" Rashad**—*Review-Journal* columnist Michael Paskevich presented Rashad with a mock award for the "Best Impersonation of a Royal Family Member" for using her Vegas debut with TV co-star Bill Cosby as an occasion to march around in stately robes and ruffed collars. As if that wasn't autocratic enough, she chewed out her backing trio in front of their Las Vegas Hilton audience in March 1990: "I don't want any talking going on. You people get paid to sing and dance." But how else were they to relieve the boredom after being onstage for another version of "Wind Beneath My Wings" (which was to the '80s what "Feelings" was to the '70s)?

**12. Tony "Who's the Boss?" Danza**—Proving that it's never too late to be anachronistic, Tony (spelled backward, it's "Y-not," he told audiences) Danza was trying to reinvent himself as a latter-day song-and-dance man as recently as April 1998. Two years before that, he told an audience at the Mirage: "I can't believe this! I'm at the Mirage and I'm usually doing this in my garage! Welcome to my experiment in terror."

"This" turned out to be a little bit of everything in the gamely, Suzanne Somers-ish attempt to live up to advance billing of "an evening of singing, dancing, and storytelling in the tradition of the greatest variety shows." As Danza commented— attempting to explain such indulgences as a 15-minute *Pal Joey* medley—"This is every Italian's dream."

# VIVE LES GIRLS

The great sage known as Redd Foxx once said, "The way I see it, Las Vegas is based on gambling, drinking, and women. That's the big three." And who could argue with an expert? But in all honesty, it's the third ingredient that separates Vegas from the Indian reservations, Missouri riverboats, and California card clubs that try to break the Strip's vice grip on the first two. The female anatomy has been a Cadillac feature of Vegas from the earliest days, a running, ubiquitous design scheme embracing everything from the anonymous cocktail waitress to the highest-paid showroom star.

Burlesque revues were part of the entertainment menu from the Strip's beginnings, though at first the gals wore pasties or dropped their tops at the end of a song, just as the spotlight blacked out. Things never would be the same after producer Harold Minsky—a name synonymous with "the quintessence of female pulchritude"—bared the first breast in a showroom. *Minsky's Follies* opened at the Dunes on January 10, 1957. *Las Vegas Sun* columnist Ralph Pearl made a few uneasy jokes about the girls in "the Naked Chest Revue" catching colds, but later conceded that the "galaxy of exotic and almost exotic gals (the latter wear clothes) make up the current and best Minsky revue ever to play Vegas."

The next year ensured there would be no turning back, after the *Lido de Paris* opened with the Stardust Hotel on July 2, 1958. The $10 million hotel was four years in construction before it came under the control of Desert Inn operator Moe Dalitz, whose "connections" back East had the money to get it finished. Frank Sennes, the Desert Inn's entertainment director, employed Donn Arden's chorus girls at both the D.I. and his Moulin Rouge nightclub in Hollywood, and he knew Arden had choreographed the *Lido* in Paris since 1946. Sennes went to Paris to check out the cabaret revue. Once he saw the *Lido,* he knew he'd found that something new for Vegas he'd been seeking.

The Stardust showroom was outfitted with hydraulic stage lifts, an 11-foot-by-30-foot swimming pool, and an ice rink that could be brought to stage level in 15 seconds. But none of the technical effects was as special as the human cast of imported showgirls. They lined the revolving stage like "a living curtain," as Pearl described the opening, before 30 more "appeared from the ceiling in elevators, and they dove into the onstage swimming pool."

Then came the kicker, as noted by the *Review-Journal's* Les Devor: "From the ceiling descend platforms, each with a bare-bosomed beauty, standing cool as you please, and before the surprise has caused nearsighted gentlemen to repair their thoughtlessness

The Dunes' long-running *Vive Les Girls* revue brought the skimpy costumes of the big Parisian production shows into a more intimate venue.

by putting on glasses, the girls are whisked upward into the rafters. ... Being bashful by disposition tends to inhibit anything but professional analysis of the plentious expanse of anatomies presented."

What follows is a rundown of the anatomies that still command attention today—the most memorable babes and bodies in Vegas history.

# Lili thrived on art

One door closes; another opens. One life passes; another is born. What would have become of the burlesque stripper had it not been for Vegas? Burlesque was on its last legs in the '50s. But fortunately for exotic dancers—and the men who like to see them—Vegas was springing to life and gave strippers its full attention.

"All through the fifties, burlesque was trying to hang on," says Dixie Evans, a retired entertainer who runs Exotic World, the mind-blowing strippers museum located in the desert near Helendale, California, off old Route 66 between Barstow and Victorville. "There may have been two or three theaters here and there, but the era was dying. All through the fifties, it was about cutting the payroll, cutting the payroll. First the chorus line, then the musicians."

Las Vegas, on the other hand, was starting to bustle. "Sure they all went to Vegas. Why not?" Evans says of the burlesque stars. Though she did not work in Vegas as much as her contemporaries, she did perform at the Embassy Club the same week that Sinatra debuted at the Sands in October 1953. "It's only natural that Vegas was scrambling for entertainment, and what are they gonna take? Some long-haired violinists or opera? No, hell no. They're catering to the gambling crowd and the fast crowd and the fast-livers, so they would want some exciting type of acts that would appeal to the people that spend money. [Vegas] was not a cultural center. It was only natural for them to hire these people."

Among the first to test the waters was the queen of all strippers, Lili St. Cyr. Lili's bath-and-towel act came to the attention of District Attorney Roger Foley the first time she played the El Rancho Vegas, in September 1951. Foley charged the dancer with a lewdness misdemeanor after watching her drop her towel while he was trying to have dinner. "There were several parties with young children in there at the time," he told the *Review-Journal*.

Lili had to move on to her next town before the matter was resolved. But Hollywood's protectors of decency proved to be equally close-minded: Her "bubble bath" routine caused Ciro's to be raided by sheriff's deputies the very next month. "I do not wish to thrive on scandal, but on art," Lili was quoted as saying.

All was forgiven when Lili returned to the El Rancho a year later, in October 1952. She showed up in justice court to plead guilty, paid a $250 fine, and was free to pursue an act described to the district attorney as—cough! cough!—a "fashion show," in which she modeled expensive clothing for dress designers. The district attorney explained to the *Review-Journal* that he was told, "The only difference between Lili's act and one seen on Fifth Avenue is that Lili changes her clothes onstage in front of the 'customers.'"

By then, D.A. Foley may have felt like the Dutch boy with his finger in the dike. Las Vegas had become something of a "fashion" capitol in the year since Lili's first engagement. The Desert Inn hosted the famous *Minsky's Follies.* The Silver Slipper's new "opera house" showcased the talents of Kalantan, billed as "the tantalizing, exotic bombshell of Afro-Cuban dancers." Off the Strip, the Embassy Club featured the likes of Antonee ("The Upside-Down Girl"), Cheyenne, Dawn Glory, and Tempest Storm, who was popular enough to merit three engagements that year.

Lili went on to become a fixture at the El Rancho. She performed there throughout the '50s, often sharing the stage with Joe E. Lewis. She was billed as "the most fabulous girl in the world" for routines such as sitting high on a throne and eating grapes in a most enticing manner to the tune of "Stranger in Paradise," or swinging out over the front row as a "Bird in a Gilded Cage," dropping lingerie on the patrons below.

But her signature piece was the bubble bath. The stage went blue as Lili took a bath in a transparent glass tub, emerged in a froth of strategically placed bubbles, then showered off in front of the customers. The act kept getting more elaborate. By 1956, as reviewer Bill Willard noted, a fireplace had been added, "before which [she would] posture sexily while using a large towel. The set turns as she dons a filmy blue negligee and lo, a very ornate bed revolves into view. Miss St. Cyr then gives the bed an exploratory spanking. She retires. Alone. Hmm."

Lili St. Cyr wasn't the only performer to work with Joe E. Lewis at the El Rancho Vegas. In May 1957, he was co-billed with "That Hungary Doll," Zsa Zsa Gabor.

Trivia

Lili—or someone close to her—had an eye for publicity. "The Anatomic Bomb" scheduled her wedding to Ted Jordan for October 1954, when the national media would be in town for the nuclear explosions at the Nevada Test Site. Two years later, another news event provided material for the show: Inspired by the royal wedding in which Grace Kelly became Princess Grace, Lili waited for her own prince to come, stripping down to a rhinestone crown against a backdrop that depicted the twinkling lights of Monaco.

Lili wasn't alone in straining the eyes of mid-'50s Vegas. There was Tere Sheehan, "The Girl in the Champagne Glass," who was part of Hank Henry's burlesque show at the Last Frontier. And Sally Rand, synonymous with the "fan dance," spelled Lili at the Silver Slipper in 1954. The former cigarette girl from Kansas City modeled her act on Isadora Duncan's scarves-and-veils routine. It was Cecil B. DeMille who supposedly

Lili St. Cyr did more to popularize the bathtub than Mr. Bubble.

changed the name of Sally's dance from "White Birds in the Moonlight" to something just a little less cryptic.

But in early 1957, the rules changed. Despite their ability to get journalists, judges, and audiences hot and bothered, none of the strippers had ever revealed anything beyond pasties and a G-string until Harold Minsky unveiled the city's first topless show at the struggling Dunes Hotel on January 10, 1957. *Minsky Goes to Paris* dropped the hint when it promised "24 Girls—24 Feathers (more or less)." The *Review-Journal's* Les Devor complained, "The artistic exposure of so many girls all at one time is hard on the neck muscles as you attempt to capture every little movement." Minsky boasted that it was the "sexiest and sauciest, most risqué show to hit this town." But he quickly added, "There is nothing 'blue' in the show. ... If pulchritude is displayed in a 'nice' way, I know of no restrictions on this art."

Not everyone was impressed. Jerry Lewis sat through headliner Brandy Martin's act obliviously eating a ham on rye, until she slinked up to him and cooed, "Don't you care what anybody says, Mr. Lewis. You just go ahead and eat."

"Pretty girls are a dime a dozen," Minsky liked to say. "Pretty girls who have talent are perhaps the scarcest commodity you can imagine." That's why, when the show

L as Vegas was so topless by the mod '60s that it even had topless lounge bands, such as the Pussycat Revue featuring Jodie Lamb (Jodie and the Pussycats? Well, they did have the ears) at the Aladdin's Bagdad Theatre in 1966. For the more musically eclectic, Ron Stanton's Topless Brazilia Jazz replaced the Pussycat Revue in September 1967, rotating with Richard Pryor.

Trivia

returned that September as simply *Minsky's Follies*, it brought bankable names like Tempest Storm as headliners. The 40-23-34 Georgia peach with flaming red hair was as popular as she had been five years earlier and would periodically headline at the Dunes for more than three years.

The topless trend set off a minor war along the Strip. Sands impresario Jack Entratter championed the more wholesome look of his Copa Girls. He warned that the topless tarts could "destroy six years of work, expensive campaigns, and sincere efforts to make Las Vegas the top entertainment resort in the world."

Instead, it became Sin City. Not that burlesque didn't eventually die in Vegas as it had elsewhere. First it took a back seat to other French revues, such as *Les Folies Bergere*, then to small lounge shows like the Tropicana's *Girl-O-Rama* or the Dunes' *Vive Les Girls*, which packed the costumes and production values of the bigger shows into an up-close and personal setting. All of them promised their tits with "class," which seemed to appease civic officials. Over time, however, the talent Minsky so valued became less important. The tease gradually left the Strip and moved to nearby "gentlemen's clubs" when the city emerged as a major convention market.

But the great names of burlesque hung on throughout the '60s. Sally Rand was still at it—making no pretense about her platinum blonde wig—in 1963, fan-dancing in Pat Moreno's *Artists and Models Revue* at the Mint Hotel. "I'll retire when they stop coming to see me," she said. (Rand died in 1979.) Tempest Storm was still on the Strip as part of *Artists and Models* at the Aladdin in July 1967. Minsky kept his shows in various venues into the '70s, occasionally trying to shed the dated burlesque image with names such as *Thoroughly Modern Minsky*. And who was still performing her onstage bubble bath at the Aladdin in *Minsky's Burlesque '70?* That's right. Our girl Lili.

# B-girls traveled light

Tura Satana and Regina Carrol had more in common than Amazonian physiques and B-movie résumés. Any surprise that both launched their careers in Las Vegas is quickly erased by a question: If you're going to be an underage dancer, where would be a more logical and lucrative place to dance?

Satana's film credits are brief but immortal. One title alone puts her into the cult

Tura Satana was able to separate her dragon lady image (left) in B-movies, such as *The Astro-Zombies,* from her long-running career as an exotic dancer in Las Vegas burlesque revues.

hall of fame. In Russ Meyer's *Faster Pussycat! Kill! Kill!* she defined the term "Dyke From Hell" as Varla, the jump-suited, karate-chopping, Amazon go-go-girl thrill-killer on the rampage. Its message? "Women aren't wimps," Satana said years later of the 1965 classic. "We were basically your avant-garde for women's rights. It showed that women weren't tied to being in the kitchen, scrubbing floors, and doing laundry."

Tura also starred for low-budget director Ted V. Mikels in *The Astro-Zombies,* released in 1968, and *The Doll Squad* in 1973. When Mikels saw her dancing in Las Vegas, he "decided I was the perfect person to try to rule the world," Satana recalled with a laugh. He cast her as the dragon lady making life tough for CIA agent Wendell Corey. In *The Doll Squad*, she said, "I got to use both my talents"—dancing and akido.

Satana (her real name, she says) was working as a security guard at the Reno Hilton in 1995 when she detailed some of her past at a Las Vegas film tribute to Mikels (a Las Vegan since 1985). She grew up in Chicago and learned martial arts from her father before becoming an exotic dancer at age 15. "There were not a lot of women into the martial arts back then at all," she said. "[But] my father and my brother were into akido; it was nothing new to me."

Tura was billed as "Miss Japan Beautiful" in burlesque revues at the Silver Slipper; Mikels said he first saw her there in 1959. Her act made a big impression, though it would be years before an agent formally introduced her to him for *Astro-Zombies*. Ten years later she was still a featured headliner, using her more familiar name, in *Minsky's Burlesque '69* at the Aladdin. "I worked at the Silver Slipper several times and stayed for months and months at a time," she recalls. "It was like being a permanent resident there. It was a seven-day-a-week job, but you'd get a chance after your show to go catch somebody else's."

Her routine involved kimonos and outsized headpieces. "The reason they used to like me in Las Vegas was you could bring your kids to my show and it wouldn't hurt," she recalls. "I twirled tassels and talked to my audience. ... We bantered back and forth, only I was taking my clothes off at the time." By the '70s, however, "Las Vegas was getting a little too wild and wooly for me." When exotic dancers went totally nude, "that ruined it," Satana says. "There's no mystery about total nudity."

Regina Carrol's Las Vegas connections are a little more mysterious. Cult movie fans know her as the big-bosomed star of the films of Al Adamson, her husband and the director of such low-budget opuses as *Satan's Sadists* and *The Female Bunch*. David Konow's Adamson biography, *Schlock-O-Rama*, quotes the director as saying that Regina lost her mother to cancer at age 15—that would have been about 1958—and she "had to dance in Las Vegas to make a living."

Carrol turns up as a dancer in *Viva Las Vegas*, but her only other film tie to the city is in the immortal *Dracula vs. Frankenstein*. Cult movie buffs agree that it's one of the worst movies ever made. The only room for argument is whether it's "fun bad" in the vein of *Plan 9 From Outer Space*, or merely painful to watch.

The plot of *Dracula vs. Frankenstein* would take pages to describe but begins, more or less, with a girl being decapitated on a beach. The film cuts to a typical rolling shot of the Strip, only this one is in daylight. (Could the movie not even afford the film stock to capture nighttime visuals?) The Frontier's marquee displays the name of Frank Sennes (who was a real showroom producer), presenting "Judith Fontain & the Show-Offs." It's the establishing shot for a production number in which Carrol, falling out of a black dress, lip-synchs with two chorus boys to the song "I Travel Light." (Boys: "Why

Regina Carrol's attempts to cultivate a Las Vegas nightclub career were captured in *Dracula vs. Frankenstein,* as well as in this "outtake" publicity still for the 1971 anti-classic.

do you carry your telephone?" She: "When I leave here, I might get a call.") An audience shot shows exactly one table occupied.

The movie leaves Vegas and moves on to occupy its place in infamy once policeman Jim Davis (later of the *Dallas* TV series) arrives to inform the singer that her sister— presumably the girl who lost her head on the beach—is missing.

There's an odd postscript to this. Most of Adamson's epics were filmed a little at a time as he raised money over the course of a year or two. However, since most references cite *Dracula vs. Frankenstein* as a 1971 release, the movie may well have been unleashed on the world by April 30 of that year.

That's when *Panorama of Las Vegas,* a weekly newspaper that existed mainly to publish strip-joint ads and topless photos the dailies wouldn't touch, announced it had acquired a new syndicated column: "The Stage of Fashion" by none other than Regina Carrol. "This glamorous star," it was promised, would provide "a new look and new views on some of the important questions and answers in today's exciting fashion world."

October, however, found the columnist writing from Hollywood in a melancholy mood brought on by "the spirit of winter underneath every autumn leaf," if not by the impending release of *Blood of Ghastly Horror:* "My thoughts are to a deeper me ... the me that at age twelve swore to be a famous lady, a mixture of Ginger Rogers and Eleanor Roosevelt." Fame, of sorts, finally came after "losing my mother to cancer, after cutting off all my hair à la Mia Farrow, after sitting alone in a room smoking old cigarette butts and eating split pea soup for the ninth day. ...

"Yes, we all want to go to Hollywood, and our only thought is, 'Make me a star!' There are no more stars like Hepburn and Cagney and Tracy. A real star is when you are sixty and still in the business, still mixing fantasy with reality, and loving every minute of it." Carrol never saw that day. She died of cancer in 1992.

# Bad girl, funny girl

Most Las Vegas performers would be quick to exploit any ties they had to movie fame. But you can understand why Dyanne Thorne was happy if people didn't draw the connection between her work in Las Vegas burlesque revues and her infamous screen role as *Ilsa, She Wolf of the S.S.*

This poster art for one of the *Ilsa* sequels depicts Dyanne Thorne as the bloodthirsty villain cult movie fans remember.

While the 1974 movie is available on video today and no longer seems so taboo in these jaded times, *Ilsa* and its two sequels acquired a ghoulish and whispered reputation in the '70s. Whenever it played in my hometown (which seemed to be often), the newspaper ad included the teaser/disclaimer, "Warning: Some members of the public may find certain scenes in this film offensive and shocking."

Thorne's title character is a concentration camp commandant who tortures or castrates her prisoners after using them as her love toys. The recognition of sets used in *Hogan's Heroes* adds a twisted surrealism to a movie that even today is too sadistic and unsettling to be the usual drive-in hootfest. (One can only imagine what the regular porno theater wankers thought whenever this X-rated feature sneaked into the rotation.)

Thorne led a Jekyll and Hyde

Dyanne Thorne (top right) was far more benign as the "talking woman" in burlesque revues like *Sex Over 40* than as the whip-cracking she-wolf Ilsa, her claim to movie infamy. The man pictured standing next to Thorne is her husband Howard Maurer. Fans of the *Vegas* TV series might also recognize Nancy Austin and Pepper Davis (seated right), who played character roles in the Robert Urich vehicle.

existence in the '70s. Before, during, and after the *Ilsa* movies, she worked on the Strip prolonging the last gasps of burlesque—which was like working in Disney movies by comparison. Burlesque producer Harold Minsky brought her to Las Vegas in 1969 to be part of his *Minsky's Burlesque* at the Aladdin Hotel after using the native New Yorker in *Minsky on Broadway.*

Though burlesque was a dying genre, it kept Thorne busy. "I don't think I was ever out of work in this town," she says. The busty performer sometimes was allowed to sing but more often was the female "straight man"—or the "talking woman" in burlesque parlance—who set up the featured male comedian's punch lines. By the time her movie *Point of Terror* played the Las Vegas Drive-In in September 1971, Thorne had wrapped a 27-week run in the Minsky show.

Thorne had completed the three *Ilsa* movies by the time she was lured back to Vegas for a dinner theater production of *Norman, Is That You?* at the Union Plaza in

1976. By then she was married to Howard Maurer, a lounge singer who also had Vegas ties: In 1966 he was one of the Brothers Cain, who worked the Sands when Count Basie was the lounge headliner. Maurer appeared in the two *Ilsa* sequels, and today he and Thorne stage specialty weddings in Vegas.

Over the years, Thorne worked in *Old-Tyme Burlesque* at the Maxim, *Burlesque a Poppin'* at the Fremont, and *Sex Over 40* at the Continental Hotel.

Though she's made *Ilsa*-related appearances at horror and cult movie conventions, Thorne tries to remind people that it's "one of many films" she has done as an actress. Still, she concedes, "It's the one that seems to have gotten the attention."

Michael Weldon's indispensable *Psychotronic Video Guide* notes that some *Ilsa* fans are "disappointed that she [Thorne] seems so normal and friendly," and few ever inquire enough to learn of her comedic background. "That's not usually their interest," she says. "People don't want to know the variety of it."

# Angelique kept on 'Trekking'

Faint brush strokes of fame colored the life of Angelique Pettyjohn, who inspired Trekkie wet dreams in *Star Trek* but spent many more unheralded years as a Vegas exotic. Had *Star Trek* and Elvis Presley not gone on to become their own religions, Pettyjohn may have remained as obscure as any other featured stripper or chorus girl who landed a bit part or two in Hollywood. But her weird fortune commands a place in cult movie—and *Cult Vegas*—history.

In 1962, the 19-year-old who was raised in Salt Lake City abandoned three years toward a college teaching degree, moving to Vegas to work as a belly dancer in *Cleopatra's Nymphs of the Nile* at the Flamingo. She would appear in a host of burlesque shows throughout the years, including *Ziegfeld's Follies* at the Thunderbird, *Vive Paris Vive* at the Aladdin, *Thoroughly Modern Minsky* at the Thunderbird in early 1968, and *Minsky's Burlesque '69* at the Aladdin during the "Summer of Love."

By then she had completed the two projects that would have the most lasting cult interest: the Elvis Presley movie *Clambake,* filmed in early 1967, and "The Gamesters of Triskelion" episode of *Star Trek,* which first aired January 5, 1968. Pettyjohn played Shahna, a "drill thrall" sent to keep an imprisoned Captain Kirk company, but later made to turn gladiator on him.

Those roles turned out to be the peak of a movie career that included a credit in the cult classic *Repo Man,* but was otherwise confined to a few exploitation films and some "adult" features during harder times. "I wanted to be Jane Fonda, and they wanted Jayne Mansfield," she noted in 1986. "My figure always got in the way."

In the way or not, her prominent 38-24-36 physique saw her through tougher times. When she wasn't peddling posters of herself in various states of drill-thrall undress at Trekkie conventions, Pettyjohn made a journeyman living by dancing topless or performing burlesque routines in Las Vegas.

"I had fifty thousand dollars saved a few years ago," she told Las Vegas newsman

Angelique Pettyjohn saw more tough times than good ones before her early death in 1992.

Ned Day during a dancing shift at the Cabaret Club in 1977. "But I was in love with a con man. He took it all and left me."

The "attention and praise" of performing made up for the parental abuse of a rough childhood, she noted in 1986 while working in the Marina Hotel's *Old Burlesque*. "Nudity didn't offend me, although the first time I walked onstage as a showgirl, I felt as if everyone was staring at my nipples."

Pettyjohn lost a prolonged battle with cancer on February 16, 1992. She died in a Las Vegas hospital at age 49, but lives on wherever *Star Trek* reruns are shown.

## Jayne couldn't help it

You know the ad slogan about being No. 2 and trying harder.

Jayne Mansfield could never be the real Marilyn Monroe, but she *could* be more of a self-promoter. Surely it was her entrepreneurial spirit more than any, uhmm, superficial traits that melted the hearts of male critics who covered the Vegas entertainment scene in the late '50s, leading them to give her kind notices even if they knew better.

The poor man's Marilyn was born Vera Jayne (which sounds a little like Norma Jean) Palmer on April 19, 1933. The low-budget 1956 rock 'n' roll comedy, *The Girl Can't Help It,* brought the pinup girl to movie life in an innocuous romp fueled by energetic performances from a host of '50s rockers, including the Treniers, Gene Vincent, and Fats Domino. The movie's release was well-timed, coming soon after Mansfield had Broadway talking about her eye-opening stroll across the stage wearing only a towel in *Will Success Spoil Rock Hunter?*

The movie adaptation in 1957 would turn out to be a big-budget exception to Mansfield's B-movie career. Like *The Girl Can't Help It,* from the same producer-director, Frank Tashlin, *Will Success Spoil Rock Hunter?* gently spoofed Jayne's own success even as it displayed her talents roundly in a sudsy bathtub. That same year, Jayne was starting to make her move on Vegas. In September 1957 she was "spotted" at the Riviera in skin-tight red pants (knee length) and a leopard-skin blouse as she strolled the lobby with the new guy in her life—muscleman Mickey Hargitay—to check out the Spike Jones show and negotiate for a nightclub act of her own.

Vegas had one thing in common with the rest of her quickly peaking career: She would never have it better than the first two times she played the Tropicana. She had just divorced Paul Mansfield, whom she had married as a Southern Methodist University teen, to marry the 6-foot-3-inch Hargitay, a former Mr. Universe who could provide the male yang to her pulchritudinal yin.

Acute packaging helped Jayne Mansfield make the most of her ample assets on the Las Vegas stage.

Perhaps recognizing the limited talents—mostly squeaks and squeals—of his curvaceous commodity, Tropicana producer Monte Prosser surrounded Jayne with specialty acts for his *Tropicana Holiday* and launched the revue in February 1958 with a big benefit dinner show that raised $20,000 for the March of Dimes.

Jayne Mansfield knew her natural talents needed the help of tireless self-promotion. Here, she and Mickey Hargitay posed with a furry co-star for Las Vegas News Bureau photographers at the Tropicana pool.

The benefit money wouldn't have quite paid for the evening's showpiece, a gold mesh metallic gown that weighed more than 12 pounds and cost a full $25,000 week's salary for Jayne as it reflected light from hundreds of tiny gold discs. But that wasn't the whole show. Audiences were treated to the sight of Mickey tossing and twirling his wife around like a sack of flour, threatening to make some man on the back row very happy.

When Jayne and Mickey returned to the Tropicana in May 1959, she had delivered son Miklos only four months prior. Yet her figure had rebounded in time for her to make her entrance in a sheer nylon gown that outdid the gold mesh. Except for the petticoats below the knees, only a few discretely placed spangles came between her and full nudity. "I wanted to be completely covered," she explained to a newspaper reporter of the self-designed gown. "If I had tried to compete with the nudes [from the French topless revues] on their own grounds, it would have been bad taste. And besides, those girls are not as healthy as I. They have been through a war and all that hardship."

Jayne and Mickey had just purchased Hollywood Estates acreage to build their famous "Pink Palace," so they were working full steam to maintain her stardom. A local columnist marveled at how the couple would spend afternoons at the Tropicana's pool, "where Jayne graciously poses for pictures to please the guests who have their own cameras." After performing the *French Dressing* revue, Mickey and Jayne would hang out in the Showcase Lounge to catch Perez Prado and sign even more autographs.

But all the glad-handing in the world couldn't sustain the novelty. Jayne, as it turned out, had made it just under the cutoff for airhead pinup girls, before the mid-'60s awakened a desire for less wholesome, more exotic fantasies. "I don't care if skirts go up and down like an elevator. Who looks at my skirts?" went one clever line attributed to Jayne in 1963. But one last prestigious big-room run—this time at the Dunes—was the beginning of the end. *The House of Love,* drawing its name from the Pink Palace, opened at the Dunes during the last week of 1960. Mickey was still onboard as the object of the presumably tongue-in-cheek number, "I'm Physical and You're Cultural."

There were some clever publicity stunts after that, such as the time the Russkies called Jayne "a philistine with a huge bust who has no need of acting talent." Rather than asking, "And what's your point?" Jayne offered to do a Russian play in Moscow. Instead, she and Mickey ended up packing it off to Europe to star in sex comedies such as *Primitive Love* and sword-and-sandal spaghetti epics like *Loves of Hercules.* By 1963, *Promises, Promises* built its ad campaign around a tacked-on nude scene, often cited as the first by a known star. It reeked of desperation. The heart-shaped pool at the Pink Palace failed to provide a cement bond between Jayne and Mickey. They were divorced that year.

*Las Vegas Hillbillys* is an amazing piece of low-rent drive-in trash, but knowing it came near the end of Jayne's road in 1966 cuts into the fun of watching her coo, "I'm hip, Daddy. That makes it ... ooh, that's so kinky." The incongruous dream sequence/musical number looks like it was part of her club act.

In September 1966, Jayne returned to Las Vegas after a five-year absence to work the downtown Fremont, a few notches down from past glories on the Strip. Mickey obviously was out of the act, but she still dragged part of her family—her poodles—into one of her routines. The poodles were in the car with her when Jayne died on June 29, 1967, after her car collided with a truck on a narrow two-lane highway near New Orleans. A Vegas fixture of longer tenure, Engelbert Humperdinck, ended up with the Pink Palace.

# Mamie got around

Beyond their co-starring roles in *Las Vegas Hillbillys* (in which they never quite were seen in the same camera shot), Mamie Van Doren and Jayne Mansfield were often linked as torpedo blondes trying to fill whatever voluptuous space was not occupied by Marilyn. The only Las Vegas location footage in *Hillbillys* is of a jalopy driving down the Strip and through the valet porte-cochère of the Thunderbird. Oddly enough, Van Doren performed there in both 1965 and 1966—"taking a break in her present filming schedule," a press release noted of the latter engagement.

By then, Van Doren had a long history on the Strip. In fact, Las Vegas paved the way to the former Joan Olander's big show-business break. In early 1951, Mamie later explained, she did a six-month stint as an El Rancho Vegas chorus girl. That bankrolled a long dry spell in Hollywood, where she finally landed a low-paying job in a production of *Come Back Little Sheba.* "Luckily, the night I was gonna throw in the towel, a Universal movie scout strolled in and caught the show. He signed me to a seven-year contract," she recalled. "I swear I must have posed for a couple of million cheesecake stills before they'd stick me in a movie."

Not that cheesecake—or tight capri pants—would fail to be her calling card. By the time she appeared in the Riviera's *Latin Quarter Revue* in October 1957, Mamie had made a big impression in three B-movies: *Jet Fighter, Untamed Youth,* and *The Girl in Black Stockings.* She'd also scored a small part in an A-picture, the Clark Gable comedy *Teacher's Pet.* Her marriage to band leader Ray Anthony made the nightclubs a natural step. Reviews of her act cited a vocal similarity to Julie London in renditions of "The Laziest Gal in Town" and "That Old Feeling." In January 1962, she was second-billed to Dennis Day at the Riviera.

By the mid-'60s, however, Mamie's career had followed Mansfield's into also-ran territory. She devoted her full energy to her headlining role in the Thunderbird's *Ziegfeld Follies,* commissioning Hollywood special-effects man Bill Tuttle to create different masks for co-star Nick Navarro to don during her number "A Good Man's Hard to Find." The masks enabled her to dance with Frank Sinatra, Maurice Chevalier, Lyndon B. Johnson, Jimmy Durante, Ringo Starr, and Vince Edwards, the title character of TV's *Ben Casey.*

The highlight of the *Follies,* however, proved that no special-effects man could compete with Mother Nature. A press release noted, "An addition to her normal nightclub routine while at the Thunderbird will be a sensational 'strip' production. Mamie has never discarded any of her clothing in previous appearances at nightclubs."

Mamie made at least one more appearance on the Strip, as an opening act for Sammy Davis Jr. at the Sands in March 1973—undoubtedly one of the oddest couplings of all time. "If that's her best or her only," *Sun* columnist Joe Delaney wrote after opening night, "someone should pay the lady and send her home."

# Flamenco meets coochie-coo

Her real name was Maria Rosario Martinez Molina Cugat Mingall. Most people just called her "the Coochie-Coochie Girl."

It seemed that no talk or variety show in the '70s was complete without Charo, the Spanish bombshell, doing her ditzy, mangled-Spanglish routine for an array of snide, yet lecherous, hosts. And it all started in Vegas. Sort of.

It is written that Latin bandleader Xavier Cugat spotted the curvy young singer—who also happened to be an above-average flamenco guitarist—in a Spanish production of *Night of the Iguana* in 1964. Deciding that she could do more in this life than perform Tennessee Williams, Cugat brought her to Las Vegas, where she became the featured star of his Nero's Nook lounge revue in Caesars Palace.

The 66-year-old bandleader had seen his heyday in the 1940s and already had been through three wives, including Vegas headliner Abbe Lane. But he still had the good business sense and aesthetic judgment to marry another young ingénue—then said to be 21—in a suite at the just-opened Caesars Palace on August 7, 1966. The band had a new focal point, one that favored skin-tight dresses, fishnet hose, and five-inch heels.

Charo and Cugie played lounges such as Nero's and the Tropicana's Blue Room for three more years. As one press release for the Tropicana noted in May 1969, "Her name is Charo, and she jingles and shakes and yells and vibrates." It was comedian Buddy Hackett who promoted her beyond "featured singer" status. At Cugat's urging, Hackett agreed to use the singer as his Sahara opening act, but told her: "You don't play the guitar. ... You play very, very good, but we're gonna save that for two years from now. You play it at home, but you don't play it in the show."

As with all his opening acts, Hackett gave Charo 100 percent co-billing. "What's the difference to me?" he later explained. "This way, if the audience never heard of 'em, they see how big the type is [and] they say, 'Look how important that person is.' Meanwhile, I'm payin' them a buck and a half."

Actually, Hackett remembers paying Charo $800. But by the end of the week, he had raised that to $2,000. "At the end of [the engagement], I bought her a diamond on a chain that hung right between her cleavage," he recalls. He took her to Cleopatra's Barge, a lounge shaped like a boat that actually sits on water in Caesars Palace. "She's wearing this diamond. The barge is rocking, that thing's swaying, those big jugs stickin'

I could be totally a guitar player, like I did at Carnegie Hall. But if I play more than two songs in my Las Vegas show, people would throw catsup. Not tomatoes, because tomatoes are very expensive. They would throw catsup and mustard, because a nightclub is not made for too much classic music.

Charo
1984

out there. ... I said, 'Now there's something I want from you.'

"'What?' she asked.

"'I want to shave your head.'

"She let out a scream—them people thought someone fell off the barge. They stopped the music."

In 1977, Charo debuted a full-blown stage act, sharing the Sahara stage in co-bills with the likes of Jack Jones, Joey Bishop, and Rip Taylor—her peer in the art of understatement. Audience members were handed red maracas at the door to shake along to the rhythms of a flamenco dance troupe. The show also included such bonuses as a "Chinese waiter" hauled up to sing "When Irish Eyes Are Smiling" and a tuxedoed chimpanzee doing a routine as Charo's "guitar instructor."

Other important things happened for the Las Vegas-based singer in 1977. She became a naturalized citizen—"I'll make a hell of an American," she told reporters—and ended the May-December marriage to Cugat with a Nevada divorce. She told reporters that the 77-year-old bandleader would live with her parents in Los Angeles. "We'll probably get drunk together to celebrate," she said.

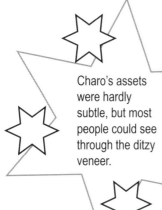

Charo's assets were hardly subtle, but most people could see through the ditzy veneer.

"I love him like my father." Within a year, she had married her manager, Kjell Rasten.

Perhaps Charo's act was so much fun because it was so transparent. Obviously a bright lady, she came up with most of the tongue-tied bimbo routine herself and could turn it on and off at will. "I don't think I am just one person," she said in 1984 while starring in the Las Vegas Hilton's *Bal du Moulin Rouge*. "I am very serious and responsible, and I am a hell of a good mother." Not that it was easy to convince people of that when she wanted to branch out: Producers have "only one image of me," she said in 1988.

After a Caesars Palace stint that same year with George Burns—when she covered Madonna's "La Isla Bonita" and Miami Sound Machine's "Conga"—Charo and her family would spend more of their days running a restaurant in Hawaii. "I don't need to work," she said. "At this point in my life, I have become selective."

# Strong legs to stand on

"Heaven is here, where Juliet lives," Romeo said of one Juliet. "She has a body that would make a bishop stamp his foot through a stained glass window," Elvis Presley purportedly said of another. That would be Juliet Prowse, the classiest dame ever to grace the Strip.

Born in Bombay, India, to British parents and raised in South Africa, Prowse brought a genteel elegance and a sense of theater to her floor shows. But what gave her the marquee value to lure audiences in the first place was her romantic link to two musical icons: Elvis and Sinatra. She met the latter after winning a small part in *Can-Can,* the Sinatra-Shirley MacLaine vehicle released in 1960. The movie brought her notoriety during its 1959 shoot, publicity releases later claimed, when it apparently outraged Nikita Khrushchev.

After touring the set during a U.S. visit, the top Commie denounced Prowse's ballet number as immoral, and a photo of the almost unknown dancer was seen in newspapers around the world. "This is what you call freedom—freedom for the girls to show their backsides. It's capitalism that makes girls that way," Khrushchev was quoted as saying.

The publicity paved the way for an even higher-profile vehicle, Elvis' *G.I. Blues,* also released in 1960. Asked about being linked to Elvis while simultaneously dating Frank, Prowse matter-of-factly told a reporter: "I've had lots of dates with Elvis, too. Frank and I are mature people. We don't go for this teen-age bit about going steady and all that jazz."

According to Prowse's publicity materials, the door had closed on a serious dance career because her 5-foot-7-inch height was deemed too tall for ballet. But she was just the right height for Sinatra, who could open doors of his own. Her debut on the Strip, in the Riviera's road-show musical *Irma la Douce,* coincided with his November 1961 Sands stint. The two announced their engagement with a Hollywood dinner party in January 1962. "We have been seeing quite a lot of each other in private," Sinatra explained.

The engagement lasted only a month, however, and many Sinatra biographers are convinced that the 46-year-old star was staging it to promote the career of the 25-year-old dancer. Whether it was a publicity stunt or a genuine romance that suddenly didn't seem like such a good idea, the attention didn't hurt. Sinatra biographer Arnold Shaw claimed the affair boosted Prowse's asking price from $500 to $17,500 per week by the time her nightclub act debuted later in 1962. The show's high point was a salute to imaginary movie musicals about Joan of Arc, Camille, and Cleopatra—the outfit worn for the latter sketch fueling publicity photos for years to come.

As Prowse told it in 1995, Vegas was really the only place to go. "I wasn't able to be used on variety television anymore, because there wasn't any. Or in movies, because they weren't making musicals. This was my outlet," she said. "I was still under contract with Twentieth Century Fox at the time. They didn't know what to do with me. They weren't making musicals; they put me in terrible movies. I got myself out of my contract. At the same time, everyone is saying to me, 'Why don't we put an act together for you for Vegas?'"

What Prowse called "the dancing, singing, everything act" became the quintessential Vegas diva showcase, defined and redefined by the likes of Ann-Margret, Mitzi Gaynor, and Lola Falana. The nightclub format was much more variety driven than today's concert vehicles. "I always loved comedy," she said. "I always felt we had to have diversity in the act." Prowse's own press materials to accompany a Flamingo run in 1968 fill in the picture by pondering whether the "real" Juliet was "the ingenious Little Girl Blue that sits alone on the stage and softly sings the introspective 'Where Am I Going?'" or "the brassy, high-stepping dynamo that leads a company of dancers through a hey-look-me-over number like 'One Person Can Beat a Drum.'" Or maybe she was the "svelt and sexy evil-eyed Apache dancer who slithers and purrs her way through 'I've Got a Spell on You,'" or "the toothy, gum-chewing chorine who camps wildly through a spoof of the Busby Berkeley era of elaborate musical motion pictures."

The showrooms "gave us a wonderful venue, a place to show off our crafts," Prowse said. "In your own show in Vegas, you had a free hand to come and go and do what you wanted to do. In my act, I loved to do the serious dancing, but then I also loved to do the comedy shtick."

Audiences and employers alike appreciated the hard work that went into two shows a night of solid dancing. At the end of a 26-week run of *Sweet Charity* in June 1967, Caesars Palace officials presented Prowse with an $8,000 maroon Jaguar.

A 10-year contract with the Summa Corporation kept Prowse in Las Vegas 16 weeks a year throughout the '70s. However, the "ball-breaker shows," as dancers called them, began to catch up to her. "They were very difficult, very demanding technically, dancewise. When you do that kind of pounding, it has to take its toll eventually, especially when you start to get middle-aged." For Prowse it meant hip replacement, disc removal from her back, and two knee surgeries. The back surgery in 1983 put an end to her headlining days, redirecting her toward touring musicals such as *Mame.*

Juliet Prowse was too tall for classical ballet—but not for Elvis, Frank, or Vegas.

"I just didn't want to do Vegas anymore and dance anymore," she said. "I didn't want the responsibility of having the act anymore. I wanted to get away from all that [and] do things where I would be recognized as not just a dancer."

Prowse did carry on in show business, but more as a

middle-rung celebrity who was never quite able to transcend the legend of her own legs. Health problems continued to plague her, and her final appearance on the Strip in the summer of 1995 came fresh from a battle with pancreatic cancer. Prowse joined a Desert Inn production of *Sugar Babies* opposite a 74-year-old Mickey Rooney only a week after chemotherapy. "When I spoke to my oncologist, I said, 'This is the situation. What do you think?' He said, 'Go for it. Try it. See how you feel.'"

It seemed to be good therapy. Desert Inn staffers who viewed the show repeatedly during its first month saw Prowse gain strength in her dance numbers onstage, and even noticed a visible change in her physique—which was at first painfully thin but later better displayed in costumes that showed off her trademark legs. (Her wigs, unfortunately, were stuck in the '70s.)

Show business is "what keeps you young," she maintained at the time. "It really does. It's because of our business—I really do believe that. It keeps you on your toes. To those of us who love performing, it's our medicine almost." Despite her courageous attitude and valiant effort in the lame musical, Prowse lost her battle with cancer—and the Strip lost a class act—on September 14, 1996.

# Las Vegas' best girl

Vegas is a city that consumes women. But Ann-Margret consumed Vegas. The "Kitten With a Whip" took all the town had to offer, from its lounges to its showrooms to its King. She could be whispery cool and velvety soft. She could be black-leather, motorcycle-revvin' hot. She rode the Vegas tilt-a-whirl for 30 years and still managed to walk away with most of her dignity and reputation intact.

Ann-Margret tricked a city that never knew quite what to make of rock 'n' roll, sneaking the primal rhythms through the back door under a cloak of pure sex. Her act grew out of TV variety-show production numbers, not to mention the diva theatricality of Garland and Dietrich. But she injected these stodgy traditions with a go-go sensibility born of an inner beat. "I always moved," she said. "Ever since I was a little kid, I moved."

In 1967, when American boys were fighting in Vietnam and the hippies were burning flags and bras on campus, Vegas was still in the grip of the squares. Ann-Margret would keep them happy with a few show tunes, a sentimental ode to mom, a lot of costume changes, and even more cleavage. But she would also roar onstage on her motorcycle and cage-dance in hip-huggers and boots to the music that moved her.

The Swedish sexpot born Ann-Margret Olsson on April 28, 1941, first sneaked into town as a lounge singer in 1960. The Northwestern University student hooked up with a piano trio headed by Scott Smith during her freshman year, and the foursome began moonlighting as a group called "The Suttle-tones." An offer to play Vegas lured them West during their summer vacation. Initially it didn't pan out; they arrived at their downtown hotel after a long drive to discover that the previous lounge act had been held over. Undeterred, they found work entertaining a well-heeled crowd at a Newport

Beach, California, yacht club. After what turned out to be a great summer, the group headed back to Nevada, playing in Elko and Reno before finally returning to Vegas to play the Dunes' Sinbad Lounge for two weeks in mid-October.

"I sang and played the maracas," Ann-Margret (who dropped her last name from fear of embarrassing her parents) told veteran entertainment writer Bill Willard in 1990. The set list included "Mack the Knife," "Bill Bailey," "Mr. Wonderful," "The Thrill Is Gone," and other standards. During their second week, New Orleans jazzman Al Hirt came in as the lounge's big headliner.

When the gig ended, the singer had already decided to return to Los Angeles instead of Northwestern: "I heard they were holding auditions for the George Burns Christmas show that was to be held at the Sahara Hotel in Las Vegas. I got an audition, and Mr. Burns liked me, so I got the job. Everything really basically started from there."

The holiday program came during an important career transition for Burns, who was establishing himself as a solo act after Gracie Allen retired to attend her health problems (she died in 1964). Uncertain of his solo appeal, straight-man Burns hedged his bet by emceeing a variety format that surrounded him with talent. (Bobby Darin had been part of the initial lineup the previous year.) Ann-Margret was given three songs and the chance to return and "sand dance"—soft-shoe on sprinkled sand—with Burns at the end of the show. The act caught the attention of *Review-Journal* columnist Forrest Duke, who wrote in his day-after-Christmas column of 1960: "Burns brings along his singing discovery for this one, 19-year-old Northwestern U. coed Ann-Margret, who almost steals the show in her allotted 12 minutes. The pretty song stylist is definite star material."

Rival *Sun* columnist Ralph Pearl, however, thought the "19-year-old doll ... offsets the strong impression she conveys with her fine and sexy tones by over histrionics. In short, too much cute mugging and eye-popping."

More people lined up with Duke. Jack Benny was always on hand for his close friend Burns' Las Vegas openings. "One night before the show, in the wings, Jack Benny asked me if I wanted to be on his television show," Ann-Margret remembered. By the end of the 10-day engagement, she not only had locked up the February 1961 Benny show, but also had signed a record contract with RCA and secured an offer to screen-test for 20th Century Fox's remake of *State Fair.*

It was there the duality that would characterize Ann-Margret began to emerge. In the acting part of the audition, Annie tested for the "sweet ingénue" part wearing, she recalled, a dress with "little rosebuds, little short sleeves, a white Peter Pan collar, and my hair pinned back on the sides with little bows." But for the singing part of the audition, she did "Bill Bailey" from her nightclub act with her hair loose and was sporting "a bright red sweater and black tights with high heels." It was her standard "uniform" for stage appearances, born of equal parts poverty and intuition.

"A funny thing happened," she noted. "After they saw the test, they immediately bleached my hair orange and gave me the other part, the part of the bad girl from the other side of the tracks."

The movie was released to little impact in 1962. But *Bye Bye Birdie* and *Viva Las Vegas* director George Sidney better understood how to fully exploit the dichotomy that the screen test had discovered by accident: Ann-Margret was a bad girl in a sweet disguise, a demure, wholesome lass who could erupt into a hair-flipping, finger-snapping fireball at the sound of a downbeat. After completing both movies for Sidney, the starlet moved on to *Kitten With a Whip, The Cincinnati Kid,* and *The Pleasure Seekers,* all showing the redhead's worldly seductive side.

The actress had a lot of livin' to do before she returned to Las Vegas in 1967. Movies such as *The Swinger* (also directed by Sidney) and the Matt Helm comedy *Murderer's Row* seem delightfully "shagadelic" now, but they were perceived as descending career moves at the time. Gradually Ann-Margret turned more of her professional decisions over to her three-year actor steady, *77 Sunset Strip* star Roger Smith. The two set their sights on Vegas, figuring a return to the live stage might be just the shot of B-12 her career needed.

Despite a well-reported temporary breakup two months prior, the couple got married in Las Vegas on May 8, 1967. "A woman can always change her mind," she told the press. The crushing blow to the men of Earth took place in a honeymoon suite at the Riviera, where Ann-Margret was not so coincidentally booked to open in July. Only a week after Elvis Presley had married at the Aladdin, the couple cruised into town in Smith's two-seater Beechcraft "Debonair." The bride wore an ultra-groovy white miniskirt with white stockings. The ceremony took place under the full scrutiny of reporters and TV cameras. The next day, both local newspapers ran a front-page photo of the bride in tears. The *Sun's* caption claimed they were "tears of happiness," but Ann-Margret's 1994 biography, *My Story,* had a different explanation: The wedding was so unlike the storybook Swedish garden affair of her dreams that the bride took one look at the journalists, wearing short-sleeved shirts and smoking cigarettes, and started to cry. "I sobbed uncontrollably that this was how my wedding day had turned out," she wrote.

Opening night on July 12, 1967, was a more universally upbeat affair, with Burns and Johnny Carson among the stars lending ringside moral support at the Riviera. The show started with a roar—literally—as Ann-Margret peeled out from backstage on a motorcycle, fronting a biker lineup of dancers. "We had twelve motorcycles onstage, and we actually started them," she recalled. "The fire department came and said, 'I'm sorry, Miss Margret, but you can't start them because of the fire laws.' It was the first time that anything like that had ever been done."

The high-energy revue was packed with numbers like Aretha Franklin's "Respect," but it also included a sweet little Swedish folk song with the English title "Violets for Mother," featuring the singer in a long white dress. Years later, she readily acknowledged that it was done "to counterbalance the image" from all those bad-girl roles. In an era when newspaper editorials were ranting about the hippies, the show also grounded its

Ann-Margret got away with working rock music—and nearly always motorcycles—into her wildly energetic stage shows even when Vegas was ruled by squares.

groovier numbers, such as "How To Be a Go-Go Girl," with a spoof of old Broadway musicals that allowed Annie to sing "42nd Street" and "Singin' in the Rain" for the squares.

That first showroom run also included a poignant visit from Elvis Presley. Columnist Duke reported that the reunion "was a joyful one with much hugging, kissing, and words of good cheer," and that Presley "introduced his new bride, a dazzling brunette who is a ringer for Elizabeth Taylor." Years later, Ann-Margret's book confided that backstage in the wee hours of July 16, she could tell that the newlywed Elvis still carried the torch for his *Viva Las Vegas* co-star.

The Ann-Margret show also introduced multimedia and lasers to the Las Vegas revue, with a five-minute psychedelic light-show prologue and movie footage on a giant screen within the show. These novelties helped draw record numbers of people, enabling the Smiths to write their own ticket on the Strip.

By 1971, Ann-Margret was a big enough name on the Strip to command a full-blown theatrical review. *A-M/PM* featured a storyline and contributions from then unknown writer/performer Steve Martin.

In March of 1971, Ann-Margret rode back into town on the newfound—and in many ways, temporary—respectability that resulted from her Oscar-nominated role in *Carnal Knowledge.* Working with Mike Nichols and Jack Nicholson instead of Joe Namath (her co-star in the biker hootfest *C.C. and Company*) apparently explains the highbrow ambitions of *A-M/PM,* which debuted at the International Hotel in late 1971. This time, director Ron Field and future *Grease* perpetrator Allan Carr helped Annie and Roger concoct the most theatrical floorshow ever attempted in Vegas. It opened with a group of people—including future comedy star Steve Martin—clustered around a piano "brainstorming" ideas for a show. This allowed the ensemble to "test" dozens of

Ann-Margret tempered her vixenish charms with a sophisticated veneer by the time she debuted at Caesars Palace in 1978. This publicity photo was used for Caesars engagements in the early '80s.

standards and, as *Sun* writer Joe Delaney noted, displayed "the many 'sides' and the attractive front and back of the talented Swedish lass."

The rest of the revue used 12 set changes and $250,000 worth of Bob Mackie costumes, as the star saluted "great ladies of the 20th century," including Marilyn Monroe and "The Lady in Red" (whom John Dillinger no doubt would have voted to exclude from the list). The show met with mixed reactions, and future Las Vegas dates would jettison much of the stagecraft.

Ann-Margret might wish she'd streamlined a bit sooner, before messing with the giant harlequin's hand that was supposed to lower her 25 feet to the stage in her next show. On opening night in Lake Tahoe in September 1972, the prop malfunctioned, the platform tipped, and the singer tumbled 22 feet to the stage. She suffered five bone fractures in her face, a broken left arm, a concussion, and a broken jaw that had to be wired shut and required her to drink through a straw.

Amazingly, she was back onstage 10 weeks later in Las Vegas, makeup concealing bruises that still remained on her face. Her father was terminally ill, she later explained, and "the only way that he would really believe [that she was better] is if I would get up on that stage."

Annie remained a top draw in Las Vegas through the '70s. Musical arranger Marvin Hamlisch even created a medley of tunes from her 1975 performance in The Who's movie *Tommy* to keep the act current. In 1982, however, the singer gave up live performing when her husband contracted a rare muscle disease. Beating the odds, Smith saw his disease go into remission and the couple resumed the live show at Caesars Palace in November 1988. The trouble was, they thought they could merely pick up where they had left off, not realizing that Las Vegas had changed in their absence.

Ann-Margret trained like an Olympian—running, swimming, and climbing the 200 steps Smith had installed in back of their beach home. But the Smiths neglected to put the same energy into updating disco-fied numbers such as "Hold Me, Squeeze Me." The couple agreed to what Caesars World President Allan Bregman termed "one of the highest amounts ever paid to any performer in Las Vegas." But they sold the hotel used goods.

By 1990, few could guess that the stunning entertainer was now 49. A testament to her beauty was the fact that the dated rear-screen video from the '70s almost matched up to the woman singing in front of it. But being tossed around by chorus boys to the tune of "Steppin' Out With My Baby" now seemed even campier than the clips from *Birdie* and *Viva Las Vegas* shown on the video screens. Two years later, the Smiths finally hired director Joe Layton to create a new show more befitting a 50-something star. With only six musicians and three dancers, it was "almost a one-woman show"— at least by Ann-Margret standards, Layton noted. But when the show opened in August 1992, *Review-Journal* entertainment writer Michael Paskevich found that it failed "to connect on an emotional level. ... Put this show in the star quality hands of Liza Minnelli,

Shirley MacLaine, or Diana Ross, and the crowd likely would have been clamoring for more. As it was, they filed out quickly."

Little was seen of Annie on the Strip after that. It was just as well. She did what she had to do—aged with dignity. But no one had to like it. An aging sex kitten may be great in the comedic context of *Grumpy Old Men,* but it wasn't the same in the showroom. Vegas would rather see its go-go girl gone than grown up.

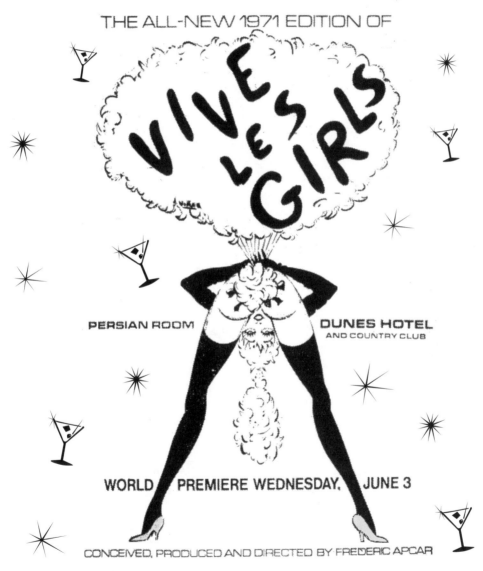

The *Vive Les Girls* show weathered the turbulent '60s. But by the beginning of the next decade, advertising reflected the more permissive—and somewhat tackier—times on the Strip.

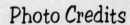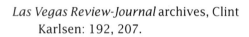

# Photo Credits

Art Nadler (www.vegasphotosbyart.com): 2.

Author's Collection: 3, 22, 53, 175, 185, 189, 197, 228, 231.

Don Knepp Collection: 49, 55, 61, 67, 127, 129, 155, 167, 170.

Harold Minsky Collection, University of Nevada, Las Vegas Library: 223.

Joe Guercio: 131, 135, 215.

Las Vegas News Bureau: 26, 89, 121, 125, 233, 243.

Las Vegas News Bureau Collection, University of Nevada, Las Vegas Library: 103, 141.

*Las Vegas Review-Journal* archives: 10, 12, 15, 19, 27, 29, 31, 39, 41, 51, 57, 65, 70, 73, 74, 76, 79, 83, 87, 91, 97, 99, 100, 105, 107, 116, 118, 139, 143, 173, 177, 180, 187, 217, 220, 225 (bottom), 229, 237, 239, 244, 245, 247.

*Las Vegas Review-Journal* archives, Clint Karlsen: 192, 207.

*Las Vegas Review-Journal* archives, Jim Laurie: 109.

*Las Vegas Review-Journal* archives, Jeff Scheid: 202.

Liberace Museum: 123, 183.

Maury Stevens Collection, University of Nevada, Las Vegas Library: 232.

Nicky Blair: 124, 153, 157, 159.

Sam Sherman, Independent-International Pictures: 227.

Sands Hotel Collection, University of Nevada, Las Vegas Library: 16, 18, 21, 63, 149, 154, 209.

Ted V. Mikels: 225 (top).

UNLV Collection, University of Nevada, Las Vegas Library: 163.

Mike Weatherford rolled into Las Vegas on Oct. 29, 1987 - the last night Frank, Sammy and Dean would stand on the same stage on the Strip. Beat down by a long drive, he didn't make it to that show. But he's seen plenty of others since then as an entertainment reporter for the Las Vegas Review Journal, the city's morning daily newspaper.

A native of Tulsa, Okla Weatherford lives in Las Vegas with his wife and daugh ter.

## Other books from Huntington Press:

*The Anointed One*
*An Inside Look at Nevada Politics*
by Jon Ralston
(ISBN 0-929712-01-3)

*The Art of Gambling Through the Ages*
by Arthur Flowers and Anthony Curtis
(ISBN 0-929712-90-0)

*The First 100*
*Portraits of the Men and Women Who Shpaed Las Vegas*
edited by A.D. Hopkins and K.J. Evans
(ISBN 0-929712-67-6)

*Fly on the Wall: Recollections of Las Vegas'*
*Good Old, Bad Old Days*
by Dick Odessky
(ISBN 0-929712-62-5)

*Hiking Las Vegas: 60 Hikes Within 60 Minutes of the Strip*
by Branch Whitney
(ISBN 0-929712-21-8)

*Hiking Southern Nevada*
by Branch Whitney
(ISBN 0-929712-22-6)

*No Limit: The Rise and Fall of Bob Stupak*
*and Las Vegas' Stratosphere Tower*
by John L. Smith
(ISBN 0-929712-18-8)

*On the Boulevard: The Best of John L. Smith*
(ISBN 0-929712-69-2)

*Quicksilver*
*The Ted Binion Murder Case*
Photographs by Jeff Scheid—Text by John L. Smith
(ISBN 0-929712-28-5)

**About Huntington Press**

Huntington Press is a specialty publisher of Las Vegas- and gambling-related books and periodicals. To receive a copy of the Huntington Press catalog, call 1-800-244-2224 or write to the address below.

Huntington Press
3687 South Procyon Avenue
Las Vegas, Nevada 89103